The Gourmet's Canada

SONDRA GOTLIEB

new press

TORONTO

1972

ISBN 0-88770-128-0 (cloth)
          0-88770-129-9 (paper)

new press
Order Department
553 Richmond Street West
Toronto 133, Ontario

Design / Peter Maher

Photo Credits: The photographs which appear between pages 148-9 are from the following sources: *Chatelaine* — photographs of GALLOWAY's, the baker and bread from PAIN DE COLLEGE, CULINA, Osso Buco, WILLI KRAUCH, and the TOMAHAWK BARBECUE; Ray Webber — photographs of tortière and oysters; Peter Varley — photographs of maple syrup, honey, and fruits; and the Canadian Dairy Foods Bureau — the photograph of cheeses.

Manufactured in Canada by John Deyell

For my mother,
who loves to cook
and
loves to eat

My warmest thanks to

Helen Wilson, and to Allan Gotlieb, my husband, for moral
support and editorial assistance. I do not know how I should
have managed without them;
Jean Holtby for typing the manuscript with patience and care;
Max and Janice Yalden for their proofreading and general
comments;
      and
Deborah Peddie, Lynn Leblanc, Joyce McDonald, Fanny Kauf-
man, Sondra Gwyn, Zoe Oreck, Kay Van Sickle, Sheila Henley,
Nicole Sakellalopoulo, Lil Tonkin, Michael Maltby, Douglas
Leopold, Florence Levers, Don Snowdon, Tuzzie Divinsky,
Louise Donovan, Ruth Erlich, Roberta Butler, Star Solomon
and Don Pepper, and everyone else I bothered in the prepara-
tion of this book.

Grateful acknowledgement is made also to members of the
federal Department of the Environment for information and
comments relating to the manuscript, to the Ontario Department of Agriculture and Food and to the authorities of a number of other provincial departments, and to members of the
Freshwater Fish Marketing Corporation, all of whom helped
me in my research.

Contents

Preface

The Gourmet's Canada is all about food in our country.

Scattered throughout the book, there are many recipes deriving from the major regions and ethnic groups in Canada, as well as a number of my own. But this is not a recipe book.

There are sections describing food shops whose products are regional, or exotic, often different from those of the supermarkets and frequently better; and other sections describing inexpensive restaurants, some of which are typical of their part of Canada or even of the particular community they serve. But this is neither a shopper's handbook nor a restaurant guide.

I discuss some of the present and historical reasons for the way we eat, but this book does not belong on the shelf of a historian or a sociologist.

I have mentioned many of the excellent ingredients that are part of our heritage and the problems we have in conserving them for the future. But this book is not an encyclopedia of food.

It is simply a personal, sometimes biased, account of the

Canadian feast, from blueberries to caviar. My own experiences of eating in Canada, my own investigations of our culinary heritage and our gastronomic bounty, recollections of food and food lore from my childhood — these are my concerns rather than historical or sociological documents.

In my gastronomic journey through Canada I had no research staff, just the help of friends who drove me around from St. John's to Victoria. I have also begged and bothered everyone I know, and all the experts I could find, for information about good places and good things to eat.

Not everyone will agree with my sentiments about food, and there is no reason why they should. But I hope this book will inform and amuse those who read it even when they disagree with me. I hope, too, by drawing attention to the gastronomic resources of this land and the wealth of its culinary traditions, to show that the gourmet's Canada *does* exist — from Peachland, British Columbia to Eel River Crossing.

Sondra Gotlieb
OTTAWA, 1972

The Gourmet's Canada

The Education of a Fussy Eater

WITHIN FIFTY YEARS, confessing to an interest in food will be like admitting, in former times, to a sexually perverted act. Now our guilt feelings arise not from moral wrongdoing, but from having eaten too much. It doesn't bother us to go to our neighbourhood movie house and stare at two or three people copulating, but how our spirits suffer, how depression reigns, if we consume two or three buttered buns at dinner. No old-fashioned sin produces the same feeling of remorse as that brought on by over-indulgence in cakes and cream.

Fat people are today's lepers. We tend to shun them because doctors — our contemporary Luthers and Wycliffes — tell us they harbour disease and death: they are ugly in our eyes and remind us of disagreeable things. The preaching of doctors has made physical well-being into a religious mania that has swept the Western world. Anyone who dwells too much on food is asking for the suffering of the social outcast as payment for his obvious attempts to pervert the good health of society. The full vengeance that will be meted out to such morbid individuals is still being devised by doctors and sociologists, who predict a future of instant light snacks instead of a good heavy three-course meal of pea soup, fried chicken and pie.

I am in the category of those pariahs-to-be who think and dream about food, as well as cook and eat it, and my gastronomic background is still strong enough to withstand the pangs of guilt I suffer when I spend the day reading cook-books and eating toasted almonds. My only plea is an early environment where emphasis on food was strong: my corruption occurred during defenceless childhood.

I was born in Winnipeg, Manitoba, and my mother, grandmother, aunts and uncles all liked to cook. They also liked to talk about food. I remember that my mother would say, when discussing a relative, "She's a nice person, but her pie crusts are doughy," and then she would wrinkle her nose. The effect of this statement, combined with her facial expression, was a powerful one for a four year old, and to this day — against my rational conscience — I tend to judge people by what they eat. I stare at other people's shopping baskets at supermarkets and I spy into friends' refrigerators for clues to their characters. It is possible that I am actually unbalanced because I can still crave butter tarts displayed in the window of a pastry shop even though I'm over-stuffed after a four-course meal in the restaurant next door.

Winnipeg was a natural breeding ground for this type of obsession. My mother's friends and relatives spent a lot of time in the kitchen and at tea parties. The work in the kitchen was necessary because of the tea parties (or perhaps the reverse was true). In any case, the tea tables were groaning about twice a week. Each lady would bring her specialty. My mother could go straight to the dining-room and guess who was at the party just by looking at the cakes and cookies spread out on the trays. In fact, specialization got to be a bit ridiculous: Mrs. Schwartzmann, even though entirely capable of baking a perfect example, would never encroach on the angel-cake territory of Mrs. Zipper; she might bake an angel cake in the privacy of her home, but she would never be tactless enough to let it be seen in public. Each pie, cake or dainty baked by my grandmother's and my mother's friends had the same personal connotation as a private family seal in Roman times. Mrs. Zipper's angel cake was her insignia — if someone else had baked *her* cake for a tea party it would have been like forging her signature.

My mother made a soup every day. I remember coming down to breakfast and, with a certain queasiness, seeing her scraping vegetables for her beef and barley soup or cabbage borsch, or taking the fat off the chicken soup of the day before. Although there is no well prepared food that I refuse to eat, soup is one of my less favourite dishes because I ate so much of it when I was a child. Larry Zolf, who also comes from Winnipeg, has similar feelings about soup. His mother used to let her soup boil so that the broth shot through the holes in the marrow bones, dissipating all the marrow and causing the formation of a geyser which spouted on top of the stove and sometimes shot right up to the ceiling. This frightened him very much when he was a young boy, and even now he refuses all soup because he is afraid it will explode in his face.

But then Larry never liked his mother's cooking. She used to go to a lot of trouble making special dishes for him, but he was the kind of son who would lift up the lid of the pot, look in, and then ask for a can of tuna.

My cousin Sheldon was difficult to feed as well. For his first eight years he lived on fruit, and then agreed to accept other food only if it was not hard to chew. His mother fed him very soft hot dogs, boiled until gelatinous and disintegrating, and a quart of mashed potatoes a day. For a time, he became quite fat, but when he entered medical school he was converted to the new dieting religion and now he eats only fruit and vitamin pills. I never see him when I go back to Winnipeg. I can't stand the sight of Sheldon peeling a banana when everyone else is eating roast beef.

But it was my uncle Morton, rather than cousin Sheldon, who was considered the fussy eater in the family. On the day of his wedding, his mother handed a little, worn pot to his bride. "I have been making Morton's cocoa with this pot every morning since he's been a baby," she said. Aunt Manya refused the gift, broke the cocoa tradition and had her first fight with her mother-in-law. But despite her firm stand with the cocoa pot, my aunt, to this day, has the problem of making my uncle's omelettes. My uncle Morton will eat eggs in only one form: my aunt separates four eggs, beats the yolks with an egg beater (neither a fork nor a mixer will do) until they are as frothy as foam, puts one-half a teaspoon of butter in an eight-inch frying pan, and throws the egg yolks in (Uncle Morton doesn't like the whites), beating all the time with the egg beater. After a certain amount of frantic effort, the eggs reach the desired state of sponginess, and the omelette is quickly transferred to a plate that has been warming in the oven. My uncle, already waiting at the table, checks the omelette placed in front of him for any faults, and then, with a certain twist, wraps the whole thing around the fork and swallows it in one gulp. No one believed my aunt when she first told the story, but one day my parents went over especially to watch the performance and they returned home awe-struck. My aunt is grateful to the RCAF for one improvement in Uncle Morton's eating habits. During his service in the Second World War, he learned to eat porridge and green peas. That is all he lived on during those years; yet before that, he would never allow either form of sustenance within eating range.

A neurotic concern with what you eat and do not eat is thus part of my origins, and to some extent, my husband's family shared the same type of background. My sister-in-law remembers that as a child she could never play on her bed because her grandmother used it for drying noodles. If any of the long strips happened to snap, Eunice fully expected to be tossed into the boiling water instead of the noodles.

Much later I left Winnipeg for Geneva, Switzerland and found myself cooking for diplomats. Geneva is less than a few dozen miles from Bresse, Ain and Bugey, and only a little farther from Burgundy, in France. These have been considered by greedy people from the eighteenth to the twentieth century — including Brillat-Savarin and Alice B. Toklas — to be the finest eating and drinking regions in the Western world. Because of my obsession with food, I was fascinated by the remarkable chickens (*poulets de bresse*), the extra rich butter and cream, the thin green beans and, of course, the wines, which were the natural products of the land.

The cooking I had known in Winnipeg, although excellent, lacked the same breadth and refinement. An excess of gastronomic nationalism does no stomach any good, so I decided to forget about maple syrup and let Geneva's Gallic traditions and culinary advantages invade my kitchen and my sauces. Vegetables, underdone meats and smelly cheeses began to mean far more to me than they ever had in Canada.

Not only are the ingredients in this part of the world extraordinary, but the restaurants know what to do with them. Some of the greatest places to eat in France are no farther than a few hours drive from one another in this region. They include the PYRAMIDE in Vienne, near Lyon (truffled fowl from Bresse and a hundred other dishes); PAUL BOCUSE in Collonges-au-Mont-d'Or, also near Lyon (*loup en croûte farcie d'une mousse de homard sauce choron* — translation: sea bass in a crust, stuffed with lobster mousse and accompanied by a bearnaise sauce with tomato); smaller, less formal restaurants like the CHAPON FIN near Bourg en Bresse (potato pancakes); and exceptionally unpretentious places such as BOURGEOIS in Priay, also near Bourg en Bresse, which serves fresh salmon trout in foaming butter sauce. These restaurants are capable of turning out the most complicated dishes perfectly — and also the most simple. A roast chicken and a plate of fresh green beans at any of these places is a revelation. It has something to do with the great characteristics of French civilization — perfectionism, attention to detail, and a sense of logic, combined with intelligence and imagination. Nothing infuriates a true Frenchman more than grandeur degraded by sloppiness.

In Paris, seventeen years ago, I had my first insight into these qualities. A waiter at one of the grand French restaurants (three stars in the *Guide Michelin*) refused to cut into our *soufflé Grand Marnier* because it was not of sufficient height. He held his serving spoons in mid-air and, without consulting us (he knew we were as ignorant as donkeys), turned on his heel and carried the *soufflé* back to the kitchen. Twenty-five minutes later he brought out another one that had reached the desired four inches above the dish.

My gastronomic interest had found the ideal place for serious research. One night I would eat *pâté chaud* (sweetbreads, little chicken dumplings, sliced truffles and mushrooms stuffed between layers of hot thin pastry) and steak with morels, and the next day I would go to the butcher shop to stare at lamb chops. The fat on the chops had all been removed except for a little rim around the edge, left to prevent the chop from becoming dry when sautéed. Each chop had its own paper frill, and the ensemble was arranged on the meat-tray like a display of Patek Philippe five-hundred-dollar watches. A vase of fresh flowers was usually placed above them on the counter. You could not ask for more respect. What I experienced then were the great classical principles of French cuisine (now, I fear, dying out), which attach great importance to the handling of food, as well as to the actual cooking of it.

Perhaps the culmination of the gastronomic excellence of the area was something called *quenelle de brochet* with *sauce Nantua,* which was defined tersely in an English translation of the French menu as "hot ground pike ball with fishy gravy". Now my grandmother in Winnipeg made a very fine hot gefilte fish — ground whitefish and pike, eggs and spices formed into balls and boiled — which she served with the broth in which it was cooked. The description of the dish, served in a small hotel restaurant in the Jura Mountains, looked familiar to me. But the translation was faulty — the restaurant owner was a wonderful cook, not a linguist. What he brought out was a large oval-shaped dumpling made of pike and cream, puffed up to soufflé proportions because of the egg whites beaten into it, and bathed in a rich pink sauce made from the shell and flesh of freshwater crayfish, thick cream, butter and white wine. There were some lumps in the sauce, but they proved to be a convoy of fresh shrimps swimming alongside.

I can honestly say that whatever I've eaten and whatever I've seen or done since that moment cannot compare with the experience of tasting *quenelle de brochet, sauce Nantua,* for the first time, at that restaurant in the Jura Mountains. Over the years I've eaten many great quenelles in this area of France and I've never failed to be spiritually moved. I've also eaten *quenelles de brochet* in restaurants in Montreal and I have never failed to be disappointed. They were closer to torpedoes than to those delectable puffs I ate in France.

It was at that special moment in the Jura countryside when I was stuffing myself with quenelles that I had an experience as rich as the sauce that accompanied it. I knew that what I wanted to do most of all in life was to eat delicious food and drink agreeable wine — in good company if possible — and perhaps write about it all some time.

I thus became the kind of person my family always mistrusted — a cosmopolitan culinary adventurer.

The
Canadian Gourmet:
Patriot and Prophet

ACCORDING TO WEBSTER'S dictionary a gourmet is "a connoisseur of the delights of the table — an epicure". If you look up epicure, you will find "one who cultivates a refined taste in eating and drinking" — this means that a gourmet must be fastidious; and "one given up to sensual enjoyment, especially in eating". A gourmet, then, is also greedy.

Can the gourmet's difficult balance between fastidiousness and greed be satisfied in Canada? It might be thought that the words "gourmet" and "Canada" are a contradiction in terms. A friend said to me "You're writing about a gourmet's Canada? That will be a short book." Nevertheless, I am convinced that the gourmet's schizophrenic desires can be fulfilled from Cape Onion, Newfoundland to Peachland, British Columbia.

Canada has not played a prominent part in the vast, growing international literature on the culinary arts. From Carême to Curnonsky and the *Larousse Gastronomique,* one finds almost nothing about Canada. There is not a mention of maple syrup in any of the classical cook-books written by the great chefs of France. You would have a hard time convicting a Frenchman that Canadians are still drinking tree sap. A recent and impressive exception to European ignorance of maple syrup is the newest three-star restaurant in the *Guide Michelin* of France — the restaurant TROISGROS, near Lyon, which has lightened and simplified such elaborate traditions of "haute cuisine" as the making of windmills out of spun sugar and the carving of begonias from turnips. The TROISGROS' iconoclasm has gone so far as to break through international prejudice and allow dishes like wild duck and peaches to be glazed with maple syrup. A touch of vinegar cuts the sweetness.

The only serious reference to Canadian cooking that I have come upon in recent international literature was an addendum on French-Canadian and Maritime cooking tagged to the New England volume of the Time-Life cook-book series. Another cook-book, published by Funk and Wagnalls, has the title *French-American Cooking from New Orleans to Quebec*. It includes (amid the hominy drop cakes, seafood okra gumbo, and creole mustard) exactly three recipes from Quebec.

The idea of a good Canadian cuisine is hazy, not only in the minds of non-Canadians, but in our own. The coffee shop in Montreal's Dorval airport has an "international menu," listing pizza as the specialty of Italy, paella, for Spain, and the hot chicken sandwich as Canada's contribution to the world's cuisine. No, Canada has not so far been considered a haven for gourmets of the world.

Many Canadians look suspiciously on anyone who shows too great an interest in food. "I eat what is put in front of me" is still considered the proper attitude of right-thinking citizens. Never complain, even when the soup is cold, the meat tough, and the mashed potatoes too heavy to be lifted on a fork. The Anglo-Saxon heritage of a stiff upper lip can be carried to absurd lengths when its manifestation is incipient *rigor mortis* caused by food poisoning! Eating is a sensual experience and our traditional *mépris* of sensuality is apparent in the many Canadians who refuse to think, talk about, or even notice food.

The word gourmet has been abused and distorted in Canada. It has come to mean a sort of gastronomic foppishness. The gourmet is thought to be a person who picks at imported gull's eggs poached in Dom Perignon '55 — the adult version of my cousin Sheldon who was the despair of his mother because he lived on cherries and air.

There is also a fraudulent use of the word gourmet in cookery-books; titles like "Gourmet Recipes for People Who Hate to Cook" are common. Restaurants abuse the word. Waterlogged chicken, meat adrift from the bone, escorted by three pickled onions forked out of a jar, is a "gourmet's delight" because a casual in the kitchen used a sugary-sweet sauterne fabricated somewhere south of Espanola, Ontario to help keep the bird afloat.

A gourmet is a person who knows and loves food. Forget about the misuse of the word in advertising, and its connotation of the over-refined, picky eater. A gourmet, his greed notwithstanding, has a lot to offer Canada. He is a seeker after excellence, and anyone in this country who craves excellence in *anything* counter-balances a Canadian weakness, the desire for an easier road, at the end of which is mediocrity. If you don't care whether the fish is fresh or the meat overcooked, you are not only indifferent to the food, but also to the natural gifts of the land.

Occupying one-fourteenth of the land mass of the world, Canada has a lot to offer the gourmet: wild rice, good beef and lamb, salmon (six kinds), New Brunswick rainbow trout, grayling from the northern lakes, pickerel and whitefish unequalled anywhere, berries (from the bakeapples of Newfoundland to the saskatoons of Saskatchewan), and real, black, sturgeon caviar.

Some of these Canadian gastronomic resources face the threat of exhaustion. For example, there used to be a great deal of caviar in Canada, but it will soon be as obsolete as the passenger pigeons that once clouded Canadian skies (until they were devoured by the hungry settlers, who couldn't eat enough of their succulent flesh). A sturgeon must be at least ten years old before the caviar (or eggs) may be used. As recently as five years ago, it was not uncommon to find sturgeon in the St. Lawrence, Rideau and Winnipeg rivers. Amateurs caught sturgeon for sport (during the thirties there was open season on sturgeon in Manitoba, and anglers could take home two a day), and commercial fishermen caught the young sturgeon for the US market — smoked sturgeon is still a great delicacy in New York delicatessens. There was no interest in letting the sturgeon age so that it would produce caviar. Caviar was something that decadent foreigners ate just before their come-uppance, the revolution.

Overfishing of young sturgeon, and industrial pollution, have now virtually stopped caviar production in this country. If there had been more gourmet-minded citizens, perhaps our federal and provincial governments might have realized that they had a very special national heritage in our caviar resource and that efficient production of caviar could be extremely profitable.

As it is, Canadian caviar is likely to go the way of Winnipeg goldeye. Smoked goldeye is sold in most fish stores and delicatessens with the description "Winnipeg," but it is a nostalgic misnomer. The goldeye left Manitoba waters long ago because of overfishing and pollution. They now come from carefully tended and well stocked lakes in northern Minnesota. That great western-Canadian gastronomic heritage, Winnipeg goldeye, is now "Made in U.S.A". (Canadian caviar and Winnipeg goldeye are discussed at greater length in Chapter 3.)

One of the purposes of this book is to make Canadians more aware of our natural gastronomic resources and their preservation. We have a lot of good food in our country but we do not take care of it or eat it all or know enough about it. Fishermen, farmers, wholesalers and retailers would be more interested in maintaining a steady supply and providing efficient distribution if good markets were available here in Canada. And good markets *would* be available if Canadians appreciated their own products. Gluttony tinged with nationalism would definitely help. The gourmet has a contribution to make in a country which has done much to squander some of its most precious resources. What is special about the gourmet is not his desires or his digestion, but his state of mind, a mind that pursues excellence in that most basic of human functions, eating. Samuel Johnson once said that if you don't mind what you put in your stomach, you're not likely to mind anything else. Insofar as the gourmet makes us conserve our extraordinarily rich resources, we should recognize him as a patriot and a prophet.

However, the consumer is not entirely at fault for the state of our gastronomic products. Distribution of fresh fish, vegetables and fruits leaves a lot to be desired. Owners of some of the finest fish markets in Ontario have told me that most fish sold in Toronto have been lying around the wholesalers' counters for at least two or three days before they even reach the retailer. Yet in the Atlantic provinces, no self-respecting person will eat fish more than three or four hours old.

Fishermen and farmers in New Brunswick, Manitoba, Saskatchewan and British Columbia raise rainbow trout commercially in breeding ponds. But people in the urban centres in Canada (where most of the trout is sold) will never taste them at their best. Trout, more than any other fish, must be eaten fresh. If you want to taste a really fresh trout in Canada you still have to catch it yourself — despite the existence of breeding farms. Fish are killed before they are shipped from these places. In Switzerland, commercial trout farms have existed for a long time, but the trout are shipped live to the fish shops and killed only upon purchase — much the way in which the best fish stores in Canada sell lobsters. No Swiss, gourmet or not, would buy a dead trout. I know of only two trout tanks in this country, at DARRIGO'S and at MISNER'S FISH MARKET, both in Toronto.

Many Canadian cookery-books wax eloquent about Canada's wild berries. If you live nine stories high in the middle of Montreal, it's not likely you'll have a raspberry bush growing on your balcony. Unless you live near a farm-

ers' market, you'll be lucky to buy anything other than
strawberries, even at the height of the raspberry, blackberry
and blueberry seasons. Supermarkets in Manitoba and
Ontario prefer to sell the large cultivated blueberries from
the United States, which have far less juice and flavour,
rather than their own provinces' smaller, wild berries.
Supermarkets are tied by very tight contracts to their US
wholesalers. Because they import most of their fruit and
vegetables during the winter season, many of them tend to
ignore the local produce during the summer, and continue
to stock beans, apples, strawberries and celery grown especially for long counter life but possessing little flavour.
Farmers who live one mile from their local supermarket
complain that they have no market for their fresh, truly
sun-ripened produce, while their consumer neighbour is
obliged to buy refrigerated, tasteless fruits and vegetables
imported from California.

Thus, we have the following situation: The farmer and
the distributor blame their lack of market on the indifference of the Canadian consumer. The consumer blames the
farmer and the distribution system for the difficulty in ob-
taining Canadian products and/or their poor condition.
All of them blame the large food retailers for distributing
US produce when Canadian is available. And I blame the
timidity and narrow-mindedness of Canadians generally.

Fortunately, the gourmet's Canada is not just a vast ex-
panse of land and water with extraordinary ingredients dispersed here and there. Canada also has different styles of
cooking, arising from the multi-national character of Canadians. Anglo-Saxons, French, Italians, Germans, Jews,
Chinese and Ukrainians have adapted their traditional
cuisines to their new homeland.

The regional and ethnic deviations in culinary ingredients are shown to a remarkable degree in specialty food
shops throughout the country. The pushcarts at the check-
out counters from British Columbia to the Maritimes reveal the depressing sameness of supermarket shopping. It is

the small specialty shop that sells different, and often better, products. The culinary diversities in our country are mirrored by those small stores that spice and stuff their own sausages or make a doughnut that has a crunchy epidermis, unlike the supermarket kind that yields and disintegrates at the first bite.

It is the very smallness of these stores that preserves the excellence of their products. M. and Mme Marcel Com who run a small but first-rate pastry shop in Hull, Quebec say that any expansion of their very successful business would ruin the quality of the baking. M. Com makes all the cakes and *croissants* himself. He was trained as a master pastry-maker in France, apprenticing over a long number of years, rather than the six-month period so many cooking schools here demand. If the Coms were to expand, they would have to depend on others to work and supervise in the kitchen. Apparently there is no one in the Hull-Ottawa area who has the training or who wishes to work the long hours necessary to keep up the quality of the pastry. So, the Coms' shop remains small, but consistent in its excellence. Size often waters down quality, because the manager or assistant lacks the technical expertise and the desire for perfection that motivates the owner. The great shame is that few young people succumb to the drive for excellence in food preparation — even when it's only the achievement of the perfect cream puff. (It must be noted that this drive for perfection in the gastronomic field very often excludes large financial gain. You only satisfy your personal goal, never your pocket-book.)

Sometimes, but not often, there is variety even in supermarket practice. Montreal, Quebec and Ottawa have certain large stores that make fresh blood pudding of excellent quality for their French-Canadian customers. You will find it on the fresh-meat counter. It's quite unlike the standard blood pudding found on the sausage counters all over Canada, which lacks texture and flavour.

Despite the sporadic efforts of the supermarkets, it is truly these little shops, run by someone, usually from an immigrant family, who is willing to work from 8 a.m. to 8 p.m. for small profit, that show our culinary heritage to its greatest advantage. The varied ethnic backgrounds of Canadians have created a demand for certain things. Toronto is bursting with shops selling goat meat to West Indians, Hungarian pastries, and espresso coffee, originally an Italian taste, now sophisticated Canadian.

To taste smoked salmon at its best, you have to go to a small specialty food shop where a lovely fresh slice will be carved from the back of a whole fish. The pre-packaged pre-sliced salmon sold in most places under various brand names (such as Nova Lax, which, by the way, comes mostly from B.C.), does not do the fish justice. The supermarkets in British Columbia and Alberta, however, sell large chunks of salmon under cellophane — an improvement over the pre-sliced variety. (Incidentally, do Nova Scotians know that El Al, the Israeli airline, calls Nova Scotia smoked salmon, which it serves to its passengers, "an outstanding star of the Jewish table"?)

Perhaps the most interesting breed of shop-keepers are those behind the counters of cheese stores. These people are not selling cheese because some big food firm has taken them off bacon slicing and put them on to cheese grating. They deal with cheese because they love it and this love often leads them to open their own shops. Their enthusiasm and knowledge about their product beats that of any second-hand car salesman. Cheese is their religion. As an example, the former owner of THE CHEESE SHOP in Montreal always has words with waiters in restaurants if he orders a Roquefort salad dressing and is given, instead, the cheaper and less subtle Danish blue. You have to have his knowledge of cheese to snuff out this common and nefarious practice.

The multi-ethnic character of Canada is also reflected in the variety of recipes that are to be found in the many Canadian cookery-books. For example, we have *Traditional Ukrainian Cooking* by Savella Stechishin, the *Canadian Mennonite Cook Book, A French-Canadian Cookbook* by Donald Asselin, and Trina Vineberg's *Family Heirlooms*, which contains Jewish and English recipes. Recipe books from the Atlantic provinces, like Marie Nightingale's *Out of Old Nova Scotia Kitchens* and the Newfoundland ladies' church-committee cookery-books, reflect the proximity of the sea, as well as the Anglo-Saxon, German and Irish backgrounds of the people.

Ancestry, then, is not the only reason for differences in Canadian cuisine. People cook what is available in their regions. Fried clams are certainly more popular in New Brunswick than in Winnipeg; Winnipeggers can eat fresh pickerel, while people in the Northwest Territories can dine on fresh-caught grayling or Arctic char. Paper cones filled with hard maple sugar and packages of granulated maple sugar are fairly easy to come by in eastern Ontario and Quebec. I couldn't find granulated maple sugar in Toronto.

In my own experience, our ethnic and regional differences can be illustrated by the culinary habits of two young girls, each of different racial and geographical backgrounds. When I was a child, my mother employed a Ukrainian maid who made the most wonderful *varenyky* or *pyrohy* (now Anglicized to the bastard word perogy), little dough-covered triangles, filled with a mixture of potato and cabbage and boiled to a texture similar to ravioli. They were more beautiful than ravioli though, because she turned the two bottom ends of the triangles into a gracious rococo curve that joined forever unto death under the envelope of filling. Sour cream eased their passing from this world. After the birth of my second child, a Newfoundland school girl named Emily stayed with us for a few months to help me over the tide of diapers. She loved cabbage and potatoes too, but her favourite way of eating them was in a purée with turnips, cabbage and potatoes all mashed in together. Later, I discovered that there is a special name for this concoction — colcannon — which has been canonized by Maritime, Newfoundland and Irish cookery-books.

Purely regional recipes are typified by a *Northern Cookbook* put out by the Department of Indian Affairs and

Northern Development. It includes recipes for woodchuck with biscuits, and stuffed moose heart. Since most Canadians live in the city and cannot easily go out and shoot game for their dinner, any recipes in my book will have ingredients that are easily procurable, and well-suited to our high-rise-dominated lives.

I am not setting out to write an historical document on Canadian gastronomy. If you want to eat what your ancestors liked, read Mme Jehane Benoit's *The Canadiana Cookbook,* Marie Nightingale's *Out of Old Nova Scotia Kitchens,* or Pierre and Janet Berton's *The Centennial Food Guide.* There are many authentic and still useful pioneer recipes in my book, like *ragoût de boulettes* and maple sugar pie. But some of my recipes bear no historical or even contemporary relationship to what Canadians eat. I put them in because they make delicious eating and excellent use of the ingredients found in our country. Perhaps the prime example of this is *bourride,* a fish stew whose origins are in Provence, France. *Bourride* is an imaginative way of cooking the firm-fleshed fish from the inland lakes of Manitoba, Saskatchewan and Alberta. History is not the prime source for my recipes. The ingredients available here and now have been my inspiration. A broader vision and practicality are more important than a sentimental adherence to the past.

Later, I will say more about books on cooking in Canada but I have something to add now about one recent book, *Capital Cookery Hundreds of recipes from the kitchens of Canada's Prime Ministers revealed for the very first time.* Unfortunately, some of the book's culinary revelations wouldn't sparkle in a cookery-book for vegetarian convicts. According to this book, our prime ministers seem to have depended greatly on soup cubes and cans of vegetables, including, horror of horrors, canned potatoes. That may be all right if you have other work during the day or if you have three children under your feet, but if your only job is feeding the prime minister of Canada, it's a disgrace to use such tasteless short cuts. There are some recipes that might do for an army mess, like chipped beef and cheese rolls, and another that could produce in the Sussex-Street guests a dehydration intense enough to masquerade as lockjaw — a dip made from peanut butter and bloater paste. Aside from the juicy bits of information, like the fact that Mr. Diefenbaker liked fish and the Pearsons' favourite food was chicken, it's a mystery why this book was even published.

A more interesting cook-book would have been one devoted to the experiences, techniques, and recipes of Jean Zonda, the former chef of Government House. M. Zonda was deservedly known throughout the gastronomic world; the meals he served during the time of the Vaniers were worthy of the standards of the White House, Buckingham Palace and even the Elysée. It would have been informative and amusing for Canadians to have been able to read his menus as chef for the Governor-General of Canada.

Many Canadians travel in the summertime — with children fighting in the back seat of their station wagon or camper truck. To relieve the tedium of these quarrels and the super-highway scenery, they might like to stop at coffee shops or restaurants that offer something better than overcooked hamburger and pie crusts that fold over and flip back at the touch of a fork, and at places that don't charge $5 a person for the privilege of eating the food. In this book, I will describe a number of places that offer surprisingly good food at reasonable prices. Now some of these places are not restaurants, or even coffee shops. A few of the fish and chip shops don't even have tables, just a few stools around a counter, but they all have take-out food. A friend of mine describes them as "quick and dirties". All of the places I describe do specialize in quick service, but they were all clean when I was in them. Naturally, there are many places that haven't been included because I've never heard of them, and I'm depending on my readers to give me names. It's impossible to go to every café and roadside stand in Canada.

I'm also interested in another class of restaurants — ones which take advantage of their geographic or ethnic surroundings, restaurants which offer on their menu fish that swim in the nearby lakes or a kind of food that is popular in their particular section of Canada. For instance, there is an excellent Chinese restaurant in the heart of Chinatown in Vancouver that serves local crab and rock cod, a place in Edmonton and Winnipeg that serves Ukrainian perogy, and a restaurant in Waterloo county that specializes in German food. In Quebec City and Montreal I've picked out examples of French cuisine, classic and French Canadian, which are the great specialties of these two cities. All the restaurants mentioned mirror the physical and human make-up of their locality. None of them has chosen Kentucky-fried chicken as its specialty because no long-standing community of Americans from the southern states (be they ante-bellum Kentucky colonels or dirt-farming Okies) exists in Canada.

What I have written is very far from a complete account of what is good to eat and drink in Canada and of the variety of our natural ingredients and our cooking. But it is a record of my observations, and as such it reveals my passions and prejudices. If anyone has anything to add to *The Gourmet's Canada* I hope they will write to me. My omissions, I am sure, are as enormous as our country. But I am convinced, and I hope this book convinces others, that it is possible to be both fastidious and greedy in this country. The gourmet's Canada *does* exist. The gourmet's Canada will flourish if we set, and insist on, high standards, and if we accept no compromises.

What to Eat
and How to Cook It
— A Cross-Canada Tour

Broiled Squirrel vs. Barbecued Chicken

IS IT POSSIBLE to write a book about food in Canada without dwelling upon beaver-tail stew and marinated "lesser snow goose" and without expounding the virtues of elk meat over moose? There are still many regions in Canada where you can eat polar bear rather than pizza (but avoid the liver, it is literally poisonous), and where you can drink tea made from scurvy grass, instead of reinforced Tang, for a more than adequate amount of vitamin C. But those places where wild game and edible plants make common table fare are far away from where most Canadians live. Not only do urban and suburban Canadians live a long distance from the woods; most of them are quite happy to live out their lives without so much as a *soupçon* of ptarmigan fricassce. Even if we city-dwellers coud obtain the delicacies of the bush, we wouldn't eat most of them. Broiled squirrel is mentioned quite often in wild-life cookery-books as a real treat. Although the main ingredient is quite easily found in suburbia, the dish has not replaced barbecued chicken for Sunday supper popularity.

Occasionally the people in charge of Elk Island National Park in Alberta feel that Canada's buffalo population is somewhat excessive, slaughter a couple of hundred, and sell the meat on the commercial market. Butchers and restaurateurs buy the meat more in the hope of publicity than in the belief that there is a large market for buffalo steak among their customers. There is a certain demand for the meat, but its price, about one-third more per pound than beef, and the lack of an adequate supply — redundant buffaloes are not an everyday occurrence — make it less than a staple on butchers' counters. I've often eaten buffalo meat myself and have come to the conclusion that it tastes just like beefsteak; in fact, I would have been hard put to tell the difference. Why pay $2.40 a pound for buffalo porterhouse when a similar cut of beef costs $1.80? However, there is a doctor in northern Ontario who disagrees with my opinion of buffalo meat. ALBERT'S MEAT MARKET in Ottawa ships him a couple of hundred dollars' worth whenever it has a decent supply. Having once lived on buffalo, exclusively, for a year, he cannot now do without it.

Sometimes special recipes are suggested for buffalo meat, as, for example, in a small booklet called *Remarkable Recipes for Sweetgrass Buffalo* published under the auspices of the former Department of Northern Affairs and National Resources in Ottawa. ("Sweetgrass" is a trademark for the finest quality buffalo meat.) Some of these recipes have enticing names such as "baked buffalo and bear pie" and "planked charcoal-broiled sweetgrass buffalo steak, Macdonald," but they are totally interchangeable with recipes for red ribbon brand beefsteak. Incidentally, you don't have to marinate buffalo to achieve tenderness.

I am aware of five current sources of buffalo meat in Canada, all of whom purchase from the government. I am including their names and addresses in the Appendix.

Wild game is not sold commercially in Canada, as it is in England and on the Continent, unless there is a glut, as is occasionally the case with buffalo. Restaurants in Europe may make their reputation on *civet de lièvre* (hare stew), *medallions de chevreuil* (venison), and even *civet de marcassin* (young wild boar), all served during the fall hunting season; but in nine provinces of Canada this is impossible because of certain laws that call all game, including migratory birds, "a free good". A free good is like water; no one in this country has the right to sell it. Thus, a hunter can shoot a deer (if it's the right season, and if he has a licence) but normally he cannot sell it because it doesn't belong to him. Game, like water, is owned by every citizen of Canada and may be consumed, but not marketed. In Europe, the forests have traditionally belonged to royal families. The wildlife is preserved by the owner of the land primarily for sport purposes; he may, of course, start to raise it commercially, slaughtering the game for butchers and restaurants.

Not all the provincial game laws and practices are the same. In Ontario, for example, the law forbids a restaurant or hotel even to mention game on a bill of fare. In Newfoundland, it seems that the practices are a little more liberal than in the rest of Canada — perhaps because they evolved in an atmosphere closer to the English thinking on the subject than the North American. Restaurants like the CANDLELITE ROOM in St. John's, Newfoundland serve partridge, caribou and moose in season. But they must have their licence (procured from the provincial government) to serve it, and they may only buy game from a licensed hunter.

From time to time Canadian restaurants serve pheasant, but the birds are raised commercially on pheasant farms, mainly in Quebec. There is a place in Ormstown, near Montreal, CLEARBROOK GAME FARMS, that raises penned caribou and buffalo for commercial purposes. The owner has several restaurants and supplies them with the fresh game-meat. Game, when shot in the wilds, has a much higher or gamier taste than penned animals. I find the taste of commercially raised pheasant rather insipid. The frozen pheasant that is offered from time to time, at high prices, by pretentious Canadian restaurants is worse than insipid — it is utterly tasteless.

Conservation experts in Canada shake their heads at the idea of a commercial distribution of wild duck, deer and caribou. They fear that if the residents in remote areas — mostly natives — were allowed to hunt for the purpose of selling to urban outlets such as hotels, or to construction camps, the animals would go the way of the passenger pigeon. They claim it would be impossible to control distribution, and difficult to maintain a reasonable supply. But perhaps the experts exaggerate the nature of the demand for game. I suspect they are obsessed with the idea of mass production, the hallmark of virtually all foods in our society, and do not realize that the market for game will always be limited. Unfortunately, they see no virtue in Newfoundland's compromise of allowing certain restaurants a small supply of game.

For those of you who hunt, and want to hunt and eat game, the first thing to remember is that porcupines, muskrats and fish ducks are only good to eat when you are lost in the woods and starving, or drunk. The second is that old game of any kind tastes terrible. Make sure that whatever you shoot is young — don't pick the biggest goose or moose as your target if you want to eat it.

To age game properly is a tricky affair. There is a difference between the state of being properly aged, and staleness — it's ptomaine. Most expert game-cooks feel that small and feathered game should be hung for three to five days at a temperature of five or six degrees above freezing. If it is frozen, it does not age; yet if it is hung too long without being frozen it will putrify.

Big-game bear is the worst-tasting wild meat, but young bear is somewhat more edible. It is like pork and requires long cooking because it may be infected with trichinosis; many people find that even after it has been cooked a long time, young bear meat can be sickening if too much is eaten.

In case you have some of the tougher cuts of venison in

your freezer and are tired of stews, here's a recipe for venison mincemeat, invented by a lady who shot the deer.

Venison Mincemeat

3 lbs. venison	1 lb. beef suet
3 lbs. apples	1 lb. raisins
1 lb. currants	2 tbsp. cinnamon
1 tbsp. salt	1 tbsp. cloves
2 tsps. black pepper	2 tbsp. nutmeg
2 tbsp. allspice	2 cups molasses
3 cups brown sugar	juice of 5 lemons
	and grated rinds
1 quart port wine	1/2 pint rum

Simmer venison for 1 hour in barely enough water to cover. Let most of liquid cook away towards finish. Grind cooked meat in food chopper and then do the same with suet and raisins. Mix with venison. Add chopped, unpeeled apples. Add all spices and all other ingredients. Simmer for 1 hour, stirring occasionally. Store in bottles.

There are many recipe books describing how best to cook wild things, whether animal or vegetable. One of the bravest and most adventurous is a little soft-cover book written by Erika E. Gaertner called *Harvest Without Planting*. Nothing seems to faze her — she recommends lichens for their caloric value, although she warns us to boil them first with baking soda because of "their purgative principle". Lilac wine (six quarts of lilac flowers) and cattail-pollen pancakes are also recommended, but the most fearsome recipe is certainly the one for making a delicious snapping turtle soup-concentrate, for forty people. I am going to quote her instructions *in toto*.

Getting hold of a Snapping Turtle might be your first worry when you expect to make your favourite soup, but will certainly not be your last — or least. To have one of these vicious beasts on your hands can offer quite a challenge. They are relatively common in many parts of Canada and we have had some up to 40 lbs. in weight. Do not lost heart when you look at the cumbersome monster with the speed of a flash in its sharp beak. The good meal that will be your reward is worth the effort. For those that shy away from sharp instruments, the easy way out could be to drop the turtle into boiling water, like a lobster, so says the cook. But Madam, how big are your pots? Then also imagine the surprise of a casual visitor being overpowered at the door with the most distinct glue factory smell. That happens when the outside scales start coming off the shell and give us an even greater sense of helplessness. To appeal to the brave nature of your mate is really the wisest course to follow. You can hand him the hatchet, a chisel, and a hammer before you make your hasty retreat, just to make sure that he will finish his part of the job.

When you see the turtle next, you hope to receive the dismembered legs and neck, good sized chunks of meat, with all the toenails still present. Scrub well, preferably with a hard brush. Put into a roasting pan with butter or margarine. Add finely chopped onions, celery stalks and carrots, together with salt, herbs and spices. Bake in a hot oven at 400° until brown, and mix well with a cupful of flour. Bake 1/2 hour longer. When the mixture is taken out of the oven, it is ready for the soup kettle, although we prefer to remove the toenails, which are very loose, first. We use either a basic stock of diluted canned consomme or better still, a home-made chicken or turkey broth. The amount needed will vary with the amount of turtle meat. Be sure that all particles are washed out of the baking pan, and add one small can of tomato paste for three regular-sized cans of consomme. Simmer slowly for 2-3 hours. Strain. Remove the skin, pick out the meat and cut it into small pieces. Replace. You now have a turtle soup concentrate, which, depending on the original size of the turtle, can make perhaps 40 servings. If you have that much, we hope that you have a freezer, for this soup lends itself well to such storage. Only thing to remember, as you are filling your container 3/4 full, is that about 1/3 in each ought to be made of the meat. When serving time comes around, dilute the soup with an equal amount of water or additional broth, bring to simmer and correct the seasoning. A dash of tabasco and/or lemon can be added together with some sherry wine. Serve. This soup is very rich and is best accompanied with a piece of rye bread or rye crackers.†

When you decide to have snapping turtle soup for your dinner, with the turtle caught alive (how does one do that?), please invite me. It's the only way I'll ever taste it.

The Atlantic Provinces—from Cape Onion to Eel River Crossing

For many reasons it's best to start in the Atlantic provinces when talking about eating and cooking in Canada. Long-settled communities like those in Newfoundland and the Maritimes have had time to develop distinctive styles of cooking that depend a great deal upon the natural products around them, whether in the sea or upon land.

Many of the Newfoundlanders are descendants of English and Irish fishermen who came to that rocky island almost three hundred years ago. Their isolation from Canada (the nearest mainland), as well as from their ancestral homes, has created a uniqueness of cuisine and language that intrigues the mainlander. Place names like Famish Gut, Herring Neck, Turnip Cove and Cape Onion reveal what Newfoundlanders have traditionally eaten — simple foods like turnips, onions, herring. And cod. Mussels, clams, salmon, capelins (a smelt-like fish), turbot, eels, crab and the blue-fin tuna share water space with the cod, but in Newfoundland, cod is king. If you look through old recipe books, usually compiled by ladies' church-associations, there are more recipes for cod, salt and fresh, than for all other fish put together. The methods of drying cod date back 300 years. The fish lie outdoors on long wooden platforms

† Quoted by permission of Dr. Erika Gaertner, the author and publisher of *Harvest without Planting.*

called "flakes," which still may be seen in the small seaside villages, or "outports," that dot the coast of Newfoundland.

The classic Newfoundland dish, fish and brewis, is composed of salt cod, hardtack biscuits and salt pork. Fish and brewis reflects perfectly the culinary facts of life in Newfoundland. Until the second half of this century, everything was imported from Canada or overseas on slow-moving boats. Thus, pork had to be salted and biscuits had to be dry and hard for keeping. (The most common imported fruits, by the way, were dates and raisins.) The biscuits and cod are soaked overnight. Then the cod is boiled, and flaked with a fork; the hardtack biscuits are drained, heated and added to the cod, and the fried scrunchions (crispy bits of pork fat) are poured over the dish. There are variations to this theme, but essentially this is it. It still is a most popular dish, along with seal-flipper pie and jigg's dinner (see p. 181).

All these dishes are still part of Newfoundland's gastronomic way of life; they may be sampled at some of the places I describe in the chapter on regional restaurants.

For cooking at home, here is a recipe from a collection from Newfoundland and Labrador, assembled by the Friendship Unit of the United Church Women of the First United Church, Mount Pearl, Newfoundland.

Fish Loaf

1 tbsp. melted butter	1 cup soft bread crumbs
1 tbsp. flour	(or mashed potatoes)
1 cup hot milk	1 chopped egg
2 cups cooked fish	2 chopped pickles
2 beaten eggs	3 tbsp. parsley

Melt butter; add flour and blend well. Gradually add hot milk, stirring constantly. Season. Add fish, beaten eggs, bread crumbs, hard-cooked egg, pickles and parsley. Pour mixture in a greased baking dish. Place in a pan of boiling water and cook 1 hour in a moderate oven. Serve hot or cold.

Two summers ago I visited Eastport, near Terra Nova National Park and not too far from Salvage, one of the prettiest fishing villages in the world. Restaurants don't obscure the landscape in that part of the world but the Eastport tourist people will arrange a meal for you in the home of one of the fishermen, provided you give them one day's notice. All the fishermen's wives bake their own bread and serve fresh berries from their little gardens. If the season is right, fresh lobster, mussels and salmon are available, but Newfoundlanders don't hold them in as much esteem as other Canadians do. You must specify that you want fresh shellfish or else you may get canned luncheon meat — which carries a certain foreign glamour to people who can eat lobster whenever they want. What we prize is often a puzzle to Newfoundlanders. A friend of mine, standing at a dock near St. John's, asked a young boy what kind of fish was being unloaded. The boy replied, "They be lumpfish," and pressing on a fish with his boot so that the roe squished out, he added, "Some say mainlanders be eating that on toast." His contempt for what mainlanders like has a certain foundation. Lumpfish roe are those hard, little, dyed-black seeds that are misnamed caviar, often featured at smart Toronto cocktail parties.

Another way to sample Newfoundland cooking is to go out on a boat with a fisherman. It's likely that he will put some fresh-caught cod, peeled turnips, potatoes, cabbage and salt pork in a little, black cooking kettle on a "firebox" filled with kindling, pour some sea water into the kettle and let the mixture cook. After fifteen minutes or so, he will turn the pot upside down, and a beautiful and delicious hot fish mould will be ready for a picnic on the boat. You'll probably eat it with hot, very strong tea and his wife's blueberry cake.

All those strange parts of the cod — fresh tongues, cheeks and sounds (glutinous bits from the back) are available at many shops in Newfoundland, and in some restaurants. One thing to remember about cods' tongues: cook them the same day or you will never want to eat them again.

Fresh local lamb is another of Newfoundland's delicacies, but, surprisingly enough, I have been unable to find any local recipes for cooking this very fine meat.

Blueberries, partridgeberries, bakeapples, and wild cranberries are also very much a part of the cuisine of the average Newfoundlander and Maritimer. These berries grow abundantly in many parts of the Atlantic provinces. Bakeapples or cloudberries grow on small plants on barren land and look something like large yellow raspberries. They cannot be eaten without sugar. Usually they are made into a sort of preserve and served on ice cream or pancakes. Most people don't like them raw because of their seediness and extreme tartness — my enthusiasm for bakeapples is restrained even when they are cooked.

These berries grow in the northern part of Canada as well. A friend of mine was recently served preserved bakeapple canapés at a cocktail party in Inuvik in the Northwest Territories at four o'clock in the morning, along with muktuk (chunks of whale fat), dried cooney, or coney (a popular term for the fish, inconnu), and sliced caribou meat. He became a convert to Northern food — except for the muktuk.

Partridgeberries are sometimes called lingonberries, and look like a blueberry, but they are deep red in colour. They make a delicious, tart, wine-coloured jam. The fruit of a dwarf evergreen shrub, they can be found on rocky open soil in Newfoundland and Nova Scotia. The Scandinavians are wild about partridgeberries and have been importing them from Newfoundland because of their own crop failure. Home-made jams from local berries and fruits, as well as the actual berries themselves, are sold at BIDGOOD's grocery store in Goulds, in St. John's South.

Prince Edward Island strawberries compare to their English cousin for sweetness and juice. If you are on the Island in July, make sure you sample them, either in a pie or plain with cream. (Many Island churches used to have strawberry/ice-cream festivals in July — *home-made* ice-cream and fresh strawberries — marvellous.) Apples from

the Annapolis Valley are of course well known all over
Canada, but the people from Nova Scotia often put foxberries in their apple pie to give it tartness. After some in-
vestigation, I have decided that foxberries are most like
cranberries, but smaller. Apple and foxberry pie can be
something very special, especially if you make it as I suggest.
(You'll never find foxberries at your local supermarket so
buy some fresh cranberries and use them as a substitute —
they do very well.) People from the Atlantic provinces
sometimes keep their berries fresh over the winter by plac-
ing them in water — barrels of foxberries, bakeapples and
water decorate the porches of many Maritime and Newfoundland homes.

Because they keep so well, Maritimers can use foxberries
in pies all year round. Here's the recipe I like.

Foxberry (or Cranberry) and Deep Apple Pie

DOUGH

1 1/2 cups flour	1/4 cup ice water
1/2 cup shortening	1/4 cup salted butter

Cut butter and shortening into flour. Sprinkle with
water and mix lightly. Roll out dough. Makes 1
crust.

FILLING

6 apples peeled, cored and sliced

1 — 2 cups of cranberries, depending on how much
you have at hand

1/2 — 3/4 cup of brown sugar, maple sugar or honey
(the more cranberries you have, the more sugar
you need)

Mix filling ingredients together and put into
buttered baking dish. Place rolled out dough on
top. Sprinkle crust with cinnamon and sugar. Bake
about 30 to 40 minutes at 375°. The fruit will cook
much quicker than the crust.

The Annapolis Valley is one of the most beautiful and fertile areas of Canada. Its fruits and vegetables are exported all over the North American continent. But one of its finest products, the Gravenstein apple, was sacrificed to the myth that an apple must be red in order to sell. About thirty or forty years ago a great many of the orchards in the Annapolis Valley were cultivating the yellowish, orangy, slightly tart Gravenstein, a fine eating and cooking apple that is thought to have originated in Germany over 200 years ago (Some people say that the Gravenstein is the only kind to use if you want a perfect apple pie.) However, someone convinced the farmers that the apple was not marketable because of its colour. The apple that would bring future profits was the red McIntosh, they were told. So McIntosh stock was grafted on to the Gravenstein trees, and the orchard owners in the Annapolis Valley, Nova Scotia — the only area of extensive cultivation of the Gravenstein in Canada — began to emulate those in British Columbia. But to this day the McIntoshes of the Maritimes have never been as successful as their west-coast rivals.

Many of the old-timers claim that the Gravenstein of thirty years ago is a far better all-round apple than any McIntosh. But then they say, "It's orangy yellow and won't sell because the customer doesn't think it's ripe enough to eat." Of course, the answer to this nonsense is the great success in Canada of the Granny Smith apple from New Zealand. It is large, tart, and green, green, green, not a blotch of red anywhere — and it sells like mad. What would happen to those rich, vinous and aromatic Gravensteins with their crisp, juicy white flesh, if they were put on the counters again? For those who must have a red apple, there is a reddish Gravenstein with some yellow ground colour, which is used for the fresh market; then there is the yellow Gravenstein, which is now primarily used for processing. Why isn't the crimson-blush strain of the Gravenstein as widely planted as the McIntosh?

The Maritimers who gather wild berries and cultivate

fruits are a rather special combination of peoples; the Scotch, Acadian and German mixture of backgrounds adds distinctiveness to the food eaten in the region. Barley broth, varieties of scones and bannock (flat, round, non-sweet cakes baked on a griddle or in the oven), and above all, the ingredient that seems to be put into most dishes in the Maritimes — oatmeal — belong to the influence of the Scotch. Oatmeal figures in recipes for meat and onions, alcoholic drinks (Atholl Brose), candies, whipped-cream desserts and, of course, breakfast porridge. There is even a recipe for using left-over porridge — the remainder goes into the meat loaf for supper. Of course, the oatmeal you use should be the Scotch variety, the kind that has to be soaked overnight and carefully stirred over boiling water, if you want a real porridge in the morning. The quick-cooking kind so popular now is only for cheaters. It is not necessary, however, to soak the Scotch-type oatmeal if you want to use it in cookies and bread; if you are ambitious, you can toast it in the oven, as the French toast almonds, so that whatever you are making will have a richer flavour.

Scotch, Acadians and Newfoundlanders used molasses as a sweetener, rather than sugar, for reasons of economy and availability. (Did you know that eating baked beans with horse-radish is a common tradition in the country areas of the Maritimes? "Cuts the sweetness of the molasses in the beans," they say.)

This widespread use of molasses and oatmeal has given birth to many thrifty and novel recipes that characterize the cuisine of the region. Oatmeal-molasses bread is per-haps the most typical recipe I could give, since people from the Atlantic provinces pride themselves on their baking, especially their bread. The wife of a well-known politician from the Montreal area spent some time in Nova Scotia about ten or twelve years ago. When she asked, at a local tea party, where she could buy some good bread or cakes — like the ones at the reception — her inquiry was met with embarrassed silence. The shortcomings of the politician's

wife were obvious to all the ladies there, who of course do
their own baking.

For those who have some Maritime-Scotch blood in their
veins, and for those who wish they had, here is a recipe for
molasses and oatmeal bread that succeeds even for the person who makes bread about once in four years. The recipe
is my amalgamation of all the molasses-and-oatmeal-bread
recipes I've read in the cook-books of the Atlantic provinces
— and it works.

Molasses and Oatmeal Bread

1 cup Scotch-type oatmeal
2 cups boiling water
1 tbsp. or 1 envelope dried yeast poured on top of
  1/2 cup warm water flavoured with 1 tsp. ground
  ginger
3 tbsp. butter
1/2 cup molasses
3 tsp. salt
3 cups whole-wheat flour
1/4 cup wheat germ or plain flour
2 cups all-purpose flour

Let the yeast sit in the water for about 10 minutes.
Make sure all particles are dissolved; if not, mix
well. Pour boiling water over oatmeal while yeast is
sitting.

Let the water and the oatmeal cool slightly, and
then add yeast, molasses, salt and butter, blending
well. Now add 3 cups of whole wheat flour and 1/4
cup wheat germ, beating hard. (Use a large bowl and
a wooden spoon.) Add 2 cups of plain flour.

It will now be impossible to beat further; kneading time has come round. You must knead for about
15 minutes on a floured board, pressing down with
the palms of your hands and turning over the
dough so that it will get smooth and elastic. It is
hard work, so if there is a willing child around give
him or her a piece of the dough to knead; it will
do it, as well as your child, no harm. When you
think you've had enough, form the dough into a

big ball, put it in a greased bowl, and brush the top of the dough with soft butter. Let it rise in a warm place for about 1 1/2 to 2 hours. (I open my oven door flat, turn on the oven to 150°, or warm, put the bowl of rising dough on the door and let the warm air from the oven waft over it.)

After the dough has doubled in bulk, punch it down, divide it into 2 parts, and put the 2 loaves into greased loaf pans. If it is now midnight, and you don't feel like waking the rest of the household at 4 o'clock in the morning for a taste of hot home-made bread, place the pans containing the dough in the refrigerator, with weights on top of the dough (cans of soup or something like that), and go to sleep. The next morning, or whenever, take the pans out of the refrigerator and allow the loaves to rise a second time for about 2 hours the same way as before.

Bake at 375° for 40 minues. The loaves should be ready if the crust sounds hollow when you tap it. It is a very crusty loaf with a slightly sweet flavour. Eat some of it immediately. This bread also keeps well (and freezes beautifully).

You might like a traditional Scotch accompaniment to your warm bread. I would suggest marmalade made from bitter oranges. Here's a recipe.

Easy Seville Marmalade

12 bitter oranges (Seville type — they appear in
   the stores in February)
12 cups water
5 cups sugar
1 lemon
Boil oranges and lemon in water until very soft — about 1/2 hour. Remove from water. Cut in little pieces, letting water simmer all the while. Add sugar to the water. Let cook for 5 minutes. Throw in oranges and lemon, pits and all, and let cook for 20 minutes or until 220°. Pour into sterilized jars.

You may cook it longer so that the colour will turn amber, but you will have less marmalade.

The Anglo-Celtic cooking traditions in the Atlantic provinces are not based only on oatmeal and molasses. All the berries and fruits that grow so well there because of the sea air are made into dumplings and puddings, called grunts and duffs respectively, as well as into upside-down cakes and muffins. The fruit can lie on top, on the bottom, or in the middle. Newfoundlanders and Maritimers are pretty much liberated on this subject.

Despite its name, Nova Scotia is also the home of a German community which settled in Lunenberg around 1793. To this day, these Germans are often called Dutch by the other Nova Scotians because of the German word Deutsch. They formed the *avant-garde* wing of the slightly more than one million people of German origin who now live in various parts of Canada, particularly Ontario and the West.

The names of recipes from the German communities of Nova Scotia have been Anglicized, or, more properly, bastardized into such terms as Solomon Gundy (from salmagundi, a marinated herring), Dutch mess (a mixture of cod, salt pork and potatoes, fried and then boiled in cream), and, of course, sauerkraut, turnip kraut and cole (kohl) slaw. Cucumbers are often served in a salad dressing made of sour cream, and soups are enriched with potatoes, sauerkraut and salt pork. I've tasted sauerkraut from Tancook Island, Nova Scotia, but I've never tasted turnip kraut, which must be pretty potent.

Another ingredient popular among Maritimers is carrots. Sweet carrot puddings, carrot breads, cakes, and even carrot jams are mentioned in many of the ladies' committee recipe-books that the churches and business associations bring out. It's difficult to say whether this penchant for carrots originated with the Lunenberg settlers and then influenced the Anglo-Celts or whether everyone in Nova Scotia just loves carrots. Putting carrots in desserts is a custom that is more common on the Continent than in the British Isles, so it's likely that the Germans in Nova Scotia brought the habit over with them 200 years ago.

Hodge-podge is a dish of vegetables which includes beans and cauliflower, parboiled, and then simmered with cream and bits of pork. The style of cooking looks Lunenberg but if corn is added to the recipe it becomes a New England succotash — a reminder of the New Englanders who came to live in the Maritimes after the American Revolution.

Before I get off the topic of vegetables in the Maritimes the most famous of them all needs to be mentioned — fiddlehead ferns. Many Canadian cookery-books describe the experience of setting out during a week in May to pick the yet-unfurled tips of the ostrich fern as an unmatched aesthetic and gastronomic event. A lot of ostrich fern grows in shady, moist woods in New Brunswick, and I dare say in many other places in the wilds of Canada. But if it's raining that week, or if you can't seem to find an adequate patch of fiddlehead near where you live, it will be necessary to resort to the frozen variety which is available in most specialty shops and some supermarkets. Personally, I don't recommend them. The frozen kind, no matter how they're cooked, are alway soggy. Even the merest warming up seems to cause them to lose any distinction they might have had when picked fresh in the wood. I have some ostrich ferns growing in my back yard in Ontario, but three tips gathered every second day would not excite even the most enthusiastic gourmet.

Although the Acadians of New Brunswick are French-speaking, they feel themselves as removed in cultural background from the Quebecois as they are from their English-speaking New Brunswick neighbours. Many dishes that Acadians eat are unknown to French Canadians in Quebec, especially those dishes that include grated potato. *Poutine rapée* is such a dish, a dumpling made of grated raw and cooked potatoes and pork fat, boiled for two hours. It is heavy — a couple of *poutines* as a morning snack should keep you happy chopping wood till sundown. They are still extremely popular in the Moncton area, as witnessed by the several drive-ins and restaurants that advertise *poutine rapée* to take out. The word *poutine* sounds almost German. Would the early German settlers have influenced the cooking style of the Acadians as well as that of the Anglo-Celts?

Pâté à la rapure, or rappy pie, as it is known to English-speaking Maritimers, is a very complicated dish that needs chicken, pork fat, grated potato and onions to make it authentic. Sometimes hare and veal are added and layers of biscuit dough are interspersed between the meat and vegetables. Rappy pie is the sort of dish that you can serve at a family festivity — it's enough of a culinary *tour de force* to attract the more indifferent cousins to come for Sunday dinner, and it is certainly sufficiently filling to satisfy the appetites of the numerous children at any clan gathering.

Chicken *fricot* is a popular Acadian dish that is easier to make than *pâté à la rapure,* but it is not commonly found in Canadian recipe books. Romeo Leblanc, who was born on a farm outside Moncton, gave me this recipe. He makes it for his family on Sundays:

Chicken Fricot

"Find two hens and chop each one in four (after they are killed). Cover them with cold water and ten chopped onions — salt to taste. Boil three hours, or until the meat comes off the bones. Put in the refrigerator until fat comes to top. Skim off all the fat.

Remove as much skin as possible from the chicken, and take out the big bones from the soup. Now put 1/2 cup of dried summer savoury in the soup. Simmer one hour. Chop 5 potatoes and 3 carrots and cook in the soup 30 minutes before dinner time. The vegetables should hold their shape and be slightly crisp.

While the soup is simmering make some baking powder dumplings and drop them in for the last 30 minutes with the potatoes and carrots."

DUMPLINGS FOR CHICKEN FRICOT

1 cup sour cream	2 tsp. baking powder
1 1/2 cups flour	1 tsp. baking soda

Mix dry ingredients and add sour cream. Form little balls for dumplings. If batter is too dry, add a little water. Drop into boiling soup, lower heat, and let simmer for 30 minutes.

Do not be shocked by the amount of savoury used. This is a very popular herb among Acadians — every family has bunches of it hanging in the kitchen. Romeo's non-Acadian wife, from Montreal, says that the amount of savoury used in the recipe is just right. She brought me a jar of *oignons salés* as a present from Romeo in New Brunswick. I've never seen this before anywhere; some of my Quebecois friends say that it must be truly Acadian. They've never used it in their cuisine. *Oignons salés* consists of the tops of green onions kept in salt and some water (they keep all winter this way). It looks like a bunch of seaweed preserved in crystals of sea salt. Acadians chop up the *oignons salés* and throw it and bits of bacon into their pan-fried potatoes. Potatoes are the Acadian staple; pan-fried is the commonest method of cooking them, so a lot of *oignons salés* are needed.

All four Atlantic provinces provide North Americans with the finest lobsters in the world — the most important income producer of all species in the Maritime waters. As I mentioned before, lobster is sometimes a great bore to people here — a bore, in the sense that it's not as much a luxury food as it is in central Canada.

Helen Wilson, the daughter of a Nova Scotia lobster fisherman, writes in her book, *Tales From Barrett's Landing,* how she hated revealing the contents of her lunch box to the rest of the kids at school: ". . . we ate lobster because we were poor. I remember that sometimes Mama put fresh boiled lobster in our school lunches and we always threw them away on our way to school. We were ashamed to let the other kids see them because they would know that we didn't have anything else to eat in the house."

Mind you, when you buy lobster in a restaurant in the Atlantic provinces the prices are not all that cheap. If you are camping, buy it directly from a fisherman or at a lobster pound.

During the summer months many local people turn their kitchens and parlours into make-shift restaurants for the tourists — with lobster as the *specialité de la maison*. If you don't mind the homey ambience, stop at a fisherman's house that has a handwritten card in the window or on the gate saying, LOBSTER — $2.50 (or perhaps $3.00), and fill yourself with boiled lobster, home-made bread, pie and tea. You just might be lucky enough to sample some home-brewed hard cider or something even harder — moonshine.

Times are changing, and lobster prices are going sky high. Next summer the prices on the cardboard in the window might be double. The demand is increasing and the lobster population, especially around Prince Edward Island, is being threatened. A new and prosperous industry has developed on the Island, the cultivation in the sea of Irish moss, for carrageenin. It has been discovered that this substance, which is extracted from the moss, makes an effective blood coagulant; because of its medical value, it has a profitable market. However, many scientists feel that the rakes used for gathering the moss disturb lobster beds and reduce the quantity of lobster wherever the moss grows. It seems as if Islanders might have to decide between lobster and Irish moss. People with whom I have discussed this from Prince Edward Island say that in the short run the moss might be more important, but in the long run the lobster industry is far more significant. Tomorrow, or next year, science will discover an even better coagulant than Irish moss, and *its* market will disappear, but the markets for lobster will always increase. Even today, the demand is greater than the supply, and the prognosis is that more and more people will want a boiled lobster for their fancy dinner.

There is a variety of lobster caught in the deep sea that up until now has never really been commercially fished. This variety can weigh up to twenty-five pounds but according to fishermen who have eaten them, they are as tasty and tender as a baby lobster. Marketing fresh twenty-to-twenty-five-pound lobsters might be tricky. Imagine a seafood restaurant in Toronto with live deep-sea lobsters of monstrous proportions clunking around in the fresh-water tanks. Hitchcock could do a lot with that scene.

If the taste of freshly boiled lobster hasn't begun to pall for you, you may want to discover the best way to cook it: Put the live lobster in some salted water — sea water if possible — bring to a boil and let it cook twelve minutes, sixteen if you're worried (lobsters lose their tenderness if overcooked). Then cool it off slightly under fresh, cold water. Crack and eat it.

Scallops are harvested on the ocean floor off Georges Bank near Nova Scotia, and in the Bay of Fundy, the well-known Digby scallop being fished in that bay. In Canada, only about one-third of the soft parts of the scallop is thought to be of commercial value. But in the scallop fisheries of Ireland, the United Kingdom, France and Australia, the roe (gonads) are marketed along with the adductor muscles (what we call scallops when we're buying fish). The orange roe has a particularly fine flavour, but if it is to be sold commercially the scallop shells must not be shucked, as they are now, directly on the boats. All scallops sold in Europe and the United Kingdom containing the roe are sold in the half shell.

As is the case with many of our fish resources, the supply of scallops is dwindling off the Georges Bank. The catch is diminishing in quantity and the scallops landed are under-sized. If too many young scallops are fished out, there will, of course, be fewer mature ones the following year and a smaller scallop production in the long run. Wholesale prices have more than doubled in four years and the Canadian contribution to the US market had declined from over ninety per cent in 1969 to slightly under sixty per cent last year.

Here is the way I prepare scallops — while they last. This is simple, yet different. The scallops are crisp, but not overdone. Although garlic adds a lot to this dish, it's not absolutely necessary to put it in if you don't like it. But don't skimp on the parsley.

Parsley Scallops

1 — 1 1/2 lbs. scallops
enough flour to coat scallops
1/2 bunch parsley, finely chopped
2 tbsp. butter and 2 tbsp. oil (more if necessary)
salt, pepper, lemons
2 cloves garlic, crushed (or more)

Rinse scallops and pat dry. Place in a paper bag filled with flour. Shake until all are well coated. Place scallops on a board or plate. Cut in half or quarters with scissors unless the scallops are extremely small. Make sure all excess flour is removed. Put butter and oil in a large frying pan; heat until it sizzles and then throw in the scallops. Cook on moderate heat from 5 to 10 minutes or until they begin to brown.

Add 1/2 bunch of chopped parsley and the garlic; stir scallops, parsley and garlic for about 2 minutes. Serve immediately with lemon wedges. Serves 4.

(An easy way to chop parsley is with the blender: Fill the blender 1/3 full of water. Tear 1/2 bunch of parsley frizz into 2 or 3 parts. Place them in blender and buzz several seconds. Drain water from parsley in a strainer. Your parsley will be expertly chopped.)

Unlike the scallops, which appear to be diminishing from the shores of Nova Scotia, the oyster is making a comeback, especially in New Brunswick. Oysters can be harvested both in a "wild state," on public beds, and from leased beds, where they are cultivated. Prince Edward Island has long been a producer of the well-known Malpeque oyster — a name that seems to be applied to all Canadian varieties. Barring disaster, natural or otherwise, a potential oyster harvest that may in a few years time be worth a million dollars annually is at this moment growing in the chill waters of Buctouche Bay in New Brunswick. Driving through Buctouche, a motorist will notice many rafts floating on the bay surface. Suspended beneath them are a number of "collectors" with corrugated surfaces holding thousands of oyster babies which were collected during the spawning season. Buctouche fishermen are studying, under the auspices of the federal government, the latest methods in oyster culture, as well as the organization of fishermen's co-operatives. The financing will continue for the next few years — after that it is hoped that the fishermen will be able to go it alone — or that the province will pick up the tab. A study made by the Woods Hole Oceanographic Institute in Massachusetts predicted that the industry had a fifty-million-dollar annual sales potential if proper methods of culture were adopted. The suspension method used in Buctouche is considered a better one than raising oysters in the bottom of the ocean: they are less vulnerable to predators and their supply of food — plankton — is greater.

There are a number of other fish of the Maritimes that a gourmet would appreciate. A great delicacy of the St. John and Hudson rivers in New Brunswick is spring shad. Fresh-caught and broiled, it's a remarkable dish. It is plentiful and cheap, and has a marvellous flavour. Fresh-caught mackerel is available all over the Maritimes and, prepared correctly (do not overcook), is also a fish to remember. Mackerel must, however, be absolutely fresh; unfortunately, it does not ship well.

Five to ten years ago the sweet little shrimps in the Bay of Fundy were totally ignored by the fishing industry. Some Scandinavian businessmen were visiting the Maritimes and convinced the locals of their market. It is now possible to buy them, shelled, frozen in plastic bags. Some of the ships in the area, and canneries, sell them fresh-cooked, with the shell on — they are sweeter that way.

Try also to get some queen crab, now called snow crab, from the Bay of Chaleur or elsewhere in the eastern part of the Gulf of St. Lawrence. They're smaller than the king crab of the North Pacific, and some consider that their flesh is more tender and better flavoured than the Pacific variety.† As with the shrimp, it's only recently that this great delicacy has begun to be marketed. When you're in the area of the Gulf of St. Lawrance, this is something that shouldn't be missed.

You should also try the smelts that are found in streams that run from the shore along Northumberland Strait (Cumberland County is one good source). They can often be picked up in baskets or scoop shovels, so large are their numbers.

It is not possible to discuss what people in the Atlantic provinces eat without mentioning their finest product. The Atlantic salmon, or salmon (salmo) salar, is in a class by itself for delicacy of taste, texture and flavour. Practically everyone who cares in British Columbia will object to this statement, but in my opinion none of the five different species found off the western coast can compare to the salmon salar in gastronomic quality. Unlike the British Columbia salmon, which dies after spawning, the east-coast salmon may return to spawn several times. Salmon salar is related to the trout family — certainly an aristocratic connection. Unfortunately, there is much less Atlantic salmon on the market than there is of the Pacific variety, and distributors and fishermen have been complaining that it is becoming scarcer every year. In fact, the east-coast salmon fishery is only about one-twentieth the size of the west-coast catch.

The reasons for the increasing scarcity are strongly dis-

† But many Maritime restaurants prefer to serve Alaska king crab because it is cheaper.

puted. Some people blame over-fishing, others industrial pollution. Some claim the salmon's fate was sealed when American nuclear submarines discovered the salmon's feeding ground between Greenland and Baffin Island, in Davis Strait; still others deny that this has been a factor. Canadians put much of the blame on Danish fishermen, who swoop down on the salmon before they spawn with equipment sophisticated enough to harvest more large fish than the number taken by the combined efforts of all of Canada's mainland fishermen.

In 1971, the Danish catch went up thirty per cent, while everyone else's plunged. The number of salmon returning to spawn in the rivers of the Atlantic provinces has dropped by eighty per cent since 1967, and the catch in these waters has decreased by a similar percentage in the same period. As a member of the International Commission for the Northwest Atlantic Fisheries, Canada has been seeking an immediate ban on all high-seas fishing for Atlantic salmon. So far, all that has been achieved is a tentative undertaking by Denmark to phase out its high-seas operation by 1976.

In desperation, the Canadian government has decided, subject to annual review, to ban salmon fishing for six years on the St. John, the Miramichi and the Restigouche rivers in New Brunswick, and in the Port aux Basques area of southwest Newfoundland. (There is no ban on most of the salmon that return to the streams of Labrador and Newfoundland because they do not go to Greenland to feed.) This step has been taken partly in the hope, naive perhaps, that such a regional ban will shame the Danes into following in Canada's footsteps and agreeing to a ban in the Northwest Atlantic.

In the meantime, is the Canadian taxpayer in effect subsidizing the Danish fishing industry? If the Danes do not agree to an international ban on high-seas salmon fishing, do we end up paying for pollution abatement and salmon research facilities that only benefit the Danes? The Danes spend no money on trying to preserve the salmon. We preserve — they scoop up the fish.

However, as noted above, there may be several reasons for the diminishing number of salmon. There is also the problem of the sports fishermen. No one is stopping them from fishing — perhaps because the industry that caters to tourists is not without some clout. It is the poor commercial fisherman whose life is disrupted. Industrial pollution kills off many of the salmon in the Canadian inland streams, and hydro-electric dams make spawning difficult. There are successful salmon hatcheries, but they cannot assure the total life cycle of the fish.

(A ban now on salmon fishing seems to be necessary. But we must not overreact, as some officials feel we did with the baby seal. Panicky public outcry, domestic and international, stopped the seal hunt. Some biologists maintain that not only was it unnecessary to ban the seal hunt; from the point of view of wild-life preservation, the hunt actually maintained a balance of nature that is now very much disturbed. Too many seals diminish the amount of certain species of fish — a worm passed on to them from the seals makes the fish diseased. Besides the upset in the balance of nature that results from the ban, the far-from-prosperous people living in that region are deprived of a traditional source of income. Now I'm going to say something that will cause sheer hysteria among animal lovers: the Canadian gourmet is missing out on something rather special too — baby seals are good to eat. Let's hope the Atlantic salmon will be preserved — but without the same hysterical treatment from the public that the seal issue received.)

There is an ironic note on the scarcity of the Atlantic salmon. The terms of the contract made out a hundred years ago between loggers and the pulp and paper companies were excellent examples of indentured labour. Yet even these companies were forced by the adamant loggers to put one condition into the contract: salmon was not to be served at meals more than three times a week! In some respects, those were the good old days.

There is a very easy way to cook a whole salmon, or even sections of one.

Salmon Cooked in Foilwrap

fresh dill (a whole bunch)
salt and freshly ground pepper
lemon slices
bay leaf
about 1/4 cup butter

Place the salmon on heavy-duty foilwrap. Arrange everything else under or on top of salmon. Dot with butter. Seal foilwrap so that no juices can seep out. Bake in 350° oven for 40 minutes or until the thickest part of the fish is flaky. Plunge a skewer into fish; if it flakes right through, the fish is right.

Serve hot, with the juices in the foil poured over it, along with extra lemon and melted butter. If you wish to serve it cold, let the fish cool before removing it from the foil.

Because of its scarcity, the Atlantic salmon is used far less for smoking than that of the west coast. Toronto smokehouses like the HARBORD FISH COMPANY smoke British Columbia salmon almost exclusively, and Willi Krauch, a transplanted Dane who runs a small smokehouse in, absurdly enough, Tangiers, Nova Scotia, often imports salmon from the west coast, even though the Atlantic ocean is not a thousand feet from his door. However, in Nain, Labrador, a modern smokehouse with kilns and freezers, operated entirely by Eskimos, exists for the purpose of processing the Atlantic salmon, trout and char that are still abundant along the northern coast. Ian Strachan, a food technologist who has organized this factory, has two of the necessary qualifications for making the equivalent of Scotch smoked-salmon, considered by gourmets to be the best in the world: A Scotsman himself, he learned the techniques of smoking salmon from experts there; also, the salmon used in Labrador is the same species of fish that the Scots use. Normally, hardwood like oak is used in Scotland for smoking the fish, but oak trees do not exactly flourish in the north of Labrador. However, blackberry bushes do, and they make the fuel for the fire of Nain's salmon smokehouse.

Using his technical knowledge and what is locally available in the way of ingredients (materials and manpower), Strachan has created a productive factory that employs sixty-five people, all Eskimo, including forty women, who do the same work and get the same pay as the men. In one operation, Ian has established a *potentially* profitable industry (at the moment it is still financed by the federal government) that satisfies the instincts of the gourmet who likes to eat well-prepared food of the region; the idealism of those who wish to see the Eskimos make the most of themselves, in the twentieth-century, materialistic, sense; and the women's liberation movement. Canadian taxpayers might be satisfied shortly as well, because Ian has sold 30,000 pounds of his smoked salmon, his total production for the year, to BIDGOOD's of Newfoundland. If he can produce more next year, perhaps the big hotels and the specialty food shops in Toronto and Montreal will get a chance to buy it. I have tasted his salmon in St. John's, Newfoundland and I find that it has more of an after-taste than Scotch smoked-salmon because of the fumes of the blackberry bushes, but the taste is pleasant, almost fruity. The quality of the salmon used is high — prime salmon, smoked as soon as it is fished out of the water, and then graded for quality and size and texture before freezing. Don't shake your head because it is frozen. Most of the smoked salmon you eat, whether it is British Columbia or Atlantic, has been frozen at one time. GOLDY's DELICATESSEN in Toronto sells fresh, unfrozen salmon that has just been smoked by the HARBORD FISH COMPANY, but the British Columbia salmon used by the HARBORD FISH COMPANY often has been frozen and then defrosted for smoking. If the smoked fish must be frozen, it should be the whole side of salmon and not just little slices — this is in order to preserve the texture and juiciness of the fish. The Labrador salmon has excellent texture, despite the freezing process. Note that smoked char, for those who have tasted it, is equally as good as smoked salmon; the taste is rich and subtle.

Smoked salmon should be served with lemon wedges, capers and buttered brown bread, and, of course, eaten as a first course.

Quebec—From Lac au Saumon to Oka

The Quebec of today retains certain characteristics that reflect its inheritance of gastronomic excellence and rural background. Some marketing facts used by sophisticated advertising agencies reveal that Quebec is truly a province "not like the others".

Quebec eats less frozen food than the rest of Canada — Quebecers still like their meats and vegetables as fresh as possible. Quebec consumes eighty times more molasses than the rest of Canada (despite the relatively high consumption in the Maritimes) — an astonishing figure. The old-fashioned rural cuisine of Quebec uses many recipes with molasses as a sweetener. Quebec drinks three times as much fresh orange juice as the rest of Canada — another sign that the Quebecois knows the difference between the natural and the denatured. Quebec prefers fruit-flavoured candies to mint-flavoured ones. I can't draw any profound sociological conclusions from this fact.

In Quebec, anything chocolate goes. Brillat Saverin, the gourmet's authority on all matters of serious gastronomy, said that chocolate cures emotional suffering, remedies feminine beauty and is helpful to those who labour in the pulpit or the courtroom. French Canadians are very sensible to like chocolate. They have more than their share of lawyers and priests, as well as beautiful women; and suffering of the spirit is not exactly unknown in their literature. *L'homme torturé* is a Quebec phenomenon.

If you are in the company of several Quebecois and conversation is flagging, bring up the subject of food. The question "What's the best recipe for *tourtière?*" will result in raising spirits as well as controversy. "You put cinnamon in *tourtière?* I have never heard of that; cloves, yes, but real *tourtière* does not have cinnamon." However, someone will remember an old aunt who lived in the Gaspé region who did just that. In the midst of such a conversation I once mentioned a rather unorthodox recipe for *tourtière* in the volume from the Time-Life series called

American Cooking: New England (it includes all of Quebec) which prescribed that tomatoes should be mixed with the meat. "Sheer vandalism, ignorance," was the response. But I knew that a few of the doubters would go home and secretly try the tomato addition in their own kitchens. All this is to show that the strong gastronomic thread that runs throughout the history of Quebec is still present. The thread is doubled: one strand is rural and regional, that is to say Canadian, and the other is urban and French, that is to say, from France.

Tourtière, ragoût de boulettes (see recipe, p. 52), dumplings or eggs boiled in maple syrup, yellow pea soup — some of these dishes are adaptations of old Norman cuisine to ingredients found in Canada 350 years ago. Given the occupations of the majority of French Canadians at that time, and until well into this century — farming, fishing and lumbering — the food had to be filling and cheap, as well as tasty. Pork and beans, pies made with three crusts, desserts of maple sugar and thick cream poured over bread, were calorically necessary for their physically taxing rural life. Of the recipes I'm going to give, four are for pies of various sorts: *tourtière, cipaille* (these two are meat pies), backwoods pie, and *tarte à la ferlouche* (sugar pie). I don't think this is because I have a weakness for pies or have simply made a bad choice of recipes. Pastry crusts are typical of the rather heavy cuisine which is characteristic of Quebec regional cooking. Perhaps that has something to do with the Canadian climate — a thick crust helps to keep warm what's inside. This reasoning doesn't seem to apply to sugar pie or to the three-layered blueberry pie of the Lac St.-Jean area, so I won't press it.

Alongside this heavy, regional style of cooking, the seigneurial class, or the upper- and middle-class urban French Canadians, produced the classical and bourgeois cuisine described in recipe books published in France. (This style of cooking influenced not only Quebec, of course, but the whole Western world.) Just as Scotch scones and roly-poly pudding were common to the cuisine of English-speaking Canada in the last century, typical French dishes such as *coq au vin, bûche de noël* and *crème caramel* were popular among the wealthier French Canadians living in Montreal and Quebec City. Far more of the long-established restaurants in these two cities serve the cooking of France than the cuisine of Quebec. In fact, surprisingly few restaurants in the province specialize in the local cooking traditions of the Quebecois; however, the number of such places has recently been increasing.

Today, of course, most French Canadians, like everyone else in Canada, live in the city and work behind desks. Their grandfather's daily intake of 5000 calories would give contemporary French Canadians a heart attack. However, individual recipes, like pea soup, *tarte au sucre, ragoût de boulettes,* and roast veal and pork, as well as *tourtière,* are still popular, as are all recipes containing maple syrup.

Pork has been a mainstay of French-Canadian cooking for over 300 years and it is still the second most popular meat in Canada — after beef. It is always one of the first foods mentioned when I ask Quebec people what their families used to eat. Pork, in a variety of forms, is the base ingredient of a number of traditional dishes such as *cretons* and *tourtière,* and continues to be a mainstay of French-Canadian cooking, whether roasted, fried or ground, eaten with beans or bread, in a *pâté,* or in many other products. My impression is that pork fat is more widely used in Quebec and in the Maritimes than it is in France.

Cretons, or *grattons,* is a sort of meat spread made from pork that is simmered for a very long time with onions and various spices, including cinnamon. It solidifies when cold and makes a very good filling for sandwiches, or a cracker spread. *Cretons* is so popular among French Canadians that big companies like Belle Fermière make their own commercial brand and sell it on supermarket counters. However, if you want to regulate the amount of fat you're eating, you can easily make a leaner variety yourself. Some recipes call for melting down four pounds of leaf lard, but this amount would do horrendous things to your cholesterol count. It's not necessary to use so much fat. Take a pound or so of ordinary ground pork (if the butcher is nice, ask him to give it a second grinding) and place it in a saucepan with two chopped onions, garlic, a teaspoon of cinnamon, dry mustard and sage or thyme, perhaps a ground raw carrot, enough water to cover very slightly, and a piece of salt pork. Simmer for one and one half to two hours, adding more water to prevent burning. You will have a good meat spread that is solid when cooled but not too fatty.

Have you ever passed by a supermarket counter in Montreal or Ottawa and noticed a plastic container holding a dark brown jelly with a layer of fat on top? This is *graisse de rôti*, another very popular spread, put out by Belle Fermière. It is made from the reduction of the juice and drippings of a cooked pork roast, mixed with some water. The jelly is not fat at all and has a very strong meaty flavour. Besides being used as a sort of butter-like spread on bread, it is sometimes added to sauces for more enrichment.

For the adventurous, I would suggest a *tourtière* with some tomatoes thrown in.

Tourtière with Tomato

PASTRY

2 1/2 cups flour	1/4 lb. butter
2 ice-cream scoops of shortening	
1 tsp. thyme	1 egg
a little cold water	

Combine as for pie crust — makes top and bottom crust.

FILLING

3/4 lb. ground pork	3 onions, sliced
3/4 lb. ground beef	garlic, ginger and cinnamon, 1 tsp. of each
1/4 lb. salt pork, cut into cubes	
3 cooked potatoes, cut into cubes	
1 can tomatoes (14 oz.)	

Put salt pork in good-size frying pan. Let it cook about 6 minutes and then add garlic, onions and meat. Stir well and cook 5 more minutes. Add tomatoes, potatoes and spices. Simmer for 3/4 of an hour. Let it cool, and then place on top of rolled-out bottom crust. Cover with remaining crust and bake in oven for 45 minutes at 350°. (You may make this in advance and freeze it before baking.)

All quantities given are approximate. There is no reason why you may not have more or less pork or beef or onions.

Another recipe that is quite easy to make and very typical of what is still eaten now in Quebec is *ragoût de boulettes*. Mrs. Lemay, my housekeeper, makes it.

Ragoût de Boulettes

2 pork hocks	1 lb. of ground veal
1 lb. hamburger or	browned flour or
ground pork	instant-blending flour
2 Spanish onions,	ginger
chopped	parsley
2 cups water	cloves
1 or 2 eggs	2 slices bread
cinnamon and garlic	
salt and pepper to taste	

Brown the pork hocks and then add the onions and water. In the meantime, combine the ground veal, ground pork or beef, spices and parsley. Take 2 slices of bread; soak them in water and squeeze them through your fingers to form a paste; add to the meat mixture along with the raw eggs. Shape into meat balls. Place the meat balls on top of the simmering hocks and onions and allow to cook about 20 minutes.

Make a paste of browned flour and a little milk or water and add it to the stew. If you don't have a box of browned flour and you don't feel like browning a little over a frying pan yourself, add some instant-blending flour to the stew.

It's best to cook the *ragoût* the day before you plan to eat it so you will have a chance to skim off the fat after it cools. The pork hocks and spices give this family supper dish a certain distinction.

A long time ago many French Canadians used to cook their meats in an iron kettle, called a chaudron, which was usually suspended over an open fire. You would have to look far and wide in Outremont today to find this phenomenon. Nevertheless, certain excellent recipes have evolved from this cooking technique.

Veau dans le Chaudron

I was given this recipe by Mme Anita Cadieux of Washington, D.C., formerly of Quebec City. Veal must be juicy and flavourful: too often it is treated as pork and cooked far too long. The secret is the retention of juices, which makes this roast veal into a whole new eating experience.

6 — 7 lb. roast of veal (preferably the rump)
1 medium-size red cabbage
1 large clove of garlic
1 cup or more, cider or beer
1 cup of chicken or beef stock
2 apples
2 large Spanish onions
salt and crushed pepper
4 cloves
2 or 3 slices of fresh side-pork

Set oven at 350°. A heavy cast-iron casserole or covered roaster should be used.

Slice the cabbage, onions and apples. Mix together, along with garlic and cloves and lots of crushed pepper. Place the vegetable-and-apple mixture on the bottom of the roaster. Pour the beer or cider and stock over it. (If you are using beer, add a few more apples.) Set veal on top of cabbage; salt and drape the side-pork slices over veal.

Cover the meat with foilwrap and then place the lid on the roaster. Roast 1 1/2 to 2 hours with lid and foil always in place. The cabbage will still be crunchy and the meat will be full of juice.

Another Quebec specialty, backwoods pie, is an interesting blend of rural wholesomeness, in the form of whole-wheat crust, and unexpected sophistication, provided by egg whites mixed with maple syrup.

Backwoods Pie

PASTRY

1 1/2 cups whole-wheat flour
1/4 cup butter
1/2 cup shortening
1 tbsp. sugar and a little ice water

Make a pie-crust shell. Place in 400° oven for 10 minutes. Make sure you prick it with a fork and cover bottom with foilwrap so it won't puff up in the oven. Let the crust cool.

FILLING

1 cup brown sugar	4 egg yolks
1 1/2 cups maple syrup	2 tbsp. butter
1/4 pint milk	4 beaten egg whites

After the first 5 ingredients are well mixed, fold in 4 beaten egg whites. Sprinkle or grate a little nutmeg over pie-crust shell. Pour liquid into shell and bake at 350° for 25 to 30 minutes. Sweet, gooey and crunchy.

Roadside stands in Quebec and eastern Ontario often have preserves for sale, and prominent among them is something called green tomato ketchup or relish. Green tomatoes are sold only in August at farmers' markets. In former times, the vegetable gardens of people living in Quebec, Ontario and the Maritimes must have been glutted with green tomatoes because every recipe book from these two parts of the country contains a way of making green tomato relish. It's good with hamburgers.

Green Tomato Relish

About 6 lbs. firm green tomatoes,
  stemmed, cut in half and then cut crosswise
  into 1/2-inch-thick slices
1/2 cup salt
2 lbs. onions, peeled and cut crosswise into
  thin slices
8 medium-sweet red peppers, seeded and cut
  into strips

1 cup brown sugar	2 tsp. celery seed
2 tsp. dry mustard	2 tsp. ground cinnamon
6 whole cloves	1 tsp. allspice
3 — 5 cups vinegar	

Spread the tomatoes (sliced) in layers on a large, deep platter, sprinkling each layer with salt, using 1/4 cup of salt in all. Cover platter and let it sit for a few hours at room temperature. Drain liquid that has accumulated around the tomatoes and transfer them to a 6-quart enamel casserole. Add the onions, peppers, sugar, celery seed, mustard, cinnamon, allspice, cloves and the remaining salt. Pour in the vinegar; it should cover the vegetables completely. Bring mixture to a boil and simmer, partially covered, for 5 minutes or until the vegetables are barely tender. Ladle the relish at once into hot, sterilized jars. Makes 3 quarts.

The Lac St.-Jean district near the Saguenay in eastern Quebec is an area where good cooking flourishes. Cécile Roland Bouchard has gathered together a number of recipes from this region, sometimes called the *grenier* or storehouse of Quebec. Her book *L'Art Culinaire au Saguenay-Lac-St-Jean* has many local recipes for specialties like *gourganes,* a big lentil used in soups and stuffings; *les perles bleues du Saguenay* or blueberries, which are large and especially good in this area; and *sipaille* or *cipâte* or *cipaille,* a meat pie made with a combination of wild and domestic food and ground pork. A great fish delicacy is *les corégones,* a type of whitefish related to the European *lavaret* or *fera.* There is also an exceptionally fine fresh-water salmon in this region, the Ouananich, which is smaller than the Atlantic salmon and particularly delicious.

Mme Bouchard's collection also includes the more traditional French-Canadian dishes such as *grand-pères au sirop* (dumplings cooked in maple syrup and molasses) and *croquignoles* and *beignes* (doughnuts and fritters), but with a Lac St.-Jean flavour. The recipes I have translated and revised from Mme Bouchard's book are typical, unusual and good, and at the same time within the capacity of those cooks who do not have access to the ingredients that are found near the Saguenay-Lac-St.-Jean area of Quebec.

Fish Chowder
from the Saguenay-Lac-St.-Jean Region
(Chowder au Poisson)

This recipe is very similar to chowder from the Atlantic provinces.

2 lbs. cod or haddock fillets, or *corégone* (ocean perch is also possible)

1 large Spanish onion, chopped	4 cups milk
2 large potatoes, diced	8 small soda crackers crumbled
paprika	
1/2 lb. salt pork, diced	2 tbsp. butter
a lot of chopped parsley	juice of 2 lemons

Cut fillets in 2" cubes. Sauté salt-pork bits. Add onion, and cook until tender but not brown. Add 2 cups boiling water and cook 3 or 4 minutes longer. Add fish and simmer 10 minutes.

In another saucepan, combine milk, crackers, butter, salt and pepper and lemon juice. Heat just to scalding: do not boil. Combine 2 mixtures and pour into soup tureen. Sprinkle with parsley and paprika. It is even better if you substitute dry white wine for the 2 cups of boiling water.

Some people claim that *cipaille, sipaille,* or *cipâte* is just a stew with meat, chicken and vegetables cooked together. But the word *cipâte* implies a crust, in fact, five layers of crust (cinq pâtes), and in the old days at least, the filling of meat consisted of game, hare, venison or partridge. A lawyer from the University of Montreal, Jean Beetz, who takes a keen interest in food, ate an interesting version of *cipaille* quite recently. It had four layers, each one with a different filling: pork, veal, partridge, and, more unusually, beaver-tail meat balls. When I asked him if it was good he said, "It depends on which layer you mean."

The *cipaille* from the Lac St.-Jean area near the Saguenay River in Quebec (similar to rappy pie from New Brunswick) contains a combination of fowl, ground meats, potatoes and layers of pie crust or biscuit dough.

What follows is my own urban version of *cipaille,* although the basics are from Mme Bouchard. It took one day to make, lasted three, and received the approval of de Montigny Marchand, whose family has been eating Quebec *cipaille* since 1680. Ideally, the duck should be wild, the "chicken" should be a partridge, and a hare should be thrown in as well. However, I live in the middle of Ottawa and do not know how to hunt. None of my friends or family will shoot any of these birds or animals for me — I asked them and was cold-shouldered. Besides, my husband refuses to eat rabbit. So, I went to the supermarket and bought one frozen Brome Lake duck, one frozen boiling fowl (impossible to find fresh on the day you need it), lots of ground meats and some chicken livers. My apologies to those who eat *cipaille* or rappy pie made only from wild game.

Cipaille

PASTRY

4 cups of flour	4 tsp. baking powder
6 tsp. butter	1/2 cup cold water
6 tsp. shortening	1/4 cup milk
1 tsp. salt	

Blend as for pie crust dough, adding liquid last. Refrigerate until ready to use. Then, divide dough into 3, 4 or 5 sections, depending on the height of your casserole, and roll out each section, making

one section larger than the rest (I use 3, because
my cast-iron container is 4 inches deep and will
only take 3 layers).

FILLING

1 large boiling fowl
1 duck (if frozen,
  defrost in warm water
  for 3 or 4 hours)
3 pork hocks and/or
  calves feet
3 parsnips
3 large carrots
5 whole cloves
3 large potatoes
1 bunch of parsley
  (chopped with
  stalks)
3 large dill pickles
1 1/2 bottles of stuffed
  olives with pimentos
  (15 oz. bottle)

1 lb. ground pork
1 lb. ground beef or
  veal
1/2 lb. chicken livers,
  gizzards and hearts
  from duck and chicken
3 large chopped onions
3 or 4 cloves of garlic
1 leek (if possible to
  to find)
3 tsp. salt
cracked pepper
2 tsp. thyme
2 bay leaves

The instructions that follow refer to the ingredients as I was able to obtain them (see page 57). If
you happen to have access to fresh fowl and game,
you should of course alter the method accordingly.
For example, if you have tender partridges on
hand, and young hare, the meat should be just
browned and then stripped from the bones in large
pieces. The full cooking should take place in the
pie. However, this is hard to do with a frozen fowl.
I compromised by throwing it into a pot and simmering it, along with pork hocks, gizzards, salt,
pepper, cloves and bay leaves, for 3 or 4 hours — or
until the meat falls off the bone easily. (At this
stage, taste and adjust seasoning accordingly.)
About 15 minutes before this chicken stock is ready,
add parsnips, carrots and 1/2 bunch parsley, including the stalks. Throw in the 3 potatoes any time
you like but remember to take them out when
they're still firm. Let them cool and then grate.
    While the chicken is boiling and the duck de-
frosting, put a good chunk of butter and some olive
oil in a heavy-bottomed pan or casserole; when it

sizzles, add the ground meat, chopped onions, celery, garlic, leek, some of the salt and pepper and thyme. Mix well, cover and simmer for about 40 minutes. When the ground mixture is cooked, add the grated potatoes and the rest of the parsley.

When the duck is defrosted, hack it in 3 or 4 chunks and sauté them lightly for about 5 minutes so that it will be easier to strip the meat from the bone. (Since the duck is more tender than the fowl, it doesn't need the long simmering.)

Take the largest piece of dough and line a casserole with it, bringing the sides up to the top if possible. Prick the dough with a fork. Spread olives and chopped pickles on it, then ground meat mixture, chicken, duck, and whole, raw livers and hearts. Add more seasoning if necessary. Add second layer of dough and repeat process. Seal with last layer.

Cut a hole in the centre of the dough and, using a funnel, pour into the pie the stock in which the chicken cooked. Be sure all the layers get moistened. Replace the piece of dough cut to make the hole. Bake *cipaille* in 350° oven for 60 to 80 minutes. It may be eaten hot or cold.

Incidentally, I mentioned using Brome Lake ducks. These birds from Brome Lake, southwest of Sherbrooke, Quebec, are known throughout Canada. There is also a steady demand for them in the United States. They have less fat and more meat than the Long Island variety, and taste better too, at least according to my palate. Unfortunately, all of the Brome Lake ducks are flash-frozen on the lake farm at the age of seven weeks so it seems that there is no way of eating them fresh.

I've already mentioned the existence of both regional and more sophisticated cooking in Quebec. By and large, the best examples of sophisticated French cooking (or, loosely speaking, classical cooking) in Canada are found in restaurants in Montreal and Quebec City. I have eaten deceptively simple dishes like poached salmon, grilled fresh Canadian lamb, and *crème caramel* that have no equal in the rest of the country.

However, *crème caramel* is offered by restaurants throughout Quebec with monotonous regularity and sometimes with not enough caramel. Here's a recipe with the proper proportions of cream and caramel.

Crème Caramel

1 1/4 cups sugar	3/4 cup water

Heat the sugar over a low fire, preferably in a wide, flat pan, until it turns brown. Then slowly pour in the water. Boil until sugar is dissolved and the water brown.

CUSTARD

1 cup cream	3 eggs
1 cup milk	1/2 cup sugar
1 tbsp. vanilla	

Combine, and then scald, cream and milk. Beat together 3 egg whites, 2 egg yolks and 1/2 cup sugar until frothy. Add vanilla to milk mixture and gradually pour it into eggs, stirring constantly.

Pour caramel (the sugar and water mixture) into a ring mold and swish it around until the inside of the mold is well-coated. Pour the custard into the mold and set it in a pan of hot water. Bake in a moderate oven for 45 minutes or until a knife inserted comes out clean. Unmold when cold. Serves 6.

Although classical *crème caramel* has always been part of French-Canadian upper-class cuisine, a more regional version exists: Take a can of Eagle Brand sweetened condensed milk, put it in simmering water for four hours and then open it up. A brown syrupy caramel milk will have formed. This was a real Christmas treat for a friend of mine. Since it's cloying, it's best eaten as a sauce for a cake or ice cream.

Still on the subject of the more sophisticated French cooking of Quebec, I rather like this fancied up recipe for roast pork.

Roast Pork with Mock Mustard Cream Sauce

3 lbs. boneless roast of pork
4 tbsp. rendered, fresh fat, or cooking oil
1 onion, sliced
1 carrot, sliced
2 cloves of garlic, if desired
parsley, 1/4 tsp. thyme, bay leaf
1 heavy casserole, large enough to hold the meat

Preheat oven to 325°. Place fat or oil in casserole, heat until almost smoking; sear pork until brown. Remove pork and most of fat from casserole. Stir in vegetables, garlic, herbs. Cover and cook 5 minutes. Return meat to casserole, fat side up. Season with salt and pepper. Cover and cook for 2 hours. When meat is done remove as much fat as possible from its juices and mash the vegetables into a gravy. Add 1/2 cup water, wine or stock. Keep warm.

MOCK MUSTARD CREAM SAUCE

1/3 cup cider vinegar
10 crushed peppercorns
1 — 2 cups whipping cream
1/2 tsp. cornstarch mixed with 1 tsp. water
1 to 2 tbsp. softened butter.

Pour the vinegar and peppercorns into a casserole and boil until the vinegar has reduced to about a tablespoon. Pour in the gravy mixture and boil the sauce down for a couple of minutes.

Add cream, simmer for 5 minutes, adding salt to taste. Beat in cornstarch mixture and simmer 2 or 3 minutes more. Sauce should be quite creamy. Correct seasoning. Add softened butter and remove sauce from stove.

Serve in a gravy boat alongside roast pork. The meat and sauce should serve 6 people.

The glaze of boredom in the eyes of some Canadians when maple syrup is mentioned is as thick as any real maple glaze spread on a cake. Yet our official attachment to that product is so pronounced that no chef, whether he be born in Paris or Budapest, can give an official Canadian dinner in honour of some foreign VIP without serving a maple-flavoured *mousse, bombe, parfait, soufflé* or whatever. This annoys some Canadians, especially those who do not eat maple syrup every day and come from parts of Canada where the sugar maple is not common. However, eastern Canada does have a lot of maple trees — in fact the dying elm is being replaced with the sugar maple — and one may as well face up to the fact that a lot of dishes are made, and continue to be made, from tree sap. The sugar maple produces a liquid that can be made into various grades and colours of syrup, as well as sugars. Roughly speaking, the finest grade of syrup is almost anemic looking in colour, and the darkest is used in commercial blends. The darker shades are usually thicker and more syrupy than the lighter.

Various textures of sugars are also made, ranging from a maple "butter" as creamy as peanut butter, to the more old-fashioned block of maple sugar that must be grated like a parmesan cheese. The latter is often sold in the spring and summer at roadside stands and farmers' markets. A more granulated variety, similar to the texture of brown sugar, is packed by commercial companies and sold in Quebec and parts of Ontario. You've often seen maple leaf candies or Easter bunnies made from this type of sugar, which again has a slightly different feel than the block kind of sugars. The only difference between them is the degree of heat to which the sap is boiled.

Maple syrup is absolutely pure; Canadian laws forbid the introduction of any artificial ingredients except in cases where these are clearly indicated on the label. It's produced nowhere in the world except Ontario, Quebec, New Brunswick, Nova Scotia and the northeastern United States, with Quebec providing somewhere between seventy-five and ninety per cent of the Canadian supply.

Many farmers in eastern Ontario and Quebec have commercial "sugar bushes" where the public is allowed to come and watch the sugar-making process and buy products freshly made on the spot. Hordes of school children are taken around during the sugaring-off period (March) and given maple syrup candies hardened on the fresh snow. In French, this process is called *la tire*, or the pull, because the syrup is pulled into long strands before it hardens. Maple products are a seasonal product and many stores advertise their fresh supply every April. Hence, in January and February the stock of maple products on the market becomes very low. In fact, the demand for maple sugar and other maple products is much larger than the supply.

Maple syrup is a bit like French wine; experts and dedicated maple syrup amateurs can tell the difference between syrups of various regions, provided they have not already been blended with syrups from other places. A friend of mine has a sugarbush in western Quebec, and his maple syrup has a very different taste from that made from trees on his sister-in-law's sugarbush near Lake Simcoe, Ontario. Invariably, at national syrup-judging events and at Canadian agricultural fairs, it is the maple syrup of Quebec that wins.

I like maple syrup, but when I was first married I miscalculated the amount that was necessary to the well-being of myself and my husband. Some supermarket was selling five-gallon cans of Quebec's premium grade at discount prices; wanting to try out the economic advantages of bulk buying, I purchased two five-gallon cans. Our flat was small and the cans took up much of our kitchen space. But I tried out maple muffins, nut fudge cakes and even duck with maple syrup, until it was a nauseous experience just to glance in the direction of the big cans sitting on the kitchen floor. After I threw out the remains of the last can, we didn't keep the stuff in our home for ten years.

Maple sugar and syrup are luxury items now. But in the last century, and even as far back as Jacques Cartier, it was cheaper to use the sap from the trees on your land than to import molasses, at that time the least costly imported sweetener. In Quebec, maple syrup was used as a glaze for hams and as a moistener for pork and beans. (I find, though, that hams that are cooked in maple syrup are not distinctively maple in taste — the strong taste of the salty ham overwhelms the subtle maple flavour. Brown sugar does just as well and is much cheaper. It's best to save your syrup or sugar for flavouring desserts where the maple taste is more pronounced.) Eggs cooked in boiling syrup were, and still are, considered a great delicacy. It would take another book to list the different kinds of cakes, puddings, muffins, pies, charlottes and ice-creams using maple sugar or syrup. The latest variation in the maple syrup theme is due to the recent successful marketing of yoghurt in Canada. Many restaurants especially in Quebec now advertise yoghurt topped with maple syrup as a *specialité de la maison*. I will try to give a few recipes that bring out the maple flavour without too much of a cloying after-taste.

But maple sugar and syrup never should have their identity hidden — we must accept the sweet flavour wholeheartedly. Here is a dessert with unashamed richness, bringing out the real characteristics of maple sugar. Maple products started out as a homely substitute for refined sugar — now they are a gastronomic luxury. Layered Maple is a voluptuous dessert which amalgamates cream, sweetness and a buttery crust that will make fanciers of maple flavour swoon. Bake this for about twelve people and cut into small, but not too small, pieces. Your guests will forget their diets for it.

Layered Maple
1 pint cream (unwhipped)
1 lb. maple sugar
my special sour-cream dough

INGREDIENTS FOR SOUR-CREAM DOUGH
2 cups flour sifted with 2 tsp. baking powder
1/4 cup butter
1/2 — 2/3 cup sour cream
1 beaten egg

Cut butter into sifted flour; add egg and sour cream. You may refrigerate the dough or use it immediately. Divide dough into 2 balls and roll out the first as thin as possible so that you can get oblong pieces from it. Each should cover the length of an oblong Pyrex dish. Prick the 2 pieces of dough with a fork and lay 1 piece on the bottom.

If your maple sugar is already granulated, spread some over the dough. If it is in a big block, grate it first. Pour some unwhipped cream over the sugar. Place the other piece of dough on top of the cream and sugar.

Repeat the process with the next ball of dough. You should get 2 more pieces of dough, each pricked with a fork. Cover the whole dish with the last piece and seal it well. Try to keep the cream within the 3 layers — it shouldn't seep to the top. Bake in a 400° oven for about 30 to 40 minutes. Watch it during the later stages so that it doesn't brown too much.

Let it cool, and slice into oozing squares. This dessert thumbs its nose at all doctors and dentists.

If you are not yet satiated with maple, try this recipe for maple sugar mousse.

Maple Sugar Mousse

2 pkgs. gelatin, softened in 1/2 — 3/4 cups strong coffee
7 eggs, separated
2 tsp. cornstarch
1 cup maple sugar (granulated)
1 1/2 cups boiling milk
1/2 cup whipping cream
salt
1 tbsp. sugar

Beat egg yolks. Add sugar and cornstarch slowly. Continue beating for about 3 minutes. Beat milk into egg and sugar mixture. Stir with wooden spoon over low heat. Do not boil. Custard should thicken enough to coat spoon. Add gelatin to that mixture and beat in until thoroughly dissolved.

Beat egg whites, adding a pinch of salt and 1
tbsp. sugar, until soft peaks form; then carefully
fold whites into warm custard. Place in refrigerator
until mixture is cold but not set. It may be necessary to fold the cooling mixture again in case it
separates.

Whip 1/2 cup whipping cream and add to
mousse. Turn the mousse into an 8-cup mold. Chill
for 4 to 5 hours or overnight. Unmold and decorate
with carmelized maple sugar.

Or try this recipe for sugar pie.

Tarte à la Ferlouche or Sugar Pie

1 cup brown or maple sugar
1/4 cup molasses (if you use molasses do *not*
use maple sugar) or 1/4 cup maple syrup
3/4 cup hot water
3 tbsp. flour or cornstarch mixed with hot water
1/2 cup raisins or nuts if desired
2 tbsp. butter
1 9" baked pie-shell

Heat sugar and syrup or molasses slowly on stove,
then add flour and water mixture (already well
mixed so there are no lumps). Cook slowly until
mixture thickens. Mix in butter and nuts and remove from stove. Pour into pie shell and put under
the broiler for about 5 minutes.

Good with unsweetened whipped cream.

If maple syrup must be regarded as Canada's most celebrated gourmet food, cheddar cheese is a close rival. Cheddar is primarily an Ontario product and I will discuss it
when I deal with Ontario's regional cooking and products.
However, Quebec produces a cheese — Oka — which I believe to be as deserving of honours as cheddar, and which
has also received international recognition. In fact *The
Gourmet Cookbook* (published by *Gourmet* magazine) lists

Oka as "Canada's great cheese". It is made by the Trappist Fathers in Oka, Quebec, and is similar in taste to the French Port Salut, soft, with a pronounced, distinctive flavour. The Fathers only produce a certain amount a year — the demand is always greater than the supply. Despite the complaints of many long-time Oka fans that the cheese does not have the same powerfully earthy smell that it had before the Second World War (there was no equal to the stink of that cheese), the Fathers claim that the same methods are still being used. And they refuse to increase their production because they feel the cheese will lose something in the process.

Many cheese-shop owners say that the refrain "Oka is not the same as it used to be" is correct, whatever the Trappist Fathers may say. Before the Second World War, Oka cheese was sold unpasteurized, and the flavour and smell accompanied the newly made product from the outset. But when the federal government clamped down, some years ago, on all makes of unpasteurized new cheese, pasteurization of Oka became an integral part of the process of making it. So Oka lost its unpasteurized smell. However, it could still smell and taste the same as in the good old days if the cheese was not pasteurized and if it was allowed to mature two months or more before being marketed. (Government and private sources consulted about this point said that as with cheddar, the maturing process kills the microbes and makes pasteurization unnecessary.) But since the demand is so great, the pressure is always on the Fathers to keep the cheese circulating on the market at all times. As a result, all the Oka sold is too young to produce the proper fumes — the real nostalgic smell of the thirties.

Oka is best eaten after sitting at normal room temperature for a number of hours. In fact, a whole Oka should be allowed to mature at room temperature for several days before the first bites are taken.

Until the beginning of the Second World War, Oka cheese was also made by Trappist Monks in St. Norbert, Manitoba, along with some other delicacies. That's all gone now, and western Canada has no steady supply of Oka cheese, since the distribution of eastern Oka is sporadic.

Would you believe that it is possible to eat a cheese that has been made in Canada since 1679? Impossible? Not at all. A small round cheese, about six inches in diameter and very smelly, is still sold in cheese shops in Quebec City and on the Island of Orleans, nearby. A family by the name of Aubertin has been passing on the secret since the seventeenth century from father to son. They live near St. Pierre on the Island and sell it, generally in the summertime, under the simple name, *Fromage Ile d'Orléans*. Their production is, of course, limited, but those who eat it swear it is one of the finest cheeses in the world.

Ermite is another Quebec cheese that is worth eating. It is a blue cheese with a strongly seasoned, almost peppery flavour made by Benedictine Monks in St. Benoit, Quebec.

After maple and cheese, I should really go on to deal with a third great natural product of Quebec — the fish in its fresh-water lakes and surrounding salt waters. However, I've already discussed at length the qualities of the Atlantic salmon and the threat to its survival (pp. 43-7). Unlike those in the Atlantic provinces, fisheries in Quebec are administered by the provincial, not the federal, government. This has been so for half a century. The Gaspé salmon has not been faring well in Quebec — no more so than salmon in Newfoundland or the Maritimes — and the Quebec government has now banned all commercial salmon fishing off the Gaspé Peninsula from Matane, 240 miles east of Quebec City, to Matapedia, on the New Brunswick-Quebec border at the end of the Bay of Chaleur. Among the treasures to be preserved is the Ouananich which, as I've mentioned, is a small fresh-water samon, and one that *stays* in fresh water. From its abundance in past centuries, when it was celebrated in Quebec literature, its numbers in Lac St.-Jean and in the surrounding rivers have steadily been reducing because of pollution, dams and other man-made forces. As for the lake trout, speckled trout, pike, pickerel, lavaret, bass and many other fresh-water fish in Quebec lakes, I wonder how many will follow the path of the sturgeon, and now the salmon, and become so rare as to be reserved for the very rich or for the museums (which is where you should really go if you want to find a jar of Quebec sturgeon caviar these days).

One further product that Quebec shares with the Maritimes is a small, very delicately flavoured shrimp which is now being marketed in increasing quantities in central Canada. I first discovered it as Matane shrimp. These shrimps have a resilient texture without being hard or tough and their taste is, in my opinion, superior to most other smaller varieties of shrimp that I've had outside Canada. Will they last?

Ontario — from Apple Hill and Maple Lake to Sturgeon Falls and Whitefish Bay

Take a large dose of American cooking, from old-fashioned New England johnny cake to the contemporary New York strip sirloin; mix with a good amount of tea (still brewed in a pot, English style); add a handful of oatmeal and some Mennonite dumplings from Waterloo County, and season everything with Hungarian paprika and Italian oregano, or "pizza spice". Stir it up, bake for 200 years (remember to add the spices only at the very end), and there you have it. Ontario cooking. You might say that Ontario cooking is unique because of the conglomeration of culinary styles that exist in this province. Historically, Americans, Anglo-Celts and Germans predominate, with Italians Greeks, Hungarians and others coming in a little later.

The Canadian Home Cook Book, compiled in 1877 by the "Ladies of Toronto and chief cities and towns in Canada" (some women didn't live in prestigious enough centres to be named in the title), kept a balance between English and American recipes. English puddings like cabinet, fig, roly-poly and marmalade puddings are made with a lot of flour and suet. Their combined weight when cooked would equal that of a team of Ayrshire bullocks. Puddings were very popular in 1877, as was Boston brown bread, Washington cake and waffles. And most Canadian cookery-books at that time, with statesmanlike impartiality, always gave one particular recipe twice, printed under different names; for example, Yorkshire pudding and popovers — the latter being American and always baked in muffin tins, the former being English and cooked with the roast beef. But the ingredients and method of mixing were always identical. The American and English ways of cooking are basic to the heart of Ontario. Now, however, English tradition has fallen off and hamburgers, Kentucky fried chicken and the American barbecue are an integral part of Ontario eating.

The strong German strain in the cuisine of old Ontario is due to the Mennonites who arrived in the Kitchener-Waterloo area (after a stop in Pennsylvania) in the early 1800's. They originally came from Switzerland, the Rhineland and Alsace. Later, they were joined by emigrating Germans who were neither Mennonites nor Amish but who identified, nevertheless, with the culture, language and food around that part of Ontario. Kitchener used to be called Berlin, but during the First World War, the English Canadians with chauvinistic fervour, made the Berliners change the name of their town in honour of the famous British general.

Edna Staebler's book *Food That Really Schmecks* describes the style of cooking of the Mennonites and Amish, which has much in common with the cuisine of their southern cousins — the Pennsylvania Dutch. Unhappily, it seems that the one place where non-Mennonites can see and taste this very distinctive cuisine is going to be destroyed. The Kitchener Market is the largest of its kind in Canada, and the Mennonite and German farm-women come for miles around with their shoofly pies, sauerkraut, pickles and jams, while their husbands bring in the home-stuffed sausages and market-gardening produce. Tourists (discerning ones) can stop on their way to Stratford on Saturdays and see a vast display of these gastronomic achievements spread out through the two levels of the old Kitchener Market.

The display includes fresh-killed white geese, plump and plucked, their feathers stuffed into pillows on sale beside them; as well as goose fat, and goose-meat spread, sold in plastic containers to people like me — I like it so much I consumed a half pound with a popsicle stick within fifteen minutes after buying it. The pig plays a prominent role at the Kitchener Market; all parts of it from head to toe are for sale, fresh, smoked, roasted and stuffed. My brother bought some pickled pork chunks floating in a brine-filled jar — he's a doctor and the sight must have made him home-sick for innards pickled in formaldehyde on laboratory shelves. We also bought baby-corn preserves, pear jam, apple butter and a bottle of "Northern Pineapple". The label on the bottle of Northern Pineapple reads: "No pre-servatives . . . Ingredients: pumpkin, vinegar, sugar, spice, packed by G. Nabrotsky, Teeswater, Ontario." It tastes neither of pineapple nor of pumpkin but more like pre-served watermelon rind.

While at the Market recently my family ate a stand-up lunch of hot, short, fat weiners, dotted with caraway seeds, spilling with juice and garnished with home-made relish and sauerkraut. Our dessert was shoofly pie — the word "pie" is a misnomer since it tastes like a light ginger cake until you reach the wet bottom, made from molasses. The gooey layer appealed to me, as it must have to the flies of by-gone days that inspired its name. Many of the vendors are of the strict Amish sect, the women wearing long skirts and aprons and the men wide-brimmed black hats. The custom-ers are neighbours, townspeople and tourists, and you will even see actors from nearby Stratford buying home-made cheeses for a picnic beside the Avon River.

The Market has a very impressive display of cheeses, from the imitation Swiss varieties to aged and new cheddar and Oka. A number of stalls exhibit great blocks or wheels of Emmenthal, Caraway and Tilsit; the Emmenthal is a cred-itable version of the original Swiss, and the others are highly edible as well.

Many people feel, as I do, that the Market is just as much

a cultural attraction as the Shakespearean Festival. However, the Kitchener city-fathers seem to think differently and the Market's demolition is imminent. The Mennonites were told they could sell their goods in a parking lot, but they refused because the Amish do not drive cars, and of course the gas fumes would hardly help the taste of the food being sold. And so Kitchener may at long last be able to take its place among the rest of those unmemorable Ontario towns — each with identical shopping centres blighting the scenery.

There is a possibility that the Mennonites and others who sell at the Market, including a gentleman who makes hot, thin Slovakian pancakes, will set up their wares about seven miles west of Kitchener. But it's not certain the land will be available because a lady who owns some of the property objects to the cars and people who would be tramping near her home.

Every region of Canada influenced by the German culture has a recipe for a cake or pudding made with raw carrots. Nova Scotia recipe books are full of Lunenberg carrot cakes and puddings, and the Mennonites of Ontario, in the Kitchener-Waterloo area repeat the tradition. Madame Benoit has an excellent recipe for carrot nut cake in the Ontario section of her *Canadiana Cook Book*. I followed her recipe carefully but after making it I felt that it needed far more spices and raisins. Here then is my version of Madame Benoit's Carrot Nut Cake (a good way to get rid of soggy old winter carrots lying in the vegetable bin).

Carrot Nut Raisin Spice Cake

1 1/4 cups salad oil (not olive oil)	1 tsp. ginger
	4 tsp. cinnamon
2 cups granulated sugar	1 tsp. each mace and
2 cups all-purpose flour	nutmeg
2 tsp. baking powder	4 eggs
1 tsp. soda	3 cups grated raw carrot
1 tsp. salt	1 cup chopped walnuts
1 cup raisins	

Set oven at 350°. Grease an angel tube pan.

Beat oil and sugar with mixer until very well blended. Sift soda, baking powder, flour, salt, and spices together and add about one-third to sugar mixture. Blend again.

Add remaining dry ingredients alternatively with the whole eggs. Mix well after each addition. Your batter will be quite thick, but the carrots will provide the moisture for the cake. Add carrots, nuts and raisins. Pour batter in tube pan and bake for 1 hour. When done, invert cake on cake rack and let cool. Freezes well.

Since sour cream is one of the most important ingredients in the Mennonite cooking of Waterloo County, this recipe for sour-cream icing has a certain logic.

SOUR-CREAM ICING

2 cups sour cream	1 2/3 cups icing sugar
juice of 2 oranges	juice of 1 lemon.

Boil ingredients to 225°. Cool and spread on cake. You might have some left for a filling.

One of the most intriguing Mennonite recipes I've come across is one for funnel cakes. It's good for cooks with latent artistic tendencies.

Edna Staebler's Funnel Cakes

2 eggs well beaten	3 tbsp. sour cream
not quite 2 cups milk	1/2 tsp. soda
1 tsp. baking powder	1/2 tsp. salt
3 cups flour	

Measure the sour cream into a cup and fill the cup with milk, then stir the milk into the beaten eggs. Sift the dry ingredients into the egg and milk mixture and beat until smooth. If the batter isn't runny, you will have to add more milk. Heat deep fat until it browns a cube of bread or reaches 375°. Pour batter into a small pitcher so it will be easier to handle.

Now comes the fun. Put your finger over the
spout of a funnel and pour about 3 tbsp. of the
batter into the funnel. Take off your finger and let
the batter run into the hot fat, swirling the funnel
around so the batter forms a lacy pattern or con-
centric circles about 3″ to 6″ in diameter. It's best
to make swirls moving out from the centre. The
frying becomes quite an art as you learn to make
quick twirls and turns of the funnel, covering and
uncovering the opening. It's not as hard as it
sounds.

Fry the cakes until they are golden brown; then
drain them on paper towels and serve hot, sprinkled
with powdered sugar.†

Let's go back to the turn of the century when Ontario
people were leaving "celery country" for "cabbage town".
The recipe books printed in Toronto at that time, like
Canada's Favourite Cook Book, used up several pages of
print teaching readers who wanted to climb the social ladder the more complicated forms of table etiquette: "Do
not mop the face with a napkin." "Never suck an orange
at the table." "Never take a piece of bread with a fork."
"Do not drink from the saucer." "Never make a hissing
sound when eating soup." One of the last admonitions belongs more to the world of Grecian-style dance, à la Isadora
Duncan: "Carry food with an inward, not an outward,
curve of the spoon or fork."

The recipe books of today on Ontario cuisine, whether
they are written by Madame Benoit or Edna Staebler, or
the mysterious group of home economists who "tested" the
recipes for the *Laura Secord Canadian Cook Book,* don't
bother to explain table manners. They feel that things
have changed and that Ontario folk are now worldly enough
to sit at a table with strangers without spitting grape seeds
in their eyes. The modern cook-books are different in other
respects too. All those steamed suet puddings have van-

† Adapted from *Food That Really Schmecks* by Edna Staebler, by permission of McGraw-Hill Ryerson Limited.

ished, except for the token Christmas pudding. Junkets, flummeries, fools made with rice, cornstarch and semolina, and other puddings and custards no longer play a prominent role in these books. Also, meat dishes like "collared calves heads" (scald for ten minutes, then scrape off the hair") and mutton and turkey that are boiled for four hours have totally disappeared from their pages.

Inexplicably enough, in many of the old Ontario cookery-books there are more recipes for oysters than for any other single item, whether fish or meat. Oysters must have been a relatively cheap and thus more common food among residents of Ontario then than they are today. Now oysters are, of course, a luxury food, costing about $1.80 a dozen. A hundred years ago they were prevalent enough to have the popular cook-books providing countless recipes for stewing, frying, poaching and saucing them. This also says something about progress in rail transportation. I suspect that 100 years ago all those fresh oysters from the Maritimes got out to central Canadian cities faster — and cheaper — than they do on today's trains.

Ontario people share the national tendency towards fancy desserts and breads rather than carefully thought out dishes from meat and poultry. In the older cook-books, recipes for the latter category tend to be simpler and less imaginative. Pork dishes are to be cooked with cabbage, apples and raisins, certainly revealing the German strain in Ontario cooking. Sometimes a pie crust is prescribed, especially for any left-over chicken that may be around, and meat loaves are a standard feature in their pages.

But the newer Canadians have added a great deal to the meat course. Modern Canadian cookery-books, reflecting new Ontario tastes, have recipes for Italian *osso buco* (see p. 83 for a recipe), Chinese sweet and sour pork, Hungarian *gulyas* (made with sour cream and paprika), and lamb with a Greek-style *avgolemeno* (lemon) sauce (see p. 84). Thus, the main course of the average Sunday dinner of the average Ontario resident in the 1970's seems to be undergoing a certain broadening, thanks, no doubt, to the great waves of newer immigrants who have come to Ontario in the post-war years. This, of course, assumes that people in Ontario still eat a sit-down Sunday dinner. As we all know, drive-in snacks and peanut butter on everything are replacing full-course meals. Perhaps the real significance of Sunday eating is in the longer lineups at the A & W, Harvey's and other "traditional" Canadian institutions.

However, for the unconventional, who still prefer a meal occasionally, I set out below some recipes from the old Ontario and the new Ontario.

The Old Ontario

Oatmeal bread sweetened with molasses is all right for poor Maritimers, but rich Ontario can afford white bread. Some people feel that it's a waste of time making white bread because brown bread is more interesting to eat and is said to be healthier. But I think the plain home-made white bread with a real crust is a classic food which, because of its simplicity, is too often ignored. This recipe produces the kind of white rolls and bread that United Empire Loyalist ladies who lived in prosperous Ontario towns might have baked on Saturday for Sunday dinner.

White Bread and Rolls

1 cup lukewarm water	1 tsp. white sugar
2 tbsp. yeast granules	1 heaping tbsp. salt
(2 packages)	9 cups flour
1/2 — 3/4 cup white sugar	3/4 cup butter
2 more cups lukewarm water	

Sprinkle the yeast on 1 cup water in which 1 tsp. of sugar has dissolved. (Use a large, warmed pottery bowl for this.) Let the yeast mixture stand for 10 minutes while you melt the butter on the stove.

When the yeast has risen to the top of the water, stir it very well so that there are no particles of yeast left.

Now stir into the yeast mixture 2 cups lukewarm water, white sugar (many people in Ontario like white bread slightly sweet), salt and the melted butter. Now add 9 cups of flour, 1 cup at a time, stirring, then beating, after each cup. By the time you reach your sixth cup you will need to throw away your wooden spoon and use your hands. The dough should be floppy and not too dry. Add 1/2 cup more water if it is.

KNEADING

Knead the dough on a well-floured surface. (You will have to add as much as another cup of flour during this process to prevent sticking.) Kneading is good exercise and will burn up the calories that you will take in when you eat the bread, hot, with butter. Remember to gather the dough in your hands and push it away with a strong motion, using the heels of your palms, turning it all the time. Keep kneading, and sprinkling flour if necessary, for at least 10 minutes. Fifteen will do the bread no harm. The dough should be smooth and elastic when you reach exhaustion.

Form the dough into a ball, put it in a bowl and let it rise in a warm spot for 1 to 2 hours. A warm spot may be the open door of your oven turned on to 150°, or your sink filled with hot water. After 1 hour make an indentation in the dough with your finger; if the impression stays, the bread has finished its first rising. It should now be doubled in bulk. Punch it down to let the air escape. Now you can let your fancy take over. Shape the bread into rolls, round breads, or loaves; or flatten it out and roll it like a jelly roll, hiding raisins and cinnamon and sugar inside. More butter mixed in with the sugar does not hurt. Place shaped dough in greased pans or muffin tins.

The second rising takes 1 to 2 hours as well. Usually 1 hour will be enough. The second rising can take place whenever you want; just put the dough in the refrigerator until you are ready. If you are worried, a weight sitting on top of the dough (which is protected by a towel) will stop the yeast from working.

After the second rising, bake the loaves or buns in a 350° oven; bread takes about 50 minutes, buns somewhat less. Both the top and bottom should be crisp, and the crust must have a hollow sound when tapped. If you think that the crust is still too soft, put it back in the oven at 250° and let it bake a little longer.

Remember, if you feel you have more bread than you need (you will get a dozen rolls and two medium loaves), wrap the excess in foilwrap, freeze immediately after it cools, and the following week, reheat in the oven. It will taste like newly-baked bread.

Ontario cheddar cheese will go particularly well with the rolls or with the toasted bread.

Canadian cheddar cheese was born in 1866 in Ingersoll, Ontario. And even though cheddar is now made in Quebec and New Brunswick, its natural home is still Ontario, which produces about fifty per cent of all cheddar made in Canada today and an even higher percentage of that exported. In addition, more small independent cheese factories exist in Ontario than anywhere else in Canada, despite the fact that their numbers are lessening every year. The unhappy headline "Local cheese factory to close" is a frequent one in country newspapers like the *Lanark Era,* the *Arnprior Guide,* and the *Smiths Falls Record News.* It spells a minor disaster for the farmers of the country who sell their milk and cream to the local cheese-makers. At the beginning of this century at least a thousand independent cheddar cheese factories existed in Ontario and Quebec. Now Black Diamond and Cherry Hill, the two best-known Canadian cheddar cheeses, are owned by foreign companies. Black Diamond is owned by a Canadian subsidiary of a British firm, and Cherry Hill by Nestlé (Canada) Limited, a subsidiary of a U.S. corporation whose parent has its headquarters in Switzerland.

Despite the diminishing number of producers, enough good Ontario cheddar remains to be classified as a gastronomic specialty of the province. It has considerably increased in price recently. Demand from abroad, particularly England, is high. The smaller independent companies often sell cheese that has an individual taste unique to each cheese maker, but the larger companies use a blend of cheeses brought in from all over the province.

A civil servant I know (and they are cautious people) invested in a cooperative cheese factory that was almost defunct, in the county of Leeds. It sells pies and doughnuts made by the local ladies, as well as cheese, to the many American tourists who come across the border. The factory used to have just a wholesale market, but since the owners have put in a show window and counter their retail operation accounts for seventy-five per cent of their sales. The cheese maker and the local people running the factory were convinced by the adventurous civil servant to age their cheese. Their sales increased from then on.

Cheddar addicts prefer the well matured cheese, and if you know where to go you may find cheese that has been ripening for three or four years. The older cheese has a much richer, tangier taste and the texture is sometimes crumblier. It may be compared to the boast of the aging prostitute, "It's the old hens who make the best soup."

Well organized cheese shops throughout Canada date their cheddar. A. L. H. FROMAGERIE at the Place Laurier in Quebec City marks the dates on a blackboard, *"Fromage Canadien: 1967 superfort, 1968 extra fort, 1969 fort,"* and so on. In Toronto, the OLD WORLD CHEESE SHOP on Yonge Street ages some of its cheddar for from nine months to a year in port wine. The final result pleases the eye as well as the palate — the wine colour leaves a delicate tracing through the block of cheese, almost like a marbling. Most places that sell cheddar, whether they are retail shops in the city or country factories, will ship orders by mail.

Although packaging and advertising for well known brands such as Black Diamond and Cherry Hill can result in increased prices — perhaps, according to some sources, as much as ten per cent — their product is no better, and is sometimes less interesting, than the other cheddar cheeses on the market.

The best cheddar is made in the summer, because when cows eat grass instead of dry winter fodder they give the best milk for cheese. Most cheese makers and cheese sellers say they can tell the difference immediately between summer and winter cheddar. In any case, cheddar, like all cheese, is best kept out of the refrigerator for five or six hours before being eaten in order for the full flavour to come out. Incidentally, a complete list of cheddar cheese factories can be obtained from the Dairy Division of the Department of Agriculture in Ottawa. The list contains outlets in every province of Canada.

There are many Canadian recipes which use cheddar cheese. I am very fond of cheddar cheese soufflé and this is my own recipe.

Perfect Cheddar Cheese Soufflé

2 tbsp. butter   1 tsp. salt
2 tbsp. flour   1 1/3 cups milk
1 1/2 cups grated cheddar cheese plus 1 tbsp. more
1/2 cup chopped dill or chives
3 egg yolks
5 egg whites

Melt butter in a saucepan. When the butter has stopped foaming add the flour and mix well. Slowly add milk, and stir until thick. Remove from stove and add egg yolks and grated cheese, salt and herbs. Beat egg whites until peaks are formed. Do not overbeat. The whites should look as if they just might drop from the beater but hold on all the same. Stir about one-third of the egg whites into the yolk mixture, and fold in the rest. Do not overfold. Place soufflé in an 8-cup container, preferably a tin charlotte-dish or an ovenproof soufflé dish. Sprinkle some extra grated cheese on top — about 1 tbsp. Bake at 400° for 30 to 35 minutes.

Here are two more recipes which I've adapted from old Ontario ones:

Yorkshire Pudding or Popovers

PUDDING

1 cup milk	1 cup flour
2 eggs	1 tsp. salt

Blend all together in blender for 1 minute. (An electric mixer is also effective.) Let mixture sit for a half-hour or more. Blend again. Time your roast beef so that it will be done 30 or 40 minutes from the time you put your Yorkshire pudding in the oven. Pour the batter into the same pan as the beef; make sure the fat is really sizzling (this is crucial) and bake at 400° for 30 or 40 minutes. The pudding should rise. Serve immediately with beef. Serves 4 or 5.

POPOVERS

Pour the hot fat from the bottom of the roast beef pan into muffin tins, cast iron if possible. One-quarter of each cup should be filled with fat. Place the tins in a 400° oven and heat until the fat is sizzling. Then pour in batter and let bake for 30 minutes. Serve from muffin pans with beef.

Steak and Kidney Pie

2 lbs. round steak or blade steak
1 1/2 lbs. veal or lamb kidneys
1/3 cup brandy
2 cups brown stock
2 cups water
flour as needed
1/2 lb. salt pork, cut in small cubes
2 tbsp. French mustard
2 large onions chopped
2 carrots
1/2 lb. mushrooms (leave caps whole)
salt and pepper
3 parsnips
a rich pastry dough, enough for one 9″ crust (prepare first and put it aside in a cool place)

Cut the beef in 1 1/2″ cubes and dredge them in the flour. Fry salt pork bits in the bottom of a heavy casserole until they are crisp. Add more fat, butter or oil if necessary and then brown meat and onions. Remove any particularly fatty pork bits.

Now heat brandy in a separate container with a handle. Light the warmed brandy and pour it over the meat, letting it burn as much as possible. Pour stock and water over meat and add salt, pepper, mustard. Let the mixture cook for 2 to 3 hours, adding carrots and parsnips about 20 minutes before you take the pot off the stove.

In the meantime, remove the filament from the kidneys and very slightly brown them in a chunk of butter. The kidneys should be quite raw in the middle when you remove them from the frying pan. Slice them up and add them to the *cooled* steak and broth mixture. If the mixture seems thin, thicken with a *beurre manie* (flour and a little butter rolled into a ball) or a paste made with flour and water. Taste for seasoning; add more salt, pepper and mustard if you think it necessary. Lightly brown the whole mushrooms and add them to the mixture.

Transfer meat and liquid to an earthenware or glass casserole and top with rolled-out pastry. Cut a hole in the centre of the pastry and insert a funnel of foilwrap so the juices won't need to spill over.

The final baking may be done a day later. Bake in a 350° oven for about 45 minutes. (You might have to use the broiler to brown the crust at the end.)

The New Ontario

Italians eat a lot of veal, and veal in Canada can be very good. It should be pinkish, not red in colour. *Osso buco* with *gremolata* is a classical Italian dish that uses inexpensive veal shanks as its prime ingredient; but wine sauce and rich marrow bones, as well as the accompaniment of grated lemon peel, garlic and parsley (the *gremolata*), make this into something very special.

Osso Buco

Allow 2 veal shanks per person, approximately
1 1/2″ − 2″ thick (if they are more than 2″ thick,
one shank each should be sufficient) .

salt and freshly ground pepper
enough flour to coat each shank
8 tbsp. olive oil
4 tbsp. butter
1 cup chopped onion
1/2 cup chopped carrot
1/2 cup chopped celery
1 large chopped leek (not absolutely necessary)
2 cloves chopped or pressed garlic
1 1/2 cups dry white wine
1 tsp. dried basil
1/2 tsp. dried thyme
1 cup chicken or beef stock (canned is all right)
1 large can of Italian plum tomatoes, drained and
    chopped
1 bay leaf

Your butcher should leave enough meat around the
veal shanks so that 1 or 2 shanks will be sufficient
for 1 person. Season meat with salt and pepper and
coat the pieces well with flour, shaking off the excess accumulation. Heat the olive oil in a large
frying pan until it begins to smoke. Brown shanks
on both sides, a few pieces at a time. Transfer them
to a large platter.

Over a moderate heat melt the 4 tbsp. of butter
in a large, heavy-bottomed casserole dish. Add the
chopped onions, carrots, celery, leek and garlic, and
cook slowly until the vegetables are lightly coloured. Then arrange the pieces of veal upright on
the vegetables, making sure the marrow won't fall
out as they cook. You may put one shank on top
of another as long as they are lying with the bone
facing up. Add wine, stock, tomatoes and bay leaf.
The liquid should come more than half way up the
sides of the meat. (More stock or wine might be
needed later.)

You may cook this on top of your stove or in the
oven. Simmer for 45 minutes to 1 hour. The veal
may be served at this stage but it tastes better if
you go to the trouble of glazing it. (The glazing
may be done just before serving.)

GREMOLATA

This is to be sprinkled on *osso buco* just before it is eaten, but it should be prepared while the meat is cooking.

2 tsp. finely chopped garlic
2 tbsp. grated lemon rind
1 cup finely chopped parsley (there is no law against increasing or decreasing the proportions of the lemon rind and garlic)

GLAZING

Remove the *osso buco* from the casserole and place it in a large ovenproof dish that will hold all the veal shanks in one layer. If you have a lot of liquid in the casserole, boil it down until the flavour is very intense. Pour some of the liquid over the shanks and glaze them on the upper shelf of the oven for about 10 minutes, or until shiny. Remove from oven; pour more of the reduced sauce over it for moisture, but don't drown the veal. Serve from the hot dish with more sauce on the side, and serve the *gremolata* separately so that each guest can sprinkle on as much as he likes. Little coffee spoons are good for scooping out the marrow.

Osso buco may be prepared the day before. It should serve 6 to 8 people.

Fresh Ontario lamb is young, tender, full of flavour, and inexpensive. A roast leg of lamb served with a Greek lemon sauce makes a memorable meal.

When roasting your lamb make sure that you do not overcook it. Ontario lamb is tender enough to be served pink.

Lemon or Avgolemeno Sauce for Ontario Lamb or Chicken

3 egg yolks
juice of 1 lemon
1 tsp. cornstarch or arrowroot
1 tsp. salt
1 1/2 cups of chicken stock, fresh or canned
1 tbsp. finely chopped parsley

In a double boiler combine egg yolks, lemon juice, cornstarch or arrowroot, and salt. Beat with a whisk, and slowly add chicken stock. Beat until the sauce thickens on the back of the spoon. It would be quicker to make this sauce directly over a moderate heat. But remember, never let the sauce come near to a boil or you will have lemon scrambled eggs. The double boiler is slower but safer.

Chopped fresh mint is excellent in the sauce instead of parsley.

Whether we talk about the new or old Ontario cooking, the natural products of the province will, I hope, always be its greatest culinary asset: the fish in its quarter of a million lakes, the game, the fresh vegetables, the product of the maple trees, the wild berries — how little we know and seem to care about conserving them, distributing them, or sometimes even eating them.

For better or worse, we can now eat fresh corn, celery, tomatoes and beans, even asparagus, during all seasons of the year. Fifty years ago fresh winter vegetables consisted of cabbage, turnips, carrots and potatoes — everything was seasonal. But there is something to be said for eating asparagus, corn and tomatoes only when they come out of the earth, rather than from hothouses. Tomatoes in wintertime are pulpy and tasteless compared with those grown in the market gardens of Ontario or of other provinces, or in your own back yard in August. The same must be said for corn. The sweetest-tasting, tenderest corn is picked, sold and cooked within 24 hours, and the best place to find the right corn is in the farmers' markets that are fast disappearing in Ontario and other parts of Canada. We don't appreciate our seasonal vegetables enough. If you don't think seasonally, you don't eat seasonally.

One of the finest vegetables grown in Ontario is asparagus, which appears for a short time in May and June. The problem is that most people don't know how to cook or serve it and some people don't even know how to eat it. Many would rather open up a tin of mushy asparagus tips even when fresh ones are for sale. Restaurants seldom serve fresh asparagus when the season comes around. I've eaten canned asparagus in June in LA SAULAIE, considered one of the best Montreal restaurants. Restaurant owners and head waiters continue to be astonished when one complains about this practice. And if you do happen upon fresh Ontario asparagus in a private home or restaurant, it will certainly be overcooked and most often served together with the main course — sometimes even on the same plate. Asparagus, like salad, should be served separately, whether before the main course, as in France (whose white *asperges de cavaillon* are the best in the world), or after, as in England. It must be firm enough to be eaten with the fingers and to be held in an upright position. Ideally, a bowl of homemade mayonnaise or *vinaigrette* sauce should be nearby for dipping. As an alternative, there is nothing wrong with pouring melted butter and lemon juice over the asparagus.

If you are a perfectionist, you will feel that asparagus should be peeled before it is cooked, just as a carrot or potato is peeled. Since the outer skin is rather tough, the inside of the asparagus often gets mushy in cooking long before the ouside is tender. If I have a small amount of asparagus, I cook it with a little bit of water and butter in a frying pan. The problem in this method is that the tips cook quicker than the rest of the stalks so a certain amount of juggling around might be necessary — for example, lifting the tips out of the water after a few minutes. Length of cooking-time depends upon the thickness of the asparagus; normally six to ten minutes simmering should be sufficient. If a lot of asparagus is used, tie the stalks around with twine, stand them up in a pot half filled with boiling water, the tips protruding out of the water, cover the pot and let them cook for about eight minutes. You must have a large pot to do this successfully. Some people find that an old coffee pot is useful for this.

When I was nine years old, my boyfriend's family used to grow corn in their back yard on the Red River in Winnipeg. Every evening during the last three weeks of August, the father, who weighed about 230 pounds and who was very interested in his supper, used to go out and pick and strip a dozen ears of corn and bring them to the kitchen to his wife to boil — three minutes only. Twenty-six years have passed by, as well as several boy friends, and I've never tasted corn quite like that. Its sweetness and freshness have never been duplicated. You might, however, find something almost equal if you go to a farmer's market in Ontario or some other corn-growing part of Canada on a morning in late August and carefully choose your corn. Purists strip each cob in order to make sure that the kernels are pale and small enough for the desired tenderness and sweetness. If you have confidence in your farmer-dealer, it is not always necessary to strip every cob before you buy it — but it's a good idea, even if it annoys him.

Remember to cook corn as soon as possible, in boiling water for three minutes. Overcooking wrinkles corn and dissipates its sweetness. Serve after, before or instead of the main course, with lots of butter and salt. Corn holders are useful — they are not, as some people seem to think, merely genteel — if you can manage to keep track of them from year to year. They are no good for anything else so they are apt to get lost, especially in February, when the taste of late August farmer's corn is a very dim sensation.

Once I tried to cook corn in their husks in the glowing ashes of an outdoor fire. It didn't work. But the next time, I stripped them and wrapped them in foilwrap and the results were fine. The corn was juicy and had a pleasant, burnt, aromatic taste.

Corn niblets are very easy to serve if you get them from a can, but it's worth scraping fresh corn off the cob for fritters. They taste 100 per cent better fresh, especially when served as a dessert with maple syrup. It takes about three minutes to scrape down enough niblets from the cob for a family of four or five — about two minutes longer than opening and draining a can of corn niblets. The result is worth the effort.

Incidentally, corn is a traditional Canadian food. It was eaten by Indians, and by the early settlers across Canada, who learned what you could do with it from the Indians. Corn has found its way into a variety of recipes, from corn rolls and corn pie to creamed corn and corn puddings. Without any doubt, the finest corn delicacy I ever ate was in a now long-defunct restaurant called Le Clair's, in St. Norbert, Manitoba. Le Clair's served corn fritters, hot, crisp, and freshly cooked — mounds of them. The owner's wife would fry them in the kitchen while the owner brought platefuls to the guests, who smothered them under maple syrup and ate them, serving after serving, like ravenous hounds.

Another common vegetable in Ontario farmers' markets is the turnip, which is available in both summer and winter. Among the turnip *cognoscenti*, the Canadian product has an excellent reputation. I have a recipe that is different and good, but you must love garlic. As a change, try the wild variety of garlic that can be obtained from time to time in Ontario markets.

Garlic turnips

2 1/2 pounds of turnips, peeled and cut into chunks (small white turnips are preferable, but the big orange kind are easier to find)
4 tbsp. butter
1/4 cup flour
1 cup chicken or beef stock
garlic

Boil turnips until tender (20 minutes or more). Drain, and mash with potato masher.

Melt butter and add flour to butter to make a roux; be sure there are no lumps. Add chicken or beef stock. Press in as much garlic as you like. I add 4 cloves — since turnips are not a delicate vegetable, they can stand the vigorous flavour of garlic. Mix this liquid with the mashed turnip. If you want to reheat the turnips before adding the liquid, do so in a double boiler.

This recipe serves 8 people. It will not be to everyone's taste but it is to mine.

I would like to write about a great many Ontario products but I'm going to discuss only two more — both are small, both dark and round, and both need to be eaten in quantities — blueberries and caviar.

Blueberries grow in every province of Canada. I always thought that the blueberries from my home province, Manitoba, were the best, until I realized that people from Ontario, Quebec, the Atlantic provinces and British Columbia feel the same way about theirs. Whatever the difference, if any, between the blueberries of each province, they all are infinitely better than those fat cultivated ones with pulpy insides, wrapped in cellophane and imported from the United States. Canadian blueberries are smaller and full of juice, and have intense flavour. You can buy the American blueberries out of season, but their insipid taste and gluey texture reveal the irreparable damage of hormones and hothouses.

Late August and early September is real blueberry time. I am fortunate to live in Ottawa where a farmers' market is smack in the centre of the city; there is always a good supply of two-quart baskets of fresh blueberries in season. On the highways of nearly every province in Canada freshly picked berries can be purchased at roadside stands. Usually those are the best kind because they are the wild ones from the woods, not from cultivated fields. If you haven't a farmers' market in your area and you only drive on six-lane super highways, you might never eat a fresh blueberry in all your life. The supermarkets are not consistent in their supply, and in Manitoba for several years there was nary a one to buy in any Safeway or Dominion store. This inconsistency in supply is a problem in the case of all berries other than strawberries. Even though Canadian raspberries are, I think, better than Canadian strawberries, you might not see a box of raspberries twice during the whole year.

About twenty years back, the KENRICIA HOTEL in Kenora, Ontario, used to serve fine, fresh, deep blueberry pie. I was there four years ago and, of course, neither pie nor restaurant are the same. The old-fashioned oak-beamed restaurant has been remodelled into a dimly-lit small-town motel dining-room, and the pie is not even a step-cousin once removed of the former one.

The most important thing to remember about cooking blueberries is not to let them lose their shape. Over-cooking does this. If you use two crusts in a blueberry pie you will have to cook the pie a long time in a fully heated oven in order to bake the bottom crust, and that will result in mushy blueberries, since they cook very quickly. The only way around this, other than cooking the berries separately and pouring them in a baked shell, is old-fashioned deep blueberry pie.

Here is my mother's recipe for deep blueberry pie.

Deep Blueberry Pie
CRUST

1 1/2 cups flour	2 tbsp. sugar
1/2 cup shortening	1/4 cup butter
salt	1/4 cup ice water

With 2 knives or pastry blender, cut butter and shortening into the flour, salt and sugar until mixture is mealy. Mix in water with a fork. Form into a ball and roll out on floured surface.

FILLING

Use 4 cups of blueberries, more if you have them. If you haven't enough, add some green apples, which will be in season at the same time. Wash the berries, add 1/2 cup sugar, and juice and rind of a lemon. Some people mix in with the berries 2 or 3 tablespoons of instant-blending flour, tapioca, or cornstarch for thickening. My mother always made a very runny pie with no thickening at all. Take your choice. I like the runny pie.

Place berries in pie dish, cover with pastry, and sprinkle top of pastry with a little cinnamon and sugar. Make a round hole in the centre of the crust and funnel it with foilwrap to prevent the filling from running out the sides. Turn on the broiler and place pie on the lowest rack of the oven. Cook for about 30 minutes.

> You must look in on your pie from time to time
> in case your crust beings to burn. If it is not done
> after 30 minutes, put the pie up on a higher rack.
> The timing really depends on the vagaries of your
> oven. This broiling technique helps protect the
> berries from over-cooking.
>
> If one part of the crust bakes more quickly than
> another, cover the already-baked section with foil-
> wrap.

I hope there will aways be people around who are willing
to gather blueberries in their wild state and sell them to
greedy city-dwellers like myself. I marvel at the fact that in
a processed and mechanized society, such manual tasks are
still done. But for how long? The exquisite raspberries of
England are virtually unmarketed because the labour to
pick them costs too much. I remember that along the roads
leading to Kenora I used to be able to buy, years ago, large
jars of small wild strawberries that, for fragrance and sub-
tlety of taste, could not even be rivalled by the *fraise du
bois* that are considered such a delicacy in France. But it's
been years since I've seen wild strawberries offered for
sale and I can only hope that blueberries won't follow the
same sorry route.

Ontario is the source of one of Canada's most precious
products — black sturgeon caviar, the real caviar. The eggs
of sturgeon can be found in many regions of Canada, including Quebec, Ontario, Manitoba and British Columbia.
But the principal commercial sources — while they last —
are in Ontario and I'm therefore going to discuss, and discuss at length, the extraordinary but sorry condition of that
celebrated product, which, in spite of its quality and its
former abundance in Canada, has been so little known and
so rarely appreciated. Actually, when I started to gather
research about caviar some months ago, my purpose was to
acquaint Canadians with their caviar heritage. Now these
notes may be a sort of memorial to a Canadian food that
most Canadians didn't even know existed. I fear that most

Canadians will be indifferent, like Duddy Kravitz in Mordecai Richler's *St. Urbain's Horseman.* "Duddy . . . ordered Beluga caviar for both of them," wrote Richler, "double portions, with a side order of chopped egg and onions for himself. For the truth was Duddy didn't care for caviar and only by mashing egg and onion into it could he make it taste almost like chopped liver."

Thanks, in part, to the Duddies of this world — I know many of them — Canadian caviar is now facing extinction. WALDMAN'S FISH MARKET of Montreal and JAN K. OVERWEEL, Toronto Fish Brokers, sold Canadian caviar regularly until 1971. Now it's a rare day when you can find a jar at either place — but try in the spring. Harry Sales of Overweel's feels that he has seen the last of Canadian caviar, at least at the comparatively cheap figure of $12.50 a pound, its retail price in 1970. (Caspian Sea caviar sells in New York for from $70 to $80 a pound.) Manitoba caviar was a staple in my father-in-law's home in Winnipeg during the thirties, and until the mid-sixties. My father-in-law would pay about $3 a pound for it and use it to stuff eggs. Now he's stuffing eggs with green pepper, since no wholesale or retail outlet carries Manitoba caviar.

However, some Canadian caviar still exists. Chef Angelo Casagrande of the CHATEAU LAURIER in Ottawa serves it for special banquets — but he doesn't always say it's Canadian. The quality is high enough to be taken for Russian. His colleague, the chef at the RITZ CARLETON in Montreal, has begged him for the name of his caviar source. A futile effort. Chef Casagrande will reveal nothing except to say that there is a remarkable fisherman from God's Lake, Manitoba who knows how to find the right sort of sturgeon, process the caviar, and satisfy the decadent tastes of the special clients of the CHATEAU LAURIER HOTEL. And, apart from the unknown fisherman in God's Lake, there still is the LAKE NIPISSING CAVIAR COMPANY, which, at one point recently, offered Canadian caviar at $28 a pound, provided you bought a dozen or more jars at a time. Not far from Sturgeon Falls, Ontario, Claude Lamontagne and Paul Benoit, owners of the Company, have been fishing sturgeon out of Lake Nipissing for the last seven years. They screen and salt the eggs in their plant and sell at least a major part of their production to Japan. The Japanese vacuum-pack it, call it Russian or Iranian, and sell it to Paris and London for astronomical prices. The stamp "Iran"or "USSR" on their cans is not surprising, since ninety-five per cent of the world's supply of caviar comes from these two countries.

Historically speaking, caviar, the most expensive food in the world, has always been associated with the rich and royal of eastern Europe. At aristocratic Russian tables, the meal began with a large choice of hot and cold "small bites", called a *zakuski*, which alway included caviar. One noble family in the nineteenth century had a cut glass bowl that held forty-five pounds of caviar. It was refilled daily. Despite its Eastern origins, caviar was known to the French writer Rabelais in the sixteenth century. But it wasn't until after the First World War that caviar became a commonplace at the tables of the wealthy in France and England, no doubt served by aristocratic Russian *émigrés* reduced to passing around *canapés*.

Beluga, the most desired sturgeon because of its large eggs, swims mainly, but not entirely, in salt water and is found primarily in the Black and Caspian seas. It may grow to an enormous size and age. One fished out of the Caspian Sea weighed over a ton, was 100 years old and yielded 400 pounds of caviar. In France a sturgeon over 16 feet long was found in the fresh water of the Gironde River in the nineteenth century. Some French caviar still exists — PRUNIER, a temple of gastronomy in Paris, will serve you some for a price. But the supply is small.

Caviar is processed by a simple method of screening from the raw eggs certain impurities which take the form of a yellow glucose matter. The eggs are then preserved with salt. The less the amount of salt, the better the caviar. The Russians put the word *malassol* on their jars of caviar, which literally means "a little salt". Despite the simple method of processing, the Russians tend to be secretive about the detail.

Experts like the editors of the prestigious and snobby

Guide Julliard of Paris claim that the choicest eggs are grey and come from the Caspian Sea Beluga. Seasoned observers of the Kremlin immediately knew that Prime Minister Trudeau was being given top priority treatment during his voyage to the Soviet Union in 1971 when grey caviar, and not black, was set before him. He and his party ate it with brown bread and butter for breakfast, with vodka at lunch to stimulate the appetite, and occasionally with sour cream, melted butter and *blini* (a thin pancake) at dinner. Despite this gracious treatment, one lesser member of the Prime Minister's entourage was heard to complain, after his seventh breakfast of caviar, ". . . wish I had some big eggs instead".

A friend, a Central-Intelligence-agent-cum-literary-editor, and I consumed vats of the grey and the black during one gluttonous night in Rome. Our experience made us ready to declare, whether to the Kremlin or to all the food snobs in France, that black was better. I will stick by this until someone presents me with the same amount of black and grey Beluga caviar again, for a serious re-evaluation. If there are any volunteers they should remember that fresh Beluga caviar costs around $70 a pound at Bloomingdales in New York, but a mere $54 for a two-pound-four-ounce crock in Moscow.

Scarcely anyone has ever heard of Canadian caviar. Mr. Bardet of CHEZ BARDET, one of Montreal's finest restaurants, and the chef of the THREE SMALL ROOMS in Toronto, were astonished when I spoke to them of it. Too often, the words "Canadian caviar" on a menu mean red salmon roe. Ironically enough, the wife of the United States Ambassador to Canada, Mrs. Schmidt, found out about Canadian caviar shortly after she came here and she serves it to her surprised Canadian guests. She used, when she could get it, at least twelve pounds a month at a fraction of what fresh caviar would cost if it came from Iran or the Soviet Union.

Canadian sturgeon carry eggs that are slightly smaller than Beluga. Claude Lamontagne says he can get as much as forty pounds of eggs from one sturgeon out of Lake

Nipissing. Most of the sturgeon he and Paul Benoit catch are around ten years old, but it's not unusual for them to find one that is twenty years of age. In addition to those found in Lake Nipissing and God's Lake, sturgeon is found in the Albany River and Lake St. Clair, and colder salt waters like James Bay. However, sturgeon living in colder salt water take a longer time to mature, and hatch eggs less often — a disadvantage from the standpoint of the Canadian caviar industry.

Canadian caviar is not considered as choice as the finest Beluga because of the smaller grains and inconsistent processing. (Canadian caviar tends to be salted more than Russian or Iranian — it keeps longer if it has more salt.) Nevertheless, caviar *afficianados*, among them myself, swear that the fresh Canadian kind is better than the vacuum-packed Russian brands found on the shelves of our specialty shops. A perfect jar of Canadian caviar, with the black or grey grains separate and just barely salted, is food for the gods.

It would seem that all you need, if you have an unabated desire for caviar, is money. But money is not enough. Caviar addicts, rich and poor, may have to undergo withdrawal symptoms because the sturgeon are disappearing all over the world.

Over-fishing of the sturgeon and industrial pollution must be controlled by stringent methods of conservation. In Manitoba during the thirties, the Nelson and Winnipeg rivers teemed with sturgeon. Bert Collins of Booth Fisheries in Winnipeg said that there was always open season on sturgeon and any angler could take home two a day. It has been two years since Mr. Collins has sold any caviar from a lake or river in Manitoba. He feels that the American demand for the young sturgeon meat, as well as caviar, has depleted Manitoba's waters. As far back as 1947, a Canadian diplomat saw a sign in a grocery store in the elegant section of Georgetown in Washington, D.C.: "finest Manitoba Beluga caviar" $8 a pound; it's a misnomer — there is no Beluga in Manitoba — but you can't blame the store for trying. Now, except for that man at God's Lake, it seems that no one finds mature sturgeon any more in Manitoba. In any case, the caviar industry is less important than the tourist industry — fish nets get in the way of speed boats and water skiers.

Claude Lamontagne claims that no young lake or river sturgeon have been tagged for the past few years in Lake Nipissing in Ontario — none has been seen. Perhaps it's the pollution from the Abitibi Mills in Sturgeon Falls, or from industries in North Bay, nearby. Or, possibly, all the young sturgeon have been fished out for their meat. Smoked sturgeon is sold for a high price on the American market. One of the stylish things to do in New York is to eat smoked sturgeon for Sunday breakfast in places like Reubens on 57th Street — no Neddicks ninety-nine cent special there. In fact, one of the fixtures of New York delicatessens is Canadian smoked sturgeon.

The future of the caviar industry is poor, not because of lack of demand, but because of lack of supply. Claude Lamontagne is prudently continuing with his profession as a chartered accountant, and Paul Benoit, who is a commercial fisherman, goes out in his boat on Lake Nipissing for other fish besides sturgeon. Professor Etienne Magnin, a professor of biology at the University of Montreal, told me that he visited the Kamouraska River in northern Quebec ten years ago and he saw sturgeon practically jumping out of the water. Fishermen were, he points out, selling them in enormous quantities across the border at pitifully small prices; today, they are difficult to find.

In the Soviet Union and Iran, the story is the same. Russian exports of caviar have averaged around 1000 metric tons per year. Iran exports are an estimated 170 metric tons. Heavy industry and over-fishing have reduced the amount of sturgeon in the Black and Caspian seas. Boris Zagolin, a Moscow State senior lecturer, says "Power dams and intensive fishing have so reduced Russia's Caspian Sea sturgeon stocks, they can no longer be restored by natural means alone." According to a Soviet journal, 66,000 tons of sturgeon were caught in 1967 in the USSR, compared with

114,500 tons in 1961. Iranian sturgeon which spawn at the mouth of the Volga River will be affected by its industrial pollution. American importers who take the bulk of their caviar from Iran say it's becoming hard to get.

All these difficulties are making Russians and North Americans turn to red salmon roe or dyed lumpfish eggs for spreading on their rye bread or ritz crackers. Most people in Canada who have eaten little, hard, black seeds on a biscuit at a cocktail party think they've eaten caviar — but it's really dyed lumpfish roe. Caviar, in the terminology of international cuisine, means sturgeon eggs (although the Russians call all fish eggs caviar).

Because of the diminishing number of sturgeon in their waters, scientists in the Soviet Union have developed an artificial caviar substitute, called *iskra*. *Iskra* is supposed to taste very much like sturgeon eggs. However, lemon juice, which is an essential when eating caviar, causes it to change colour. I get some sort of satisfaction from that fact.

On occasion, as I mentioned earlier, I have had Canadian caviar of astonishingly good quality. But I have purchased Canadian caviar from the same supplier — LAPOINTES in Ottawa — during the same period that was so salty, so glucose-like, so poor, that I considered it to be inedible. This is no fault of the retailer, but one of the main problems in marketing Canadian caviar is that the quality is inconsistent.

Fresh Canadian caviar is usually sold by the pound in Mason jars, screw-top jam jars. (Choose your jar carefully. Much of the screening and salting of caviar is done by hand, so each jar is different. Make sure your jar is not too salty or yellow.) It's odd that the caviar is never vacuum-packed and merchandised in fancy little pots, as the Russian is. There's not even a label on the jars, such as mother's preserves might have. It took me weeks to find out about Claude Lamontagne and Paul Benoit. When I asked the retailers the sources of their caviar, they generally mumbled, "Oh, some fishermen up north." This lack of sophistication in marketing is another reason why Canadian caviar is so little known.

If you get hold of some Canadian caviar, and if you can restrain yourself from gobbling it all up at one go, you can store it, theoretically at least, for quite a long time. A refrigerator set at thirty-five to thirty-eight degrees will keep caviar for a year, *if* the door is not being constantly opened. Harry Sales, who has been selling caviar for over twenty years, says it can be frozen without damage to the grains. Claude Lamontagne and Paul Benoit freeze much of their shipments to Japan. But connoisseurs of caviar like Helen and George Papashvily, who wrote *Russian Cooking* for the Time-Life cook-book series, and the knowledgeable *Guide Julliard* of Paris, claim that the cellular formation of the grains will burst at freezing temperatures.

If you are curious enough to want to find out if caviar freezes, buy the twelve jars from Claude Lamontagne and freeze one. If you discover that frozen caviar is not as good as the fresh, you've only lost the price of one jar in the interest of Science.

Here is how you eat caviar — if you can afford it. By the way, caviar is always eaten raw; never cook it.

Caviar — Classic Style

lots of caviar, with wedges of lemon on the side
finely grated egg yolk
finely grated egg white, on another dish
finely grated raw onion on yet a third
fresh thin toast

Mix according to taste on your toast. (Don't use too much onion.)

My Mother-in-law's Caviar Recipe

Boil some eggs. Remove egg yolks after cutting the eggs in half. Mash egg yolks and add as much caviar as you wish to them. Place caviar and egg yolks back into halved whites.

Serve with whole green onions and lemon wedges and rye bread.

The Prairies — from Duck Bay to Blueberry Mountain

I was born in Winnipeg, and our proudest boast (perhaps it was just the wishful thinking of impressionable natives) was that our railway yards were the largest in North America — we were the greatest railway centre of the world and Chicago was facing oblivion. Gastronomic lore centred on the train journeys taken by farmers, immigrants and hobos, during which all dined on "CPR strawberries". In the east they were called prunes.

The fact that people had to travel long distances to get to their destinations, the cold weather, the bitter wind, and the general bleakness of the surroundings all conspired to make most prairie settlers stick close to their homes. The result was a strong interest in the culture of the kitchen. Many of the Ukrainians, Mennonites, Icelanders, Jews, Germans and Scots borrowed one another's transplanted cooking styles, even if a certain degree of suspicion existed among them.

A good example of this mingling of cuisines was my own mother's experience when she went out to teach school in northern Manitoba after the First World War. Even at the age of nineteen she had already imbibed, physically as well as spiritually (she was what was then called "pleasantly plump"), the techniques of her mother, who had a reputation for culinary *panache* among the kosher set in Winnipeg. In northern Manitoba she stayed with a couple who had just emigrated from England. The husband was a former officer in the Indian Army and had to leave England because his family disapproved of his marriage to a low-born nurse from Liverpool. I guess he was a sort of remittance man because they lived off a very small cheque sent to them from England, the monthly stipend from the Manitoba government for my mother's board and room, and the food that his most unprofitable farm supplied. His wife was laughed at by all the neighbours because she was the only one in the region who put a cloth on her table for supper. My mother didn't mind that — or sharing her bed with the one-year-old baby who wet it nightly — because Mrs. Bell's interest in eating went beyond tablecloths.

When my mother rode her team of horses back to the Bells' farm after a day at the one-room school house (most of the students were of mixed Indian and Scotch blood), clotted cream scones with blackberry jelly, seed cake and pressed chicken were spread on the much-maligned lace table-cloth for tea. Mrs. Bells' shock at housing a real live Jew (nineteen years old, female, and afraid of horses) was overcome by her terrible loneliness and my mother's delight in her cooking.

It was a prairie phenomenon, this hospitable offering of English cakes and pressed chicken in Birch River, Manitoba, to the local school teacher, who was brought up on chopped liver and borsch 300 miles to the south. My mother, far from rejecting the new food, has been baking Mrs. Bell's scones, Yorkshire puddings and steamed puddings for the last thirty years. There's a sad footnote to the story. Mrs. Bell's North Country family began to prosper in England, while she and her semi-aristocratic husband desperately tried to scratch a living out of their farm. Weather, loneliness and lack of experience in farming drove the Bells to mental and financial desperation, and the last years of their lives were extremely sad. My mother remembers Mrs. Bell opening a Christmas present from her prosperous family — a red velvet party dress — and bursting into tears. What she needed were flannel sheets but she was too proud to tell them. She used to write her family glowing letters about her glamorous existence with her upper-class husband in the north of Manitoba.

Mrs. Bell died long ago but at least one happy memory of her has been preserved in an unexpected place. My mother was asked to contribute some of her gastronomic specialties to Winnipeg's Hadassah cook-book. Printed next to the sour-cream knish dough, poppy-seed *fluden* and farfel toasties are Mrs. Bell's fresh-fruit trifles, seed cakes and Banbury tarts.

A story from the Lac-du-Bonnet region of eastern Manitoba provides a classical example of these western, cross-cultural, gastronomic appropriations, circa 1960. Two high-school girls, one of Norwegian-English background, the other Icelandic, were going out with second-generation Ukrainian boys. A friend of mine walked into the kitchen of one of the girls and discovered them making, not Icelandic recipes or a Scandinavian specialty, but mountains of perogies, "enough to feed all the Ukrainian male population from Lac-du-Bonnet to Beausejour" (see p. 106 for a recipe). The girls wanted to please their boy-friends and were trying out the effectiveness of the adage about the way to a man's heart.

Throughout Canada, one of the richest sources of recipes are the little paperback cookery-books put out by local ladies' benevolent associations. And a certain bond exists between a book of recipes of the Ladies Auxiliary of the Kingston Peninsula Volunteer Fire Department in New Brunswick, a Ukrainian cookery-book from Saskatchewan and a collection of recipes put together by the Pioneer Women in Winnipeg. Some might draw back and point out, even in this age of the concept of universal man, that the mind boggles at invoking, in the same sentence, salt cod dinner cooked with milk and pork fat, brain and bacon *pashtetky*, and gefilte fish. But the similarities are of several kinds: Most of these cheaply produced little recipe books have some little homily printed at the beginning — the ingredients for a happy home, the observation that a woman's work is never done, etc. And one invariably gets the feeling that some of the recipes aren't telling all. There seems to be a Mrs. Birnbaum in every ethnic group in Canada. Mrs. Birnbaum's dishes were considered the most *raffinée* by the gastronomic *cognoscenti* of Winnipeg. Her cherry preserve was an elixir that was used as an antidote to eastern European melancholy. But when her contributions to the Hadassah cook-book appeared in print they looked

stark. A few ladies tried them with no success. Obviously
Mrs. Birnbaum had omitted an ingredient or a vital technique that made all the difference. Judging by some of the
sparse technical information in the ladies benevolent
cookery-books of those regions, I have the feeling that Mrs.
Birnbaum lives under various names in Misery Point, Newfoundland; Lac St.-Jean, Quebec; Wawanesa, Manitoba,
and Gravelbourg, Saskatchewan.

Other parallels come to mind. Certain recipes appear in
these ethnic cook-books that belong to none of the traditional styles of cooking. "Chinese" chicken and almond
casserole and ginger-ale salad have made deep inroads into
Mennonite cooking, kosher cuisine and the recipe books
of ladies' clubs in the Maritimes. Finally, it should be noted
that in all of the various charity recipe books in Canada
there is an emphasis on sweets. The largest section of recipes
in all of the books deals with cakes, pastries and desserts.
Canadians of all racial backgrounds appear to share an un-
conquerable sweet tooth. The dishes that involve the most
labour, take the most time, and seem worth the most effort
to those compiling their books, come at the end of the meal.

Here are Mrs. Bell's scones made with sour cream in
Hadassah cook-book tradition.

Mrs. Bell's Scones

2 cups flour	3 tbsp. sugar
2 tsp. baking powder	1/3 tsp. soda
3/4 tsp. salt	5 full tbsp. butter
1/3 cup currants	1 egg separated
2/3 cup thick sour cream	cinnamon

Sift flour before measuring, then sift together dry
ingredients. Rub in butter and then washed and
dried currants. Mix yolk with cream. Add to make
soft dough. Mix well and knead lightly 2 or 3
times on lightly floured pastry board or cloth. Pat
out 1/2" thick. Cut in circles about 4" or 5" in
diameter. Mark out into quarters with back of
silver knife. Brush lightly with unbeaten egg white.
Sprinkle a little sugar and cinnamon on top. Bake

in 425° oven 15 to 18 minutes (or less) until well raised and golden brown.

My mother is particularly talented in making blintzes. Blintzes are very much like French *crêpes*, but more homely. You can shape them into triangles or roll them into sausage-like envelopes. You can put almost anything into a blintz. Most people like them with cottage cheese or meat filling — but never combine the two in one blintz.

Here is a Hadassah cook-book blintz recipe, revised by my mother (whose red-pencilled corrections in the back show that she sees Mrs. Birnbaum everywhere).

Blintzes

DOUGH

1 cup flour	1 1/2 cups water
3 eggs	a little salt

Beat eggs, and add water and salt; stir in sifted flour, beating until smooth. Slightly grease a hot 8" frying pan. Pour just enough batter in to make a thin sheet. Cook only one side of blintz. Cook until firm enough to turn, baked side out, on a pastry board.

Many Jewish people were raised to the sound of grandmothers banging out the blintz skin. This was done by rapping the overturned frying pan on a pastry board. You can keep two frying pans going at the same time: while one is being rapped, the other cooks.

Notice that water, not milk, is used. It makes for a thinner blintz dough. Thick blintz doughs are crass.

FILLING

1 lb. dry cottage cheese
a bit of sugar
   (a couple of tbsp. if
   you like a sweeter
   filling)
2 eggs
melted butter

Mix it all up.

Place 1 tbsp. cheese filling on one end of the blintz skin and roll, folding in the ends. Very gently cook the blintzes in a buttered skillet until they look a little brown — but not too. Serve hot with sour cream and strawberry jam. You can make the blintz skins in advance and brown them later in the oven, or use the top of the stove.

One of the glories of Winnipeg dessert cookery was something called a Russian butter cake, which used to appear at every bar mitzvah and charity tea. It had to be rich and moist — the home-made chocolate pudding in between layers softened it to the right degree. As children we used to hang around the tea tables searching out this particular delicacy, which was cut up into small pieces and dispersed among the frugal almond crescents and "nothings" (so called because they were made with "hardly any" flour). We thought these last goodies suitable for gall badder and ulcer cases and other sickly conditions.

Russian Butter Cake

1 cup butter	2 cups bread flour, sifted
1 cup white sugar	1/4 tsp. baking soda
1 egg	

Cream butter and sugar well; add egg. Add the flour and baking soda; mix well and divide the dough into 5 portions. Pat out dough into 8″ layer-cake tins. If you only have 2, you will have to bake the dough over a period of time. The best kind are those with a little lever attached to help remove the baked dough. Otherwise use foilwrap.

Bake the dough for about 10 minutes in a 375° oven. Remove the layer from the pan after it has completely cooled. It will be very brittle, so handle carefully. Continue to do this until you have 5 baked layers.

FILLING

1/2 cup sugar	2 tbsp. cocoa
1 tbsp. cornstarch	2 egg yolks
2 cups milk	1 tsp. vanilla
1 tsp. butter	

If you are like me, you may substitute 1/2 cup of rum for 1/2 cup of the milk. But put it in towards the end of the cooking.

Mix egg yolks, sugar, cocoa and cornstarch. Put into double boiler and cook until thick. Add vanilla and 1 tsp. butter. Spread filling in between layers (all layers must be cooled). Ice with chocolate icing of your own choice. Put into refrigerator for at least 48 hours. It must be very moist. But, cake should be removed from refrigerator 3 hours before serving, to soften.

Some people use apricot filling because chocolate is so rich, but I think chocolate is best.

My Mother's Chocolate Icing

Melt 3 squares unsweetened chocolate. Cream 1/2 cup butter, 1 whole egg and 1 cup icing sugar in electric mixer. Add 1 tsp. instant coffee and cooled melted chocolate. Beat for at least 5 minutes. Add 1/2 tsp. almond flavouring.

Another recipe that is excellent but much simpler is Mrs. H. Sokolov's honeyed nuts. She called them "expensive but good".

Honeyed Nuts

4 tbsp. honey — Manitoba buckwheat honey does
   very well
1 lb. nuts, preferably almonds
1 tbsp. cocoa   1 tbsp. butter

Boil together until mixture is very slightly burnt. Mix thoroughly until nuts are covered with honey. Pour on damp wooden board. Undo in clusters while still hot.

Jewish cooking, aside from the traditional religious rules, is very like another prairie cuisine — Ukrainian. The two culinary styles originated in Slavic countries, and although

Ukrainians use a lot of pork and add butter and cream to their meat dishes (strictly forbidden in kosher cooking), many recipes are identical. Both groups share a penchant for little envelopes of pastry of varying textures, made with a multitude of fillings. The most popular are *kreplach* (a Jewish name) and *pyrohy* (Ukrainian), now known throughout the prairies and British Columbia among all races, as perogies. Cabbage, mashed potato, chopped meats, cottage cheese, liver, *kasha* and blueberries are used by both groups as fillings.

A lady who is expert at making this delicacy told me that the secret of a tender *kreplach* or perogy dough is mashed potatoes.

Kreplach or Perogy Dough

2 scant cups flour
1 tsp. salt
1 egg
1 small mashed potato
enough lukewarm water to make a soft dough

Mix the flour, potato, salt and egg. Add some water to make a soft dough. Let stand for 1/2 hour.

Prepare a filling as directed below.

Roll dough until quite thin on a floured board. Cut rounds with a large glass or biscuit cutter. Or cut into squares with a knife. Put the round or square in the palm of the hand. Place a spoonful of filling on it, fold over to form a half-circle or triangle, and press edges together with fingers. The edges should be free of filling, and well sealed.

Drop a few perogies into a large pot of boiling water. Do not cook all of them at one time. Make sure they do not stick to the pot. Boil for 10 minutes or until puffy. They must rise to the top.

Drain and put in a dish with melted butter. Keep adding the perogies to the dish, shaking them along with more butter so they won't stick together. The dish of buttered perogies may be kept in a warm oven while the last ones are being boiled.

Serve with sour cream or, if you prefer, Ukrainian-style, browned buttered bread-crumbs.

CHEESE FILLING

2 cups dry cottage cheese
1 egg slightly beaten
1/2 cup sour cream
salt

Mix until the filling holds its shape.

Kasha or buckwheat groats played the same role for the Ukrainians and Jews as oatmeal did for the Scotch. It was their staff of life. A good many members of the two ethnic groups (along with the Scotch) fortunately emigrated to a place where buckwheat grows like mad — the western provinces. Not only could they indulge in their taste for *kasha* in Canada; the favourite sweetening agent of the Jews and Ukrainians — honey — is a western Canadian specialty. One could say that the gastronomic culmination for Canadians of Jewish and Ukrainian origin is Red River buckwheat honey, premium grade.

The Red River flows north-south and so did some of the gastronomic traditions. In fact, it would have been hard to say where, at the turn of the last century, Manitoba and Saskatchewan stopped and Minnesota and North Dakota began. Immigrants wandered over the border, settled for a few years or longer on the American side, and often returned to become residents of Canada again. My husband's great-grandfather, a Baron de Hirsh emigrant who settled in southern Saskatchewan (in Hirsch, to be precise) in the early 1890's, was one of those who wandered south for a while; his son opened a mill for grinding buckwheat groats in St. Paul, Minnesota. He couldn't sell the stuff and my father-in-law remembers a steady diet of *kasha* and milk for breakfast and *kasha* and gravy for dinner, until they all gave up in despair and went north again, this time to Manitoba.

Buckwheat grits or groats — I shall refer to them as *kasha* from now on — are not difficult to prepare and are very good to eat. A casserole of *kasha* and macaroni shells used to sell out in the first hour of the Winnipeg Symphony Ladies International Food Fair. You can buy *kasha* at any Jewish or Ukrainian specialty food shop and at supermarkets that have a large Jewish or Ukrainian clientele. In Quebec it is marketed under its French name, *sarrasin,* and the flour is used to make buckwheat pancakes. Lately, health-food stores have started to stock it because of its nutritional value. *Kasha* grains come in different sizes: the health-food people prefer the large because it's less refined, but many *kasha* lovers think medium size is best for cooking.

This is the recipe that was so popular at the Winnipeg Symphony Fair, but I think it's too starchy; and I suggest that mushrooms be substituted for the macaroni. This dish can be used as a change from potatoes or rice.

Kasha and Mushrooms

2 cups kasha   1 or 2 tbsp. fat if desired (butter,
1 egg   chicken fat, or drippings)
2 tbsp. salt
about 4 cups boiling water, or enough just to cover
    kasha
onions
mushrooms

Put the dry kasha in a shallow pan on low heat. Mix in the raw egg and dry the mixture thoroughly over the stove, stirring frequently. The kasha should begin to smell nut-like, but be careful not to scorch it.

Put the kasha in a casserole; add fat, salt and boiling water. Cover and cook at 400° for 15 minutes. Lower the temperature and cook a little longer — until the kernels are separated and fluffy and the water has evaporated. Mix some fried mushrooms and onions with this.

Instead of water, substitute boiling chicken soup or consommé for a richer taste.

If you would like to learn more about the stomach culture of the eastern European Jews of western Canada, I suggest you read Fredelle Bruser Maynard's *Raisins and Almonds*. The book contains some poignant memories about how baking and cooking added stability to a family always on the move in the small towns of Saskatchewan and Manitoba. Jewish culinary traditions in Canada are, of course, not all derived from eastern Europe; nor are they limited to the Jewish communities of western Canada. Trina Vineberg's *Family Heirlooms* will give you an account of a very different kind of Jewish culinary culture — this one derived from the cooking traditions of England and transplanted to Montreal.

One of the most exhaustive and authentic cookery-books found on the shelves of Canadian bookstores is *Traditional Ukrainian Cookery* by Savella Stechishin. Mrs. Stechishin, a home economist, gathered her recipes from the wide membership of the Ukrainian Women's Association. Titles like "Tender Bulochky" from Wroxton, Saskatchewan, "Plain Krendli" and "Crackling Korzhiyky" — both specialties of North Battleford, Saskatchewan — reflect something of the nature and style of the Ukrainian communities that are spread across the western provinces.

Of the approximately 475,000 Canadians who regard themselves as being of Ukrainian origin, it is the large concentrations in Winnipeg, and in towns throughout the West, who have succeeded in maintaining a vigorous and flourishing culinary culture. In order to reach the cultural mainsprings of the rural, but sophisticated, Ukrainian cuisine we can travel to Two Hills, Alberta for the best *boiled bublyky,* and to Krydor, Saskatchewan to eat a fine *spice medivnyk*. There, living amid the winter snow and summer wheat, are Ukrainian women with at least four different kinds of recipes for perogy dough — depending on whether the filling is plum or cabbage (yeast dough is best for plum) or something else. Some of them know how to make *saltseson,* a pressed loaf made from two pig's ears, one pig's stomach and one cup of fresh pig's or calf's blood. Mrs. Stechishin realizes there might be a few slackers among the younger women and remarks, "The making of *saltseson* is quite troublesome but it is really worth the effort."

She has preserved many invaluable and unusual recipes using honey, cottage cheese, rhubarb, beets and *kasha* — all ingredients common to the west of Canada. Perhaps the essence of the Ukraine and the Canadian prairies merge together in this enchanting recipe for "Rose Petal Preserves," made from the wild rose of the prairies or Betty Bland, a hardy cultivated rose originated by Dr. Frank Skinner of Dropmore, Manitoba (the Luther Burbank of Canada, he has developed more new strains in plant life than any other Canadian). This is a version of Mrs. O. Wolchuck's recipe from Saskatoon.

Rose Petal Preserves

To avoid washing the petals, pick them after a good rain. Pick the petals of the fully or partly opened roses, pulling them with one grasp; while holding them in the hand, cut off the yellow tips that have been attached to the crown of the blossom. These yellow ends must be removed because they have a bitter taste. Spread the petals on a clean wire screen to let the stamens and pollen fall through, and then pick the petals over.

Scald with boiling water and drain. As an alternative method, omit the scalding, sprinkle the petals with some sugar and crush with the hand to remove bulkiness. Sprinkle very generously with lemon juice; otherwise, the petals will turn brown. Use equal quantities of sugar and petals. Use 1 part water for 3 parts rose petals. Combine sugar and water and bring to a boil. Add the petals and simmer, stirring frequently, for about 10 minutes. Add more lemon juice if necessary.

Remove from stove and let the preserves stand overnight. Then bring to a boil once more and cook until syrup is thick and clear. Pack into hot sterilized jars.

Uncooked Rose Petal Preserves
from Mrs. Wolchuck

Follow the directions in the preceding recipe for Rose Petal Preserves but do not scald the petals.

Sprinkle the petals with some sugar and lemon juice, and crush them well. Chop small quantities until fine, and mix 1 cup of chopped petal pulp with 2 more cups of sugar and mash some more in a bowl. It must be as smooth as possible before you seal it.†

Ukrainians consider rose petal preserves unequalled as a filling for yeast-raised doughnuts, called *pampushky*. When the early Ukrainian pioneers arrived, their "longing for rose petal preserves" was satisfied by the abundant prairie rose and the Betty Bland.

It is not possible to discuss prairie Slavic cuisine without mentioning *beet borsch*. The best I've ever tasted was at my grandmother's house one Passover. She made it with a base of fermented beets, or "rusell" (as she called it), that she kept crocked for about two or three weeks in her basement. It had an intensity and sourness that the more common flavourings of lemon or vinegar combined with sugar, cannot equal. Savella Stechishin says in her book that "Ukrainian connoisseurs of good borsch insist that beet 'kvas' or fermented beets is absolutely necessary to give personality to borsch." How many Ukrainian and Jewish families in the Prairies have crocks of fermenting beets in their basements today?

For a perfect and authentic *beet borsch* here is how to make "kvas" or "rusell".

Pure Beet Borsch Made from Kvas

Wash and pare 12 beets, cut into quarters, place in an earthenware container and cover with boiled water cooled to lukewarm. Cover and keep at room temperature for a week. Remove the scum and check to see if the beets are fermenting — the liquid should be a little cloudy. Stir well and replace cover (don't keep the cover on too tightly). When the liquid is wine coloured and sour tasting you can use part or all of it for borsch.

† Adapted from *Traditional Ukrainian Cookery* by Savella Stechishin, reprinted by permission of the author and Trident Press Ltd., Winnipeg.

Heat as much of it as you like and boil some potatoes and onions with it. Additions of lemon and sugar, as well as salt and pepper, enhance the flavour.

Eat hot or cold with chopped cucumber.

Ordinary Beet Borsch with or without Rusell or Kvas

5 beets, not pared
2 lbs. flank steak, short ribs, or any soup meat
2 onions
1 tin of tomatoes
3 large carrots
celery stalks
1 potato per person
about 2 quarts water or enough to cover everything in the pot
flavourings — salt, pepper, garlic, lemon, tartaric acid crystals and sugar. If you have fermented beets, by all means put them in.

Let all this cook about 2 hours. Take out the beets, slice them up and return to the pot. It is impossible to say how much tartaric acid crystals, lemon juice and sugar the borsch will need. It should have a sharp, not too sweet, taste, not insipid. The lemon juice should be added towards the end.

Beet stems and tops add greatly to the borsch. Chop the tops and stems into lengths of 1″ and put them in. Cook another 20 minutes and flavour the soup to your taste. Add potatoes one half-hour before eating. Serve with a dab of sour cream on top.

Molasses might be the favourite sweetener in the Maritimes and, according to some figures, it is even more popular in Quebec, but honey, as I mentioned, belongs to the prairie provinces. Unfortunately, the honey squares covered in chocolate that used to be made by the Trappist Monks of St. Norbert, Manitoba are now just a memory. But you will find western honey in liquid, creamed and block form. You will find the clear variety — light, thin and mild — as well as buckwheat honey — amber coloured, heavy and sweeter. Three-quarters of the total Canadian crop of honey is produced in Manitoba, Saskatchewan and Alberta, mainly from alfalfa and clover. The quality is high and noted for its uniformity. Nothing compares with the rich flavour of prairie buckwheat honey, especially when baked in a Ukrainian honey cake from Edmonton.

Sour Cream and Buckwheat Medivnyk (Honey Cake)
(an adaptation from Mrs. M. Nowosad)

1 cup honey
  (preferably buckwheat honey)

1/2 cup butter	1 tsp. baking powder
1 cup brown sugar	2 tsp. ginger
4 eggs, separated	1 cup thick sour cream
3 cups sifted flour	1 cup chopped walnuts
2 tsp. baking soda	1/2 cup raisins

Bring honey to a boil and cool. Cream butter and add sugar. Add egg yolks one at a time and beat until fluffy. Beat in honey. Sift flour and dry ingredients. Add alternately with sour cream to the honey mixture. Stir in nuts and raisins. Beat egg whites stiff and fold into batter. Spoon into buttered tube pan.

Bake at 325° for 50 to 55 minutes. Lower the temperature for the last 15 minutes of baking to 300°.

I haven't done justice to the countless recipes from the West, whether of Ukrainian or Jewish origin. Those I have chosen seem to be typical, and reasonably easy to cook, as well as delicious to eat. And they arouse such personal nostalgia. I used to go to Luxton School in the north end of Winnipeg, where most of the pupils were Jewish or Ukrainian, while the teachers, like most teachers in Winnipeg at that time, were Scottish. The only time the parents and teachers ever faced one another was at the annual Home and

School Tea. While the students passed tea cups and eaves-
dropped on conversations, the teachers attempted to trap
the parents of the worst and best pupils. (The mediocre
ones like me were pigeon-holed as "daydreamers" and not
fussed about.) About three weeks before the tea the mothers
were asked to bake a little "square" (that was the term
the teachers always used) for the event. The teachers were
always afraid, for some reason, that if they didn't organize
and mark down what each mother was baking well beforehand, there would be nothing to eat on the day of the tea.
A sort of gastronomic roll-call would take place before the
tea, and invariably, suspicion and confusion would cloud
the face of the Scottish teacher as each pupil gave the name
of his or her mother's contribution.

We were ignorant of the Winnipeg Scotch terms for these
delights and would reply, almond *pyrozhky, mondlebroit,
moon* cookies (actually *mohn* for poppy seed, but some of
us were already Anglophones) and *teiglach* — becoming
lame with embarrassment when Miss MacKay or Miss
Dunbar or Miss McNeil asked for more explicit descriptions. We knew that our teachers didn't stuff *their* cakes
with poppy seeds, or use Mazola oil in their shortbread.
Our revenge came soon enough though. On the day of the
school tea, the teachers were always overwhelmed by the
full force of the manifestation of eastern Europe's culinary
resources. I remember a giant cornucopia made from
shaved almonds filled with a cream pastry flavoured with
ground almonds. It was brought by a nine-year-old girl,
who had carried it from her house to the school basement,
a distance of one mile, in the usual twenty-five-degrees-
below-zero weather. She knew if she dropped it on the way
she could never go back home again!

Less spectacular, but just as rich, were the variety of
tortes filled with prunes and apricots, paper-thin strudels
set with turkish-delight jewels, and the 100 different kinds
of cookies, twisted and turned every which way, made from
honey. The new teachers at Luxton (there was always a
large teacher turnover at that school) were impressed but

aghast at the extravagance and showiness of the baking, and those who had to bear with the unfamiliar ways and the loud mouths of the Luxton school pupils for a few years, would take a certain pride in the "team spirit" of the mothers, many of whom spoke no English. Unconsciously, the mothers' rule-of-thumb was the worse the English, the more lavish the contribution; in this way they made up for social inadequacies. There were exceptions to this rule; my own mother always let me down because she felt no need for self-expression at the Luxton Home and School Tea. Her contributions were the aptly-named "nothings".

A large proportion of Canada's one million citizens of German origin can be found spread out across the Prairies, both in the cities and in the small towns. Like the Ukrainians, Jews, Hungarians and other eastern European groups, they like to eat, and they too have preserved and adapted much of their cooking culture. In Steinbach and Altona, Manitoba, as well as in rural Saskatchewan, the Sunday night communal dinners are gastronomic events at which local residents and strangers alike can experience the whole gamut of German cooking. I've already described the German cooking that centres around Lunenburg, Nova Scotia and Kitchener-Waterloo in Ontario, so I won't repeat now what I've already discussed, particularly since the Mennonite cooking of the Prairies is essentially the same as the Mennonite variety of Ontario. But lest anyone think that the Mennonite cooking of the Prairies is a dying art, I should record that the *Altona Women's Institute Cookbook*, now called the *Canadian Mennonite Cookbook*, has run through fourteen printings and, according to the Altona publishers, sold more than 50,000 copies.

The Icelanders, perhaps the smallest ethnic group on the Prairies (they number about 30,000), have, along with other Scandinavian descendents, also left their mark on the cooking traditions of the region. The Icelanders, Swedes (some from Minnesota) and Norwegians brought their particular cooking skills to many small settlements in the West. The Manitoba government is so aware of its Nordic heritage that in an advertisement recently placed by its tourist people in the *New Yorker*, Americans are invited to visit "picturesque" Icelandic fishing villages on the shores of Lake Winnipeg. The good people of Gimli might be a little startled by this folkloric description. But it was true, nonetheless, that before the Second War Winnipeg had more people of Icelandic origin than Reykjavik, the capital of Iceland. What did this mean gastronomically?

During a certain period the Scandinavian settlements along the Winnipeg River used to smoke their own sturgeon, caught in the River. A lady from Lac-du-Bonnet told me about her Swedish grandmother whose kitchen smelled deliciously of cardamom — a traditional Scandinavian spice for flavouring home-made bread. The odour was so agreeable that a heel of a stale loaf was deliberately left in the bread box to prolong the perfume. Herring in sour cream and fruit soups (stewed, dried fruits, puréed and thickened with cornstarch) were served at lunch with home-made yoghurt. The Scandinavians have always been great coffee lovers so many of the housewives used to buy green coffee beans and roast them to their own taste in their ovens. The odour of roasting coffee mingled with cardamom must have made the kitchen the most wonderful place to be on a winter's night. Icelanders, Norwegians and Swedes who lived in the western provinces all liked one dish in particular — very thin pancakes, a little like French *crêpes*, that were stuffed with whipped cream and fresh berries. They also appreciated all milk products, and fish from the yet-unpolluted lakes. According to my sources, pork was popular with the Swedish people, while lamb was the favourite of the Icelanders, who would take a flank, roll and pickle it and then serve it in thin slices, like a spiced beef.

Waffles, meat balls, and our old Maritime friend, dried cod, called *lut fisk*, a great specialty at Christmas, formed part of the prairies' Scandinavian cuisine. A Swedish friend told me that she hated *lut fisk*; it looked like a piece of plywood before it was treated with baking soda and lime. After the treatment, its appearance changed; in this finished state, her family renamed *lut fisk* Lux Flakes, because of a certain similarity in taste. A personal not a general opinion.

No account of western cooking should overlook a particular culinary delicacy, not as common now as it was at one time — gopher stew. James Gray, in one of his books about the West during the Dirty Thirties, *Men Against the Desert*, describes the gopher phenomenon.

"Why shouldn't gophers be good to eat?" they [the farmers of Saskatchewan and Alberta] demanded. "They exist almost exclusively on a diet of grass and grain, and there is no reason why the meat of a grain-fed gopher should not be as good as the meat of a grain-fed steer."
[But] it took a lot of them to make a meal....
After being skinned, cleaned and dressed, gophers were cooked in just about every way a rabbit could be cooked. When simply popped into a pot and boiled they excited few appetites. This undoubtedly led to experiments with gopher stew. If gopher quarters were mixed in with vegetables and chicken, there were those who insisted that no one could tell chicken and gopher apart. . . . In addition to stewing, the gophers were canned in the same way as canned chicken. One farm family . . . came up with gopher pie. The meat was simply placed in a pan, covered with a crust and baked in the oven. Another favourite dish was smoked gopher which was regarded by some as the ultimate delicacy of the Dirty Thirties. The meat was hung on sticks in the bright sun with a fire going constantly to smoke the gophers and keep off the flies.
Pickling gophers was common throughout southern Saskatchewan. A school teacher visiting a farm home east of Canuck arrived just as the farm wife was completing the pickling of a 10 gallon crock of gophers. Preserved in brine, they helped stretch the winter's food supplies. . . . Some children developed a strong liking for gophers that were breaded and fried like chicken. . . . †

Now I am going to talk at some length about one of the greatest and least appreciated gastronomic resources of this

† Reprinted by permission of the publisher, Western Producer Book Service.

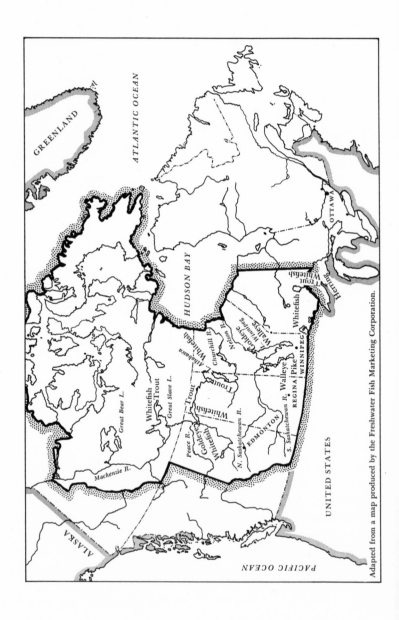

region — its fresh-water fish. Look at the map on page 118. Twenty per cent of the world's fresh-water is contained within the zone whose boundaries are roughly the western Alberta border extending northwest, the northernmost parts of the Northwest Territories, the western shore of Hudson Bay and a north-south line bisecting Ontario. This marks the boundary of the Freshwater Fish Marketing Corporation, which was set up by the federal government in cooperation with the provinces concerned to be the sole buyer for export, out of the province of origin, of all species of fresh-water fish from commercial fishermen in north-western Ontario, Manitoba, Saskatchewan, Alberta and the Northwest Territories. The Corporation, which operates out of Winnipeg, was established in 1969.

Despite pollution, the tourist industry and over-fishing, it is obvious that there is still a vast quantity of fish around. And at least twenty varieties of fish in this area are market-able. Others, like the beautiful grayling in Canada's north-ern waters, which are delicious when freshly pan-fried and are supposed to smell like thyme (they don't), are the preserve of sportsmen. But when was the last time you ate buffalo fish, inconnu, redhorse, sheepshead or even red or gray mullet? The Corporation is anxious to market as many of these lesser known species as possible. But it even has trouble selling whitefish, walleye and perch. Some of its problems are due to the difficulty of distributing fish caught in areas far from marketing centres. Quick-freeze techni-ques are essential and not yet widely available. But the Corporation's greatest problem is psychological — Canadi-ans hate fish. It is laughable to compare the tiny number of retail fish outlets in the prairie provinces (and everywhere else in Canada, for that matter) with the amount of fish potentially available. The Quebecois share the western dis-like of fish. Since the Roman Catholic Church dispensed with meatless Friday, fish sales in Quebec have dropped thirty-five per cent. If we need some more statistics to prove the point about the Canadian attitudes towards fish, here are some: Canadians consume only 13 pounds of fish per

capita per year. Compare this with a per capita annual consumption of 180 pounds of meat and poultry.

The frightening phrase "mercury pollution" has scared
off the limited number of Canadians who actually liked
pickerel and whitefish — the traditional stand-bys of the
prairie lakes. Whitefish has been far less affected by mercury than pickerel, according to the experts in the Fresh-
water Fish Marketing Corporation. They say that the
mercury problem has been pin-pointed to the South Saskatchewan River, Cedar Lake and the northern shores of Lake
Winnipeg. Most of these waters are now open again for
fishing. And for the last two years, every shipment of fish
has been monitored by government inspectors. In any case,
a lot of skeptics feel that the mercury scare has been edging
on the hysterical. There have been no documented cases of
fatal mercury poisoning from fish in Canada. There was a
lady in the United States who died after eating only swordfish three times a day for two years — she wanted to lose
weight. Try eating an exclusive diet of *anything* for that
amount of time and your insides will react. If you consumed
carrots as she ate swordfish, your complexion would glow
bright orange; it's called carotenemia — look it up in any
medical book!

However, if you have to diet, whitefish makes a fine food
— delicate, subtle and firm in taste. Here's a recipe for what
is hardly a typical prairie soup, but our lake fish are perfect
ingredients for it — an exotic but impressive dish.

Whitefish or Pickerel Bourride
This is a kind of soup made with garlic mayonnaise.

COURT BOUILLON
2 fish heads, bones and trimmings
3 cups water
2 cups dry white wine
2 large onions, thinly sliced
1 leek (optional)
2 tbsp. wine vinegar
the fresh peel of half an orange
2 bay leaves

1 tsp. fennel leaves
2 tsp. salt
fish — 5 lbs. of whitefish or pickerel cut into 3″ chunks 1″ thick

In a large saucepan bring all the court bouillon ingredients to a boil except the fish; cover and simmer for 30 minutes. This part may be made in advance.

AIOLI

3 tbsp. fine dry bread crumbs
1 tbsp. wine vinegar
6 chopped cloves of garlic
7 egg yolks and 1 whole egg
1 tsp. salt
1 1/2 — 2 cups olive oil
juice of at least 1 lemon

Soak the bread crumbs in 1 tbsp. vinegar for a few minutes, then squeeze them dry. Put 1 whole egg, 3 egg yolks, garlic, bread crumbs and salt in blender. Buzz slowly; add about 1/2 cup olive oil, blending all the while. A mayonnaise-like mixture should form. Add another cup (or more) of oil, and the lemon juice. (Add more lemon juice or vinegar if you think it necessary.)

Save half the sauce for serving with the fish and add the 4 extra yolks to the remaining half. (The aioli also may be made in advance.)

COOKING THE FISH

After the bouillon has simmered for 30 minutes, and about 15 minutes before serving, bring it to a boil again and add prepared fish. Simmer uncovered for about 8 minutes. Make sure the fish doesn't overcook. Remove the fish from the broth with slotted spoon.

Correct the seasoning of the broth. Strain and remove 1 cup of broth from the pot. Add the cup of broth in driblets to the aioli, beating all the time. Carefully pour this mixture back into the pot of soup and heat until the soup thickens — 4 or 5 minutes. Do not let it boil or you will have scrambled eggs with garlic.

Serve the fish in the soup or separately and pass the extra aioli around. Serves 8 people.

Because of the Canadian indifference to fish, and the difficulties of transportation, two or three species of fish that practically choke certain lakes have never been harvested. It is the goal of the Freshwater Fish Marketing Corporation to make North Americans eat red and grey mullet and fresh-water cod, even if they have to put them in a deboning machine, chop them up and reconstitute them into fish sticks. Canadians may soon be able to eat mullet in the form of a fishcake called "Chimo". Personally, I prefer to eat fish as they come out of the lakes, but the Corporation feels that fish that tastes like something else may be the saviour of the fresh-water fish industry of Canada. Notwithstanding the twenty species of marketable fish in fresh-water lakes, the catch up until now has been restricted to the conventional whitefish, pickerel, sauger, trout and northern pike. If Canadians cared more about fish, we might see some more of the lesser known species on the market some day.

Arctic char is perhaps our most distinctive Canadian product, since it can be found nowhere in the world except in Canada. When it's fresh, it's extraordinarily good, but when it's frozen, it becomes, like its cousin the trout, just plain ordinary. There are real problems in distributing the char commercially. While it can be found landlocked in some eastern lakes, it is mainly spread throughout the remote northern areas of Canada — in places like the waters off Herschel Island, Ellesmere Island, the Territories and the Labrador coast, and in many rivers running into these waters.

The commercial importance of the char has increased greatly in recent years in response to southern interest. Even now, smoked char is beginning to be sold in Newfoundland, and it certainly rivals the smoked salmon of the same region. But I think it's a pity that like fine lake trout (much of which is fished commercially from Great Slave Lake and the waters of northern Saskatchewan), char is rarely marketed fresh. I find it hard to believe that the potential demand for this fish can't lead to its commercial distribution in a fresh state at prices that would make it worthwhile.

One point that I find confusing is the terminology surrounding this fish. There is a superb delicacy known as *omble chevalier* that, so far as I am aware, is found only in the lakes of Switzerland (particularly Lake Geneva) and the neighbouring French lakes (such as Lake Annecy). *Omble chevalier* is very much like *truite saumonée*, only the flesh is firmer and finer and the taste — remarkably enough — is even more delicate than that of its trout cousins. The arctic char belongs to the same general family as the trout — the Salmonidae — and Arctic char is sometimes translated or referred to by experts as bearing the French name of *omble chevalier*; or sometimes *omble de l'arctique*. But often Canadian trout, not char, is given as the French equivalent of *omble*; for example, brook trout is called *omble de fontaine*. To make matters even more confusing, still another fish, a cousin, I believe, to the salmonidae, the excellent Arctic grayling, is sometimes called *omble de l'arctique*. In fact in two authoritative works of the Fisheries Research Board of Canada, *Freshwater Fisheries of Northwestern Canada and Alaska* and *Fishes of the Atlantic Coast of Canada*, each by a different author, the Arctic grayling is styled *omble de l'arctique* by one, while the other gives the identical name to Arctic char. If the terminology is confusing, there is one point that is not: the Canadian char, when caught and served fresh, is the equal, in my experience, to the European *omble chevalier* at its best.

Since arctic char is so close to a salmon, cook it in the same fashion (see the recipes on p. 46 and p. 140).

The Winnipeg River used to be a good source of sturgeon and its caviar but it has now disappeared from the commercial market. (The fate of Canadian caviar is discussed in the Ontario section.) As for sturgeon, from May 1, 1969 to April 30, 1970, only slightly over 16,000 pounds of sturgeon were acquired from fishermen in Saskatchewan, Manitoba and Ontario and sold in interprovincial and export trade. Of these 16,000 pounds, only 60 were sold fresh.

Another delicacy from this region — Winnipeg goldeye — has achieved international renown over the years. The goldeye is frozen, then thawed, dressed and soaked in brine; it is artificially stained so as to attain an orange-gold colour, following which it is treated for several hours in the hot smoke of burning oak logs. The taste, essentially, is that of the smoke of oak wood and it's a very good taste indeed.

But as I mentioned earlier, Winnipeg goldeye is rare enough to be practically unobtainable. Some are still caught in that enormous shallow lake, which used to be so full of them, and a diminishing number can still be found in various lakes in Saskatchewan and Alberta and the Territories, such as in Lake Claire, west of Lake Athabasca. (Lake Clair in Wood Buffalo National Park, Alberta, used to be the major source of goldeye in Canada for a number of years after the Second World War, but the lowering of the water level as a result of the building of the Athabasca Dam killed off most of them.) The general story is that the goldeye were not conserved: they were caught too young, and other regulations for their protection were not enforced against the impoverished fishermen who barely made a living on the shores of western lakes. Now, the goldeye sold at fish shops and delicatessens in western Canada comes from Minnesota.

Smoked tullibee is widely available, and many people claim you can't tell the difference between tullibee and goldeye except for the teeth — goldeye is toothless, tullibee is not. Some of Manitoba's *cognoscenti*, including my father-in-law, would never eat a smoked goldeye without its head. If there was no head, there was a strong presumption that the creature was not goldeye but tullibee. My father-in-law always maintained that tullibee was inferior to goldeye. In fact, many westerners would not eat tullibee because it was widely believed that the fish had worms. My personal opinion is that smoked tullibee can taste as good as goldeye and is, in fact, very good indeed.

The growing rarity of Winnipeg goldeye is particularly sad because it was such a proud symbol of western hospitality. The visitor who had to make a short stop in Winnipeg sometimes had to face smoked goldeye at breakfast, lunch or dinner for the length of his visit. While the fish is an extraordinary delicacy if carefully selected, prepared when very fresh and not overcooked, the smoked goldeye that used to make its way on to restaurant menus in Canada (and still does, occasionally) is rarely worth eating, and serves only as a reminder of how good the fish can be if properly done. Meanwhile, the production of tullibee in Canada seems likely to rise. Over one million pounds were sold in interprovincial and international trade last year; most of this was from Manitoba and Alberta. On the other hand, during the period of the sixties, total production of goldeye was down to about 200,000 pounds per year.

The story of the decline in the number of goldeye has implications for the other fish of the western lakes. There is statistical evidence of the decline in the yield of whitefish in Lake Winnipeg. In 1969, sixty per cent of the whitefish caught commercially were very small — under one and a half pounds — harvested before maturity. The same thing seems to be beginning to happen in pickerel fishing. After being almost entirely closed to commercial fishing for two years, all of Lake Winnipeg is now re-opening, except for a small area near Grand Rapids. Fishermen are now setting out from villages along the west coast of the lake — Hnausa, Riverton and Hecla — to fish again for whitefish, pickerel and sauger. But strict quotas have been set for the number of fishermen allowed to operate and the size of the catch. The problem is that proper conservation measures have not been taken in the past because of our long indifference towards our great fish resources in western and in northern Canada. Fish have been caught too young, stocks have not been replenished, other regulations have been ignored, and the result is that a once tremendously abundant resource is beginning to be seriously threatened. Fortunately, federal and provincial authorities, alarmed by the fate of sturgeon and goldeye, now seem to be showing a determination to stop the erosion of our fish resources and save our heritage for future generations.

One of the most exotic products of western Canada is wild rice. The early French explorers of Canada called it *folle avoine*, but it is more commonly known in French as *riz sauvage* or *zizanie*. Did you know that there is a Rice Lake and Zizania Lake in Ontario, both of which have taken their names from wild rice growing nearby?

In eastern Canada, wild rice can cost as much as $8 a pound, depending on how big a rent the shop is paying; it has sold for even higher prices. In Manitoba, the rice is somewhat cheaper but it's not sold at what you would call bargain-basement prices. Traditionally, it has been the Indians' prerogative to harvest wild rice from "natural stands" on Crown lands in the province of Manitoba, and the Indians still use it as food. Actually, wild rice grows in any swampy sort of land and is found in Ontario, Quebec, New Brunswick and Saskatchewan, as well as in Manitoba. But most of the natural stands are in Manitoba, and until a few years ago Indians from that province were the only ones to harvest wild rice for commercial gain; they supplied a large part of the world market, which is principally in the United States. However, much of the wild rice processed in Manitoba and exported from there now actually comes from western Ontario, where the quality of the grain is also good. Asian-style rice paddies have been established; mechanical pickers are used and the result is a much higher yield of harvested rice than any hand-gathering done by the Indians.

Wild rice, by the way, is not a true rice but a kind of wild grass — Canada's only native cereal. Its nut-like flavour and crunchy texture goes especially well with fowl. It could become very popular if the price were lower. The company that produces Uncle Ben's Rice in the United States conducted a survey about two years ago on the potential market for wild rice. The survey showed that the company's market for rice would increase from the present one per cent of the population to fourteen per cent if wild rice were to drop in price — a nice market for anyone.

Twelve thousand acres of wild-rice paddies have been cultivated in Minnesota with very successful results: the yield has been very high, prices are now beginning to drop slightly, and more people have become interested in buying wild rice. In Manitoba, certain private companies and scientists have been experimenting with these same high-yield methods, with varying results. If proper agricultural methods are followed, such as the use of suitable pesticides and disease-resistant strains, and if measures are adopted to prevent "shattering," the falling of the grain before it is ripe enough to be harvested, Manitobans have the potential for a ten-million-dollar annual crop of wild rice. Of course, it may mean that the Indians hit the dust again — another traditional occupation lost to the white man's civilization. Far less manpower is needed for the new mechanized harvester; and Indians who sell hand-picked wild rice will not be able to compete with the lower prices that will be possible for the American and Canadian companies that own the artifically made rice paddies. Whatever is good for the white man seems to be disastrous for the Indian.

Unfortunately and for reasons I don't understand, wild rice is almost always served mushy — practically on the verge of disintegration — whether you eat it in an expensive restaurant or in someone's home. It is not necessary to soak wild rice overnight before cooking; nor is it necessary to keep it boiling for an hour, as some recipe books advise. If properly cooked it will have a nutty, sweet flavour and its texture will be firm, almost crunchy.

Wild Rice

Rinse out rice in a fine strainer. Use 4 cups of water to 1 cup of rice; add as much salt as you think necessary. Boil for 35 to 40 minutes and drain. Serve with sautéed mushrooms and celery, mixed in at the last moment. The rice may be reheated in the oven, but be careful about overcooking the first time.

Yet another fine natural product of the western provinces is the wild berry. One of the most plentiful and delicious of the wild berries is the Saskatoon berry, known in other areas as the Juneberry or serviceberry. In Saskatchewan, it can be found throughout the southern part of the province. A map showing the precise areas of concentration is contained in a small book called *Saskatchewan's Sportsman's Gourmet Guide,* by Henrietta Goplen, along with maps showing the distribution throughout the province of the blueberry, buffaloberry, high-bush and low-bush cranberry, pinchberry, raspberry and strawberry. This information, along with similar kinds of data on game and fish in the province, and recipes as well, makes this small book a useful source of information that is otherwise hard to come by. Each province should have such a book.

The range of growth of the Saskatoon berry is amazing; sometimes it remains as a knee-high shrub but it can also stretch up as high as sixteen feet. The berry, however, is always the same. The fruit is purplish in colour, with ten soft seeds inside that in no way detract from the sweet taste of the berry. Dried Saskatoon berries and wild buffalo meat were the classical ingredients for pemmican — the gastronomic staple of the Indians and Métis. But it is the fresh berries that are the most delectable to eat. They should be treated like blueberries and cooked in pies, cobblers and muffins. For muffins, cook the Saskatoons beforehand and drain off the sauce before adding them to your muffin batter. The seeds will give the muffins an almond-like flavour.

Muffins and Saskatoons

Sift 2 cups of flour with 2 tbsp. sugar, 1/2 tsp. salt,
1 tbsp. baking powder and 1 tsp. soda
Stir about 1 1/2 cups drained berries into flour.
(When you stew the berries, use 1 cup of sugar to
3 or 4 cups of berries.) Gently add 1 beaten egg and

2 tbsp. melted butter. Add 3/4 cup buttermilk or
sour milk to flour and berry mixture. Just dampen
ingredients — too much stirring is not good for
muffins. The dough will be sticky. Fill greased
muffin tins half way and bake for about 18 minutes
at 400°.

Another berry that's abundant in Saskatchewan and
Manitoba is the chokecherry. When you eat it, you feel like
choking. I taste its extraordinary tart flavour every time I
see the word. In the prairie autumn, branches of the large
trees that produce the chokecherry bend down like willow
trees, so laden are they with long strings of drooping berries. In the Winnipeg farmers' market, you can see barrels
of them in the early fall. Chokecherry jelly served with
turkey is something to experience, and to remember.

An outstanding product of the Prairies is beef. The best
beef in Canada comes from Alberta and northeast British
Columbia. Alberta beef, to me, has a better flavour than
eastern beef. Most Westerners agree with me, of course, but
for different, although not conflicting, reasons. Some say
the difference in quality is because of the breeding. Western
animals are usually a cross between Hereford and Aberdeen
Angus, a breed mixture that is supposed to reach maturity
quickly and withstand the cold weather at the same time.
It's a very large animal, raised for beef, not dairy, purposes.
Eastern herds, until now, have been mainly pure-bred Hol-
steins raised for dairy stock; some easterners are now
changing this practice.

A second theory has to do with care and feeding. Western
herds roam freely on ranges and feed on real grass. The
exercising of the cattle causes the fat to marble right
through the animal — and much of the flavour is found in
the fat. Eastern cattle are often penned animals, fed on
mixed grain; the fat doesn't marble through as thoroughly
as in western herds, and of course the feed is different. This
theory has a certain logic, in that penned creatures of every
kind, from pheasants cultivated on farms to trout raised in

breeding ponds, have less flavour than their wild counter-parts, who exercise freely and feed on a variety of vegeta-tion.

The steaks I have eaten in restaurants in Calgary taste better than steaks I've eaten anywhere else in Canada. And aside from the quality of meat used, this fact has something to do with the hanging, or aging, process. Although most butcher shops and restaurants claim that their beef is pro-perly hung, it's not an easy thing to check. In any case, beef that goes directly to the slaughter house, is hung, and then goes to restaurants in the same city to be hung again, tastes better than beef that is shipped longer distances.

Hy Aisenstat, President of *Hy's of Canada Ltd.*, steak restaurants in the West, claims that the best-tasting beef is fed on a hard cereal grain the last sixty days of its life. The tenderness factor is achieved (according to Mr. Aisen-stat) by hanging the dressed beef in a cooler with circu-lating air at a temperature between thirty-one and thirty-four degrees fahrenheit for approximately three weeks.

A new breed of beef for Canada, the Charolais, is be-coming popular, especially in Alberta. The Charolais breed, "the big white cattle," is one of the oldest beef breeds known today. Records show that they were a distinct breed as early as 1760 in Charolles province in France. They are prized in France for their tender meat. "Un coeur de Charolais" is a standard phrase on French menus if the restaurateur wishes to indicate the high quality of his steak. The Charolais' popularity in Alberta has been growing since 1965 when the government first allowed the full bloods in, directly from France. Their great advantage to the breeder is their large size and rapid weight gain. Cows weigh in excess of a ton, and bulls are often well over 3000 pounds when mature. I look forward to the day when I can sink my teeth into a born-in-Canada Charolais steer (after it's been slaughtered, dressed, hung and cooked).

Aside from t-bones, rib roasts, sirloins, briskets, short ribs and stew meat, there is a cut of the steer that is popular among cowboys and farmers but does not appear too often on the counters of butcher shops. "Prairie Oysters," the testicles of calves, removed in order to convert would-be bulls into steers, are said to have almost magical properties. Men who have eaten them swear that their virility has been favourably affected. A small fortune might be in store for the enterprising merchant who can corner the market on prairie oysters, freeze them and start on an advertising campaign that promises rejuvenation, just as ads for hormone creams pledge to banish female wrinkles. Calves' testicles are supposed to be delicious grilled on hot coals on an open fire and served with baking powder biscuits for breakfast — they are what you call a "pick-me-up". But what happens to the women who eat them?

> *How to cook a two-inch sirloin steak in the oven*
>
> Heat oven to 400°. Pepper and salt the steak, and dot the top and bottom with a lot of butter. Put steak in middle part of oven on a cast-iron pan, and bake for 10 to 12 minutes. Turn it over and bake another 10 minutes — if you like a rare steak. Bake it 10 minutes more for medium to well done.

Before I leave the Prairies, I have to observe that it's only fitting that the buffalo meat now marketed throughout Canada comes from Alberta. Elk Island National Park has a herd of 600 Buffalo, and Wood Buffalo National Park has the biggest herd in North America. For a few observations on recipes and on the meat itself, which, in my opinion, is very good but not noticeably different from beef, see the introduction to this chapter.

British Columbia—from Trout Lake to Peachland and Oyster River

The magic beings who hand out wealth, mild weather and physical beauty emptied their pockets when British Columbia came by, cap in hand. And the gastronomic good fairy, apparently infected by her colleagues' enthusiasm, waved her wand around a few times as well. Fruits and vegetables have a longer growing season here than anywhere else in Canada. Five kinds of salmon, as well as crabs, prawns and oysters, live in the neighbouring waters, and fine-quality lambs are raised on the salt marshes of Vancouver Island and the Gulf Islands of the Strait of Georgia. Many retired British people live on Salt Spring Island (perhaps the most beautiful of the Gulf Islands) and raise sheep. The wool is used by the Cowichan Indians to make their heavy waterproof sweaters. The lamb is delicious, but hard to find in butcher shops, even in Vancouver. But most important of all, British Columbia is the home of a special group of people who put good cooking high on the list of life's essentials and do justice to the ingredients that flourish in the province. Thirty thousand Chinese live in British Columbia — the second-largest Chinese population in North America. It doesn't matter whether you are in an Italian, French, Greek, German or Canadian-style restaurant in Vancouver, the cook is probably Chinese. If you walk down Pender Street, the heart of Chinatown in Vancouver, even in January, you'll see the smallest and most exquisite heads of spinach, the largest fresh bean sprouts in the country, and bunches of broccoli that look like green Queen Anne's lace.

British Columbia has the ideal climate for the most diverse vegetable gardens in Canada, and it's the Chinese, more than any other British Columbians, who take advantage of this. Only on Pender Street do you really see the remarkable results of man's imagination working with sun, rain and soil.

If you don't know how to cook the wide choice of vegetables that the province produces, it doesn't matter too much, because any of the Chinese restaurants in Vancouver will feed you well and cheaply. In my chapter on cheap restaurants I've suggested the names of a few that I particularly liked. Like the French, the other nationality that thinks that cooking is an art, the Chinese like to eat out. (During President Nixon's visit to Peking, someone wrote that the only occidental culture that the Chinese could comprehend was the French.)

Cooking the Chinese way mystifies a number of people, but there are only two basic concepts involved: chop, and stir while frying. Vegetables are finely sliced and then barely cooked. They must be hot and crunchy at the same time; you do this by throwing them into a "wok," a Chinese cooking utensil, or into an ordinary cast-iron frying pan at a high heat. The vegetables are cut so thin that they barely need to be cooked at all.

Try this recipe for lemon chicken, which I culled from a Chinese nurse, living in Geneva, Switzerland but born in Trail, B.C.

Lemon Chicken

4 whole chicken breasts boned and skinned, and chopped in 1" crosswise slices
2 tbsp. light soy sauce
1/2 tsp. sesame seed oil (peanut oil or corn oil)
1 tbsp. salt
1 tbsp. gin
3 egg whites beaten frothy
2 tbsp. cornstarch
1 cup of water-chestnut flour, (available at any Chinese-food specialty shop — use cornstarch here, too, if you are not a purist)
1/2 cup white vinegar
fresh ginger, peeled and sliced, as much as you like
3/4 cup sugar
2 tbsp. water
1 cup chicken broth
3 lemons, juice and finely chopped rind
2 cloves garlic, sliced
1/4 head iceberg lettuce, shredded
3 small carrots, cut into thin strips
1/2 cup shredded canned pineapple
3 green onions, cut finely
1/2 large green pepper, finely cut

Place chicken in shallow bowl. Combine soy sauce, sesame seed oil, salt and gin; pour over chicken. Let sit for 30 minutes. Drain chicken and throw out marinade. Add chicken pieces to beaten egg whites and toss to coat. Place the water-chestnut flour on a plate and coat the chicken with the flour.

Add peanut oil to a frying pan or wok to a depth of about 1/2" and heat until it sizzles. Add the chicken a few pieces at a time. Brown on both sides and drain.

Place sugar, vinegar, broth, 2 tbsp. cornstarch mixed with water, lemon juice and rind in a large pot. Bring to a boil, stirring until mixture thickens and becomes clear. Keep drained chicken warm in a 200° oven.

Add vegetables, ginger, garlic and pineapple, to hot sauce. Remove from heat and pour over chicken. Serves 4.

In British Columbia, as elsewhere in Canada, every cultural group borrows from the other, especially in the field of cooking. Don Pepper, a former fisherman from Alert Bay, British Columbia, gave me this example. Cabbage and rice (he claims) is a particular dish cooked by the fishermen from that area. The method is basically stir-fry. Some pork and beef are finely sliced and placed in a frying pan with ginger and soy sauce. In another pan, round cabbage (not the Chinese kind) is chopped up and also stir-fried. The two are combined and served with rice. One curious fact about this special taste of the Alert Bay fishermen — none of them is Chinese.

I've stressed the good fortune of British Columbians in having the Chinese tending to the gastronomic resources of their province. Yet there is another exotic group that also flourishes in the province.

It's the English.

Nowhere else in the North American continent have the English been so successful in transplanting their afternoon teas. On the lawns of Stanley Park, in Vancouver, on a summer's afternoon, tea is served, with scones and jam. In cottages on Vancouver Island and the Gulf Islands of the east coast "tea and crafts" signs are prominently displayed.

Of course, the Empress Hotel in Victoria is the great tea mother of them all, but during the summer, ladies who weave, school teachers using the family silver, and other tea buffs from Victoria, Sydney and the Gulf Islands do their bit to maintain the British Empire off the western coast of North America. Sydney, on the southern tip of the Island, rather than Victoria, is the place to go to see English cottage gardens with roses and currant bushes. Currant jam, red or black, is the correct accompaniment to scones for afternoon tea. Never, never serve marmalade.

There are other things on Vancouver Island besides tea and scones. On Swartz Bay, north of Victoria on the east side of the Island, little places serve take-out clams, prawns and oysters, and if you drive across to the very beautiful Gulf Islands, the same seafood will be offered by very modest roadside stands. If you want to cook the fish yourself, buy them fresh from the fish-packing plants on the Gulf Islands.

Lulu Island is near Vancouver Island but has more sunshine. The rain clouds, for complicated meteorological reasons, float past Lulu and only let go when they reach Vancouver. The growing conditions on the island are fantastic and "truck," or market, gardening is the way of life. Lulu Islanders try to avoid labour costs by putting "Pick your own" (raspberry, asparagus, corn and cucumber) signs in front of their farms.

Because farmers' markets of any substantial size are not found near the city of Vancouver (there is a small one in New Westminster), picking your own is the way to ensure the freshest supply. Mylora Farm on Lulu is one of the oldest organic farms in Canada.

The two berries that people from British Columbia identify as their own are the loganberry and the salal berry. Both are particular to the Pacific northwest — the loganberry's only other home is in Tasmania. You might describe a loganberry as a large, elongated raspberry. The *Britannica* says it is a cross between a blackberry and raspberry — naturally crossbred in Judge Logan's garden in 1881. A

British Columbian friend says, "They may be like raspberries, but they're bigger and better." The salal berry is small and dark, something like a blueberry, and was once an Indian staple. Except for the most discerning jam and pie makers, most people tend to overlook the salal as a fine edible.

Another berry that can be found throughout the Pacific Northwest is called, appropriately enough, the salmonberry. It's a species of wild raspberry — very large in the North — that comes in three colours, yellow, bright red, and dark red. The golden yellow salmon berries have a better flavour — something like caramel — than the red ones. They make good jams and preserves.

Before I go on to fish, I must comment on the McIntosh and Delicious apples that overrun British Columbia orchards. I am not a Delicious fan myself — they're too sweet — but they do have a wide appeal, and they make a very tidy packet for those who grow and sell them. The McIntosh is a Canadian invention. John McIntosh, a farmer living in the upper St. Lawrence Valley in Ontario over 150 years ago, found the apple tree on the land he was clearing. McIntosh has, to my regret, edged out all other Canadian apples in production and sales. It grows from the Okanagan to the Annapolis Valley; other varieties, perhaps less red, less sweet, but still flavoursome, have been sacrificed to the stampede of the McIntosh. The McIntosh is a good-tasting apple, especially when it's just picked, but it does seem to lose its crispness and flavour as the winter goes on. Many apples, if they retain their firmness, have a flavour that is just as good, and even more interesting. I've already praised the texture of the Gravenstein. Russet is a good-sized apple for children, who always throw away half their Delicious. The flavour is subtler than most, and it's a far better apple for baking than the McIntosh. McIntoshes, cooked, have a tendency to lose their apple taste and sink into undistinguishable sweetness. I wish that growers would diversify their stock and give consumers a chance to eat all the varieties of excellent apples that grow in this country.

Besides salmon, which I will discuss later on, the waters aronnd British Columbia provide a harvest of halibut, tuna, flatfish or flounder, sole (a variety of flounder), some pompano, red snapper, excellent sturgeon, and lots of herring, which British Columbians don't eat — as one fisherman put it, herring's not for eating, it's for trading. Red snapper and pompano bring high prices at fancy restaurants. Delicious Canadian sole — although not of the same family as the European — is plentiful off the west coast of Vancouver Island and in Queen Charlotte Sound. The lemon sole in particular, is a lean fish with a very delicate lemony flavour and closely resembles in shape and colour the lemon sole of European waters. Canadian Dover sole, although very palatable, is not popular with the fishermen. It is slippery to handle and does not fillet as easily as the lemon sole, which is usually the species marketed as sole fillets. Dover sole, of course, should be served whole, grilled or sautéed, and then filleted by the waiter or eater. It seems to me that some fresh BC Dover sole would have a nice market in the luxury restaurant trade which imports fresh and frozen Dover sole from Europe. I would like to see Canadian sole served fresh, whole and filleted at the table, in Canadian homes and restaurants. Someone should convince a few enterprising fishermen to harvest it.

Pacific cod for fish sticks is a substantial part of west-coast fishing industries. Other species, commonly called cod but not really related, are black Alaska cod (sablefish), rich in vitamin A and generally marketed as a fine smoked fish; ling-cod, an excellent fish for deep-fat frying (a staple in good fish-and-chip shops); and rock cod — the Chinese do miraculous things with this fish, especially the yellowtail variety.

The varieties of shellfish that come from Pacific waters are legion. In deep waters can be found the Alaska king crab, the Dungeness and the snow crab. Opinions differ but many rate the flesh of the Dungeness as the tastiest in North America. Among the varieties of Pacific shrimp, most notable are a large prawn that can reach nine inches in length, a very small pink shrimp that is extremely tasty, and a side-striped shrimp that grows up to five inches long. Native oysters are gathered off the coastal rocks of British Columbia. They are exceptionally delicious and quite small but their size makes them difficult to harvest and they have been overwhelmed in importance by a transplanted oyster, a Japanese variety, which has flourished here for many years and has gone wild in various areas of the Pacific Northwest.

British Columbians like the smaller, butter clams better than the larger, razor variety. They clean them in two washings of fresh sea water and oatmeal. The latter is supposed to remove the sand. Although abalone is found mostly off the California coast, enough gets near British Columbia to make fishermen look out for it. Usually they cling to rocks, and are immediately recognizable by their ornate and elegant shell. Treat abalone like wienerschnitzel: they must be pounded, then sliced thin, and fried in butter. Sea urchins, not considered a delicacy in Canada, are highly prized by the Japanese for their gonads or roe. Japanese fishermen flash-freeze them on their boats off the waters of British Columbia and treat them with special chemicals for the market in Japan.

The salmon in British Columbia is quite different from the Atlantic type. In fact, there are five species: sockeye (best for canning), pink, chum, coho, and red spring, or chinook. All Pacific salmon die after one spawning, in contrast to Atlantic salmon, which may spawn several times. Each of the five species of Pacific salmon differs in its life history; the pinks, for instance, live only two years and reach a weight of little more than four pounds, while the giant chinook can reach 120 pounds or more and live up to seven years. The coho and red spring salmon are considered the best fish for the fresh and frozen market, while sockeye is used almost exclusively for canning. The fishermen who catch salmon prize white spring as the best eating fish. Its marketing value is not as high as that of red spring and coho because of its white flesh. Salmon may be sold frozen, smoked, canned, or fresh, but the consumers insist that its colour be red-pink. Nobody throughout the country is psychologically prepared to pay $1.90 a pound for salmon with white flesh.

By the way, the smoked salmon available in this part of the country is the best I've tasted in Canada.

British Columbia red spring salmon and Quebec maple syrup are considered by the Canadian External Affairs Department as "gastronomic good-will ambassadors," and very often Canadian diplomats abroad will stock their larders with frozen slabs of fish and jereboams of maple syrup in order to beguile the natives. About fourteen years ago, when the temperature of the cold war was more extreme than now, friends of mine who were members of the staff of the Canadian Embassy in Moscow managed, with great difficulty, to find some high-ranking Russians who were prepared to come to their place for dinner. In order to flaunt their diplomatic coup they also asked a couple of ambassadors from the Western Powers, one of whom was a Hohenzollern prince, four feet tall. The Canadian wife, young and nervous, was saddled with Sonya, a maid-cum-spy who came with their flat, courtesy the Soviet government. (I believe the Canadians had to pay her wages, thus supplementing the NKVD budget.) Sonya was good at listening at doorways and reading other people's mail, but she was unsure about cooking and decorating the great thawing fish on the kitchen counter. Sonya spoke no English, and the wife's Russian was rudimentary. For reasons that she now finds hard to explain (it might have had something to do with impressing the dwarf prince), the wife wanted the fish garnished with three slices of lemon in its mouth. She thought she managed to convey the idea to Sonya. When the moment came, in walked Sonya, dressed up in a frilly cap and black dress, the red spring salmon garnished with hollandaise and three slices of lemon in her mouth.

A good way to serve frozen British Columbia salmon is

as an entrée for a dinner party, especially if you are inviting aristocracy.

This dish tastes very much like smoked salmon and should be served the same way, only more lavishly, since it is a cheaper dish.

Gravlax

1 whole salmon, about 6 or 7 lbs. (ask your fish dealer to saw through the frozen fish lengthwise to make two slabs)
2 bunches of fresh dill (or dill seed if fresh is unavailable)
1/2 cup coarse salt (or pickling salt)
1/2 cup sugar
4 tbsp. peppercorns (crushed), preferably white

Defrost fish. Place half of fish, skin side down, in a glass, enamel or stainless steel baking dish. Chop dill and place it over fish. Combine sugar, salt and crushed peppercorns in a separate bowl. Spread this mixture over dill. Top with other half of fish, skin side up. Cover with aluminum foil, and on it set a heavy platter or a board larger than the salmon. Pile the platter or board with several cans of food — they act as weights. Refrigerate 3 days.

Turn fish every 12 hours, basting with liquid marinade that accumulates and separating the halves a little to baste the salmon inside. Replace the platters and weights each time.

When the gravlax is fully marinated, remove fish from liquid; scrape away dill and seasonings and pat dry. Place separated halves, skin side down, on a carving board and slice the salmon halves thinly on the diagonal, removing the skin as best you can.

Serves 10 to 12 people.

Gravlax is served as a first course, or as part of a cold buffet, with toast, brown bread and a cucumber salad. A fresh dill and mustard sauce is the classic accompaniment.

Mustard Sauce

8 tbsp. French mustard (Dijon type)
1 whole egg
2 tsp. powdered English mustard
6 tsp. sugar
salt to taste
4 tbsp. white vinegar
2/3 cup vegetable oil
as much fresh chopped dill as you like

In a small bowl mix the mustards, sugar, and vinegar to a paste. Add whole egg, beating hard. With a wire whisk, slowly beat in the oil until it forms a mayonnaise. Stir in fresh dill.

You may keep this in your refrigerator for several days; just beat it up again before serving.

The same sauce can be made in a blender: Add egg, mustards, sugar, salt and vinegar to blender. Then pour in oil while blender is working.

British Columbians and Yukoners make a sourdough bread which is a regional specialty dating back to the time when the miners and trappers could not get ordinary yeast to grow in the cold. They added wild yeast plants to the starter dough. If replenished every few days with flour and water, the starter will keep for months. It should always smell slightly of sour milk, but never of mould.

Sourdough Starter

2 cups flour
2 cups water (warm)
1 tbsp. yeast

Mix well, then put in a warm place or closed cupboard overnight. In the morning it should be bubbly or frothy; it is then called a sponge. Take out 1/2 cup of the sponge, place it in a scalded pint jar with a tight cover and store in the refrigerator for future use. This is sourdough starter. The remaining sponge may be used for bread, pancakes or muffins.

At the end of February each year, Whitehorse has a Sourdough Festival: the locals eat sourdough pancakes, dance on the streets, and drink quite a bit. Sourdough hotcakes have a good tangy taste but they can be disastrous. My Alert Bay fisherman told me this story about the cook on his boat. The cook was a failure at making hot cakes; the fishermen looked forward to huge breakfasts, especially sourdough pancakes but his hot cakes were a little too filling. One of the members of the crew felt that they could be used for a purpose other than nourishment: as the ship was mooring, the cook discovered all his hot cakes strung along the side of the boat, acting most efficiently as bumpers between the dock and the boat.

Great
Gourmet
Specialty Shops

FROM BIRTH TO death, our lives are rounded out by the supermarkets. We can see our total gastronomic existence unfolding before us as we pass by the supermarket shelves with the non-allergenic special-formula milk, and pea purée, pause briefly at the pre-packaged Sloppy Joe and hamburger-buns section, fly by the pot roasts of middle age, and stave off, or at least ease, extinction at the patent drug counter with its laxatives and Vitamin E.

It is a secure but monotonous way to nourish ourselves. Those who seek a certain adventure in life and who have taste buds that respond to sensations other than sweet-and-sour and peanut butter might be interested in this chapter about specialty food shops in Canada. It describes a way of life that is nineteenth century in its devotion to the philosophy of hard work and in its dependence on the family structure. Perhaps it is a way of life that is already almost obsolete, and that is why I want to record it. Any shopkeeper who takes a craftsman's pride in the bread he makes, or in the manner in which he pickles his ham, is an old-fashioned idealist who cares more about individual quality than big profits.

Generally speaking, the people who own specialty food shops are first- or second-generation Canadians who work all day, six or seven days a week. Most of these shops are family enterprises — it would be financially ruinous to pay a stranger to put in the time and effort needed to keep up the excellence of the product and the service. I have yet to see a first-class specialty food shop that does not have as its source of success and continuation a husband and wife, father and son, sisters and brothers, or other family combination working behind the counters.

The correlation between European immigrants, delicious food, and the much-maligned nuclear family is also notable when you go to a restaurant in Paris or Rome. Most good restaurants in Europe are owned by families who take a direct and personal interest in their trade. In Canada, restaurants seem to be organized on the basis of several invisible backers, who also do other things for a living (mayors, apparently, go in for owning restaurants), and an indifferent manager, who feels he's not getting enough money for his work. That is why there are not enough "good little French," or Italian or Canadian restaurants in this country. For years, the European tradition of families being the source of good things to eat has crossed the water but more often it has taken hold in our specialty food shops rather than in the restaurant trade — it takes less money to open a food shop than a restaurant.

The family owners of these shops make their work their life, but since they make something exceptional, the work they do has a meaning for them which is probably missing in the work of a supermarket clerk or manager. The specialty-shop owner is responsible for his product and takes a personal pride in its excellence. He likes his work because he sees the goal of his labour, whether it is a better blintz, a superior apple tart or the freshest fish in town.

There are a few exceptions to the rule that most better-food shops are owned by recent immigrants, or their children. WILLE'S BAKERY in Victoria, which sells some of the finest bread (sourdough and French) in Canada, is a family business that has passed down to the present baker, a great-grandson. PETER DEVINE in Ottawa and DIONNE'S in Montreal are respectively Anglo-Saxon and French-Canadian owned shops that date back over 100 years. ROGER BIDGOOD, who owns a flourishing grocery-cum-Newfoundland-specialty-food shop, comes from a family that has been living in the small town of Goulds, Newfoundland ever since anyone can remember.

Despite its being a nineteenth-century anomaly, somewhere on the edge of your town there is a stand selling icecream in flavours unknown to the ubiquitous Dairy Queen . . . or a shop that makes better butter buns than anyone else . . . or a delicatessen which uses a secret recipe for spicing sausages. If you are camping through Canada and you want to buy something other than bread that tastes like sliced Kleenex, and sanitized cheese, for your dinner, you can find, if you are persistent, some shops that specialize in offering products different from, and better than, the average grocery store or supermarket. Your city has, supermarkets notwithstanding, a whole sub-culture of food shops that sell something unusual and good — the result of individual endeavour, not mass production. Depending on where you go in Canada, you can buy home-cured bacon, rabbit cooked in red wine, and cakes made with real cream — not a guck that could double as shaving foam. But do not expect to buy Ukrainian perogy in Newfoundland or fresh clams in Regina.

Each region has its own peculiarities. Store-bought cakes and bread have always carried a stigma of shame for the daughters of the Maritimes. As little as fifteen years ago a decently brought-up girl was as ignorant of the whereabouts of the town bakery as she was of the town brothel. Or so she had to pretend. A really first-class bakery is still hard to find east of Quebec City. Ditto for fruit and vegetable shops. The battered fruits displayed on Maritime and Newfoundland counters are victims of cultural apathy. Many Maritimers have their own vegetable gardens, but their range goes mainly from cabbages to turnips.

Toronto is interested in pastry shops, more so than Montreal. But Montrealers can find a must-be-eaten-the-same-day

flûte in most of their delicatessens, and even in super-
markets. What Toronto calls "French bread" compares to
Montreal's slim, elegant *flûte* the way off-the-rack at the
Miracle Mart compares to a Dior gown.

The West has a surprising number of specialty food shops,
and they seem to be cheaper than those of Montreal and
Toronto.† Even though Vancouver is brimming over with
prosperity, eastern inflation has not hit its delicatessens,
pastry shops and ethnic trading posts. Napoleon creams and
sausage rolls cost less in the West. Is it the cost of real estate
or is it western generosity?

In narrowing down the list of places to go in this chapter
I have had to leave out as many specialty shops as I've described. I write only of some of the most exceptional ones
that I found, starting in Newfoundland and moving across
Canada to Vancouver Island.

Newfoundland and the Maritimes

There is an exception to the lack of good fruit in the Atlantic provinces — the berries in the summertime. Prince
Edward Island strawberries have a stronger, sweeter taste
than that of any glamour queen from California. Deep red
partridgeberries (a small, tart berry that makes wonderful
jam) and golden bakeapples (a seedy, yellow berry, also
used as a preserve) are hawked by children beside the roads
in Newfoundland and Nova Scotia.

Although the sea is all around you, fish markets are not
at every corner. Most people buy fish directly from the
fisherman at the wharf, or from a fish pedlar. And remember, fish, in Newfoundland, means cod. Halibut is halibut,
salmon is salmon, but "fish" is cod. The question "What
kind of fish do you have?" makes no sense to a Newfoundlander.

---

† A word about prices: I have not attempted, either here or in Chapter 5,
to provide complete price lists, since they can, and do, change so quickly.
Sometimes I include the price of a few items, by way of example, but
these, too, may be different by the time this book is published.

NEWFOUNDLAND

St. John's

For a gastronomic and sociological experience go to Bidgood's Food Centre at Goulds, just outside the city in
St. John's South. (After your stop at Bidgood's, drive right
on to Petty Harbour to buy lobster at the lobster pound —
and for the view.)

The rabbits, ready for skinning, hanging from the porch
at Bidgood's give notice that the ingredients for a Newfoundland dinner are here. Whether it is rabbit for rabbit
pie, seal for seal-flipper pie, or salt cod for fish and brewis
(hardtack biscuits and salt cod, soaked, dried, and fried),
Bidgood's has it. Basically, it's a general store that carries
everything from hardware equipment to fresh meat and
fish. There are packages of something called "sounds,"
which are bits of cod taken from the backbone and fried
with onions and scrunchions (crispy pork fat); as well as
fish, potato and onion patties, freshly made up every day
and ready for the frying pan. All the Newfoundland fruits
are there, both fresh and flash-frozen, from blueberries to
wild damson plums. If you worry about vitamin-D defici-
ency, you can cure it with a lump of fresh cod liver. Fresh
salmon is available in season.

Some Other Items

Bidgood's canned lobster
Bidgood's canned salmon
Fresh Newfoundland lamb
Salt beet *à la maison*
Brookfield ice-cream (the honey-scotch and grape-
  nut flavours were new to me)
Pickled cod heads
Partridgeberries
Turbot salmon
Doyle's ginger wine
Beef Iron and Wine (ostensibly medicinal, but an
  old stand-by for Maritime hang-overs when the
  "government stores" are closed)

STOCKWOOD'S FINE FOODS, 316 Freshwater Road in St. John's, is one of the few places in the city for bakery bread and raisin buns.

NOVA SCOTIA

Halifax†
In the old shipping days of Halifax, the green coffee beans came right off the boats from Peru, Mexico or Columbia and were roasted by certain shops near the wharf which catered to the Haligonian interest in a good cup of coffee. The JAVA BLEND COFFEE & TEA SHOP, 1540 Hollis, is the only one left that continues this tradition. Peter Dikaios, the new owner, roasts the beans in a Kaiser Wilhelm pot-bellied coffee machine that came from Germany over eighty years ago. He periodically tests the "doneness" of the beans by scooping them up and looking at the colour, the surest method he knows. All his customers are familiar to him because "you come once, you come back again". The smell is intoxicating. His special blend sells for $1.20 a pound.

Fish in Halifax should be fresher and better than most places in Canada. Yet there are only two fish stores of note. BOUTILIER'S, 1670 Bedford Row, has been in business seventy years and sells small, medium and large oysters at varying prices, starting from $1.25 a dozen. Besides the usual sole and halibut, BOUTILIER'S has live and boiled lobsters ($1.95 to $2.39 per pound), and dulse, that strange, dried seaweed which many Maritimers eat like potato chips.

FISHERMAN'S MARKET, Ferry Wharf, sells mussels and clams and fish for freezers.

ASTROFF'S DELICATESSEN, 1514 Dresden Row: Cheese, sausages, crusty bread, submarine sandwiches.

† The specialty shops listed for Newfoundland and Nova Scotia are practically all from the St. John's and Halifax regions. I am sure there are plenty of other good specialty shops in these two provinces. I would welcome information on places that could go in future editions of this book.

GALLOWAY'S in Vancouver offers an abundance of candy and nuts . . . or how about some gorgeous glazed fruit from an East that is more familiar to Vancouverites than mysterious Toronto.

If you are in the company of several *Québecois* and conversation is flagging, bring up the subject of food. The question "What is the best recipe for tourtière?" will result in raising spirits as well as controversy.

Lorenzo Richard, owner of PAIN DE COLLEGE in Memramcook, N.B., used to make the bread at St. Joseph's College, now the University of Moncton. A former student said the only good food he ate at the College was the bread.

Pastries from CULINA, Quebec City. Madame Lea Gaspard, the proprietress, makes all her pastries from butter and only fresh fruit is used in her tarts.

Many farmers in eastern Ontario and Quebec have commercial "sugar bushes" where the public is allowed to come and watch the sugar-making process. Hordes of children are taken round during the sugaring-off period and given maple syrup candies hardened on the fresh snow.

It has been said that the bravest man in the world was the first person to eat an oyster. Now the problem is to keep up with the demand.

The favourite sweetening agent of Jews and Ukrainians — honey —
is a western Canadian specialty. Unquestionably the favourite, for
Canadian descendants of these two groups, is Red River buckwheat
honey, premium grade.

Toronto has a large Italian community and Ontario has good veal, so Osso Buco, a classical Italian dish, is an outstanding part of the *New Ontario's* cuisine.

By late summer, fresh, truly sun-ripened, produce is available at markets and roadside stands in various parts of Canada. Unfortunately for local farmers and consumers, many supermarkets, even at that bountiful time of year, continue to stock refrigerated, tasteless fruits and vegetables imported from California.

Canadian cheesemakers are of course internationally known for their native cheddars, and for Quebec Oka, but a number of them also turn out creditable versions of Swiss, Dutch and Danish cheeses.

Willi Krauch in his smokehouse in Tangier, Nova Scotia. Outside the shop a hand-lettered sign says "Willi Krauch, Danish smoked salmon recommended by Craig Claiborne of *The New York Times*".

What attracts me to the TOMAHAWK BARBECUE (in Vancouver) are the Yukon-style bacon and eggs — the back bacon fans over the hashed brown potatoes like a deck of cards spread out by a Las Vegas croupier.

THE CAKE BOX, 5190 Blowers St.: Old-fashioned cake doughnuts that crunch when you bite them.

CANDY BOWL, 5505 Spring Garden Road: Absolutely everything in the line of manufactured candies and chocolates. It is an outlet for Ganongs and Moirs, who are the big candy people in the Maritimes. There is also a good choice of imported sweets, jams, teas, and coffees. (Other locations.)

HOUSE OF SPICES, on the Village Square (a big shopping complex): Mr. Vishna Mitter packages his own spices and sells various Indian flours.

EATON'S basement, in the Halifax Shopping Centre: A huge variety of Indian spices, limes, chili and pickles. The British element in Halifax is very much in evidence, with its English taste for good curry, and the pappadums* and chapati flour* that go with it. There is also a vast assortment of British marmalades and biscuits, and Pegotty pie (whatever that is).

Chatford
CHATFORD'S LOBSTER POUND has live lobster available for cooking.

Sauerkraut from Tancook Island is a great Nova Scotia delicacy. Most supermarkets carry jars of it in season. According to local fishermen, the juice of the sauerkraut is especially good for curing hang-overs.

Tangier
About fifty miles from Halifax, in Tangier, you can see a hand-lettered sign saying "WILLI KRAUCH, Danish smoked salmon recommended by Craig Claiborne of *The New York Times*". As you come in from the sunlight to the darkness of the smokehouse, a man looking like a gnome out of a Nordic myth is doing something at a very low bench. He is slitting the stomachs of eels that are coiled in baskets below the racks of dried smoked mackerel and

---

* Terms marked with an asterisk are included in the Glossary.

salmon. Some people have a prejudice against eels, so Mr. Krauch provides certain assurances on his business card, which reads

Smoked extra large Atlantic salmon	$3.40 a lb.
Smoked barbecued mackerel	.90 a lb.
Smoked eels (smoked in a separate smoker)	.25 a lb.
minimum 3 lb. order	

The salmon is a little saltier than I like, but Craig Claiborne raved about it. The mackerel and eel are juicy and full of flavour.

PRINCE EDWARD ISLAND

Prince Edward Island has some great bake shops. All the following specialize in home-made bread, cookies and finger cakes:

Charlottetown
ENTERPRISE BAKERY, 205 Grafton; MRS. KENNY'S HOME BAKERY, 35 Bayfield; RUTH'S HOME BAKERY, 132½ St. George; WORTH'S BAKERY, 37 University Ave.; MRS. RODD'S HOMESTYLE BAKESHOP (All Mrs. Rodd's baked products are sold through ELLIS BROTHERS' SAVE-EASY SUPERMARKET.)
   THE CANDY CORNER, in the Royalty Mall Shopping Centre: Candies from all over the world, and a large assortment of cheeses and cold meats.

Montague
MONTAGUE BAKERY: Marvellous baking powder biscuits, and home-style bread that is distributed in a number of local grocery stores.

Souris
Go to the fish-packing plant for fresh queen crab in season.

NEW BRUNSWICK

Moncton

Moncton, near the Shediac vacation land and fifteen miles from the sea, is the centre of Acadia — an economically depressed, French-speaking part of Canada which is treated with indifference by Quebec, as well as by the rest of the country. The CNR has its railway lines going right through the main thoroughfare of the town.

People in Moncton like sea food. Fried clams are as popular here as hot dog stands in Winnipeg. Great numbers of clams, or quahaugs, an Atlantic specialty, may be found in the MONCTON FISH MARKET, 211 St. George St. Live lobster and fresh salmon are available in season. You also find shrimp, oysters, and crab — sometimes fresh, sometimes frozen — from Caraquet and Buctouche, New Brunswick. The store also has a supply of capers, wine vinegar and curry powder — hard-to-find items in Moncton.

The only delicatessen in Moncton belongs to an amicable Italian lady, Catrina Toffolo, who opened her store in 1971. THE EUROPEAN VARIETY DELICATESSEN, 388 St. George St., has good rye bread and serves mini submarine sandwiches, for a quarter, on very crisp buns (from the HOME BEST BAKERY, 629 Main), as well as imported cheeses and sausages. The store is large and bright but it is an uphill fight for Mrs. Toffolo to get the local people interested. The Delicatessen also carries Melita coffee and distilled water.

THE PASTRY SHOPPE, 193 St. George St.: The specialty of this house is chocolate-chip squares at $0.80 a dozen. It also has oatmeal and brown bread on the week-ends, makes its own milk bread every day, and has nice walnut butter-tarts and meat pies.

THE DONUT SHOPPE, 37½ Archibald St.: Home-baked beans, and home-made marmalade at $0.39 a jar. Also doughnuts.

Memramcook

PAIN DE COLLEGE: The baker at this shop used to make the

bread at St. Joseph's College, now the University of Moncton. A former student said the only good food he ate at the College was the bread.

Shediac
ROSINA PASTRY SHOPPE

Saint John
The City Market in Saint John is considered by Maritimers to be unequalled in New Brunswick, or probably anywhere else in the Atlantic provinces. Fresh berries are available in season, and fresh fish, including oysters and lobsters, and fresh dulse from Grand Manan. There is always home baking.

FENWICK'S, 430 Ridge Row W., in the City Market: So famous for their cheddar cheese that Lord Beaverbrook had it sent to him in England.

Cocagne
The E. P. MELANSON LTD. Cannery near Shediac sells fresh lobster and scallops, in cold packs (the meat is removed from the shell and put in a plastic bag).

Penobsquis
(seven miles from Sussex, between St. John and Moncton)
GINGERBREAD HOUSE: Fresh gingerbread.

QUEBEC

Quebec City
People in this city take food seriously and buy cheese, coffee, bread and pastry that are second to none in the land. A cheese square called *fondue de fromage* is a local specialty. It's made from a mixture of white sauce and grated cheese covered with bread-crumbs. People buy the squares

already made up and reheat them in their ovens. They are sold at all the shops I discuss below.

Mme Lea Gaspard is the proprietress of CULINA, 2510 chemin Ste-Foy (west of Vallon Highway), probably the finest delicatessen and pastry shop in the city. A Belgian, she and her son provide Quebec with long French loaves, or *flûtes, croissants,* authentic *galantines*, terrines* and *pâtés.* Her *grande oeuvre* of that particular group is sweet-bread *pâté,* which must be ordered in advance. She also pre-cooks *coq au vin, coquilles St. Jacques* and a myriad of sauces from *béarnaise* to mayonnaise. All pastries are made from butter, and only fresh fruit is used for her tarts. For simple tastes, take-out submarine sandwiches are available, made from her own rolls and meats. I don't want to gild the lily, but she also has a licence to sell beer and wine. Apple turnovers are $0.25 at CULINA, *croissants,* $0.15, puff-pastry dough with creamed seafood, $0.45 cents each.

Place Laurier (la rue de Vieux Quebec) is a shopping centre that looks like all others, but it does contain a very good delicatessen called LE MONDE DE LA SAUCISSE. The meats are supplied by Sepps in Montreal. Next door is one of the best cheese shops in Canada, A LA FROMAGERIE, run by George Gingras. M. Gingras carries vintage Canadian cheddar (1967), parmesan from the Argentine, Morbier from the Jura, La Cranée from the Pyrenees, freshly grated Gruyère, and ricotta that is fresh every Friday. The most interesting cheese comes from just across the St. Lawrence from Ile d'Orléans, where it is made by the Aubin family. Because the cheese smells quite a bit, M. Gingras has to fetch it himself — some of the postmen have refused to deliver it.

DELICATESSE CARTIER, 108 St. Cyrille: Though not of the same exquisite quality as CULINA, this shop has a huge selection of cooked meats, sausages, and pasta dishes — all cooked in its own kitchen. Lasagna was $3.25 for four servings when I was there. What I liked best were the mushrooms in tomato sauce and the *pâté de campagne* ($1.50 a

pound). There's a good selection of olives in bulk, and uncooked meats cut in the continental manner. Other items
include pizza, Italian-roast coffee beans, cooked scampi, and
salads.

The pastries at KERHULU, 22 Côte de la Fabrique, are not
what they used to be, but their chocolates, especially the
truffles and liqueurs, merit a wider fame. Eating KERHULU
liqueur chocolates is risky, like all interesting enterprises.
You must place the whole chocolate in your mouth at once,
and resolutely bite through the sugar-coated lining. Beware of holding it outside your mouth, unless you are wearing a bib.

Two places to buy specially roasted and blended coffee,
and tea, as well as special coffee makers, are at J. B. ROUS-
SEAU'S two locations, 605 rue St. Jean, Plaza Laval in St.
Foy, and Place Laurier, La rue de Vieux Quebec. M.
Rousseau's family have been tea and coffee importers since
1867. You can meet and talk to M. Rousseau himself at rue
St. Jean.

J. A. R. LEMIRE ENR., 1150 Cartier, Uppertown: Suck-
ling pigs all ready to serve, Quebec lamb from Charlebois
all year round, specialty foods, and a wide choice of fresh
vegetables.

BARDOU ET FILS LTEE., 1040 Cartier and 48 1/2 Couillard: Pastries, fresh fruit baskets, widest assortment of fresh
vegetables in town, and *charcuterie.*

Sherbrooke
PATISSERIE LIEGEOISE, in the Shopping Centre, 2291 King
St. W.: Supplies for picnics, fresh French bread, sausages,
wonderful pastries and excellent cheeses. There's a self-
serve liquor store in the same shopping centre.

Knowlton
(near Brome Lake)
Jehane Benoit's gourmet shops, NOIRMOUTON FARM SHOP
on Main Street in Knowlton and at R.R. 4, Sutton, five
miles out, in the Eastern Townships, are open every day of

the week. The fresh Canadian lamb from her farm, as well as the lamb patties and pies, are worthy of her name. She also sells home-made apple pies, jams and jellies.

Val Morin

North of Montreal, on route 11 near Val Morin and Val David, late-spring skiers can buy maple products of all kinds from outdoor stands along the road. The most elaborate (it has a roof and refrigerator) is CHEZ CLAUDE, right beside the Belle Neige ski tow. CHEZ CLAUDE sells maple syrup, sugar, *pain paysan,* home-made jams and pickles, and apple cider and apple beer.

Montreal

There are three solitudes in Montreal (*pace* Hugh Mac-Lennan) — gastronomically speaking. There is French, of course, with classic French cuisine like *vacherins, pâté au cognac* and *bouchées à la reine* more in evidence than traditional French-Canadian dishes such as pea soup and *ragoût de boulettes* (see p. 52 for a recipe). In fact, many of the shops seem to be owned by people who left Normandy three years ago rather than three hundred. Then there is the "ethnic" world centred around St. Lawrence St., with Hungarian, Jewish and Italian specialties predominating. Finally, there is the Anglo-Saxon taste, nourished on scones from EATON's and fortified by delicacies from THE CHEESE SHOPPE, formerly owned and still operated by Mr. Machonnachie, who learned his trade in Aberdeen.

THE CHEESE SHOPPE, 611 de Maissonneuve W., is situated just around the corner from THE BAY, in accordance with the dictum that Westmount ladies don't go east of that institution. Mr. Machonnachie has been in the cheese business since 1915 and knows more about the subject than anyone else in Canada.

The cultures are beginning to mix, gastronomically, at least. THE BAY, that Anglo-Saxon bastion on St. Catherine and Maisonneuve, has just opened a *French* gourmet shop in the basement near the Metro entrance. Their meat *pâtés* are *à la maison* — try those flavoured with cognac and madeira. You'll also find a multi-cultural clientele at DIONNE's, 1221 St. Catherine St. W., a fancy-food grocery shop that dates back over 100 years. The shop carries fresh oysters, trout, meats, and good quality fruits and vegetables, as well as a huge selection of imported delicacies. Ready-cooked *pâtés* are also available.

Côte des Neiges near St. Mary's Road has a strong French enclave. The DUC DE LORRAINE pastry shop is famous for its *vacherins* and its rich ice cream and parfaits, with flavours of chestnut, walnut, and real orange. I saw the fresh orange halves lying on the wooden table in the kitchen. Its *croissants,* though smaller than usual, are very buttery. The house specialty is *croquembouche,* a mountain of richly filled cream puffs artistically glued together with caramelized sugar — about $23 for a mountain serving twenty people.

Next door is the NORMANDIE-CANADA CHARCUTERIE, 5024 Côte des Neiges, which makes home-made *pâtés, terrines,* servings of *coq au vin* that have been pre-cooked and frozen, and rabbit in red wine. Homesick Frenchmen come here for the rolled and larded cuts of meat, fresh celeriac, tiny green beans, and Boston lettuce. All the butchers wear oxblood coloured jackets and come from Normandy. *Pâtés* made from duck and cognac cost about $0.79 for half a pound. They are cooked and sold in individual foil cups with a jelly covering.

The service at the French food shops is efficient but somewhat haughty. The spirit of de Gaulle stands behind those counters.

While you're on Côte des Neiges, stop at No. 5709, CORONET CHOCOLATES. It has European-style chocolates, the best in Montreal. They're hand-dipped.

The shops in the very ethnic St. Lawrence area are less austere than the temples of gastronomy on Côte des Neiges. At the MONTREAL HEBREW DELICATESSEN, 3895 St. Lawrence, Bob ("I manage everything here") will give you a piece of home-spiced tongue or corned beef off the tip of his slicing knife. The shop smokes turkeys, ducks and geese — $0.35 a pound if it's your bird, and $1.60 if it's theirs. Don't ask them to smoke a ham. No delivery service. Also try SEPP's DELICATESSEN at 3769 St. Lawrence: Excellent sausages and pickled meats and *pâtés*.

Not too far away, at 3855 St. Lawrence, is THE OLD EUROPE, a spacious delicatessen which stuffs *krakowska*, *kabanes*, *debrecener*, *shabai*, and *chorizo* sausages. All sausages are home-made, represent four countries, and have no chemical additives. There's another branch of THE OLD EUROPE in Alex Nihon Plaza, selling ham salami at $1.69 and veal weiners at $0.99 a pound. They will deliver.

Don't leave St. Lawrence without a visit to WALDMAN's FISH MARKET, 74 Roy St. Fresh squid, frogs' legs, periwinkles, oysters, snails and conches decorate the counters — a remarkable display. How do you eat conches? Ask the Chinese gentleman in the corner pawing over the live pincer crabs. Besides all of the above, there's fresh salmon, rainbow trout and, when it's available, Canadian black sturgeon caviar. The quality and diversity of the fish is unique, and the same might be said for the clientele.

THE ST. LAWRENCE BAKERY, 3830 St. Lawrence, makes excellent rye breads, bagels, and challa or egg bread. At LA CASA DEL FROMAGGIO, 6592 St. Lawrence, you will find imported cheeses and home-made sausages from the different regions in Italy.

Climb up the stairs inside VAN HOUTTE's establishment, 272 St. Catherine St. E., and watch the man roasting coffee beans from the sprawling gunny sacks at his feet. VAN HOUTTE's mail their roasts and blends all over Canada. ("Our clientele does not come from the neighbourhood.") The coffee is priced from $1.10 to $2.50 a pound (pure Columbian). Worth a trip just for the smell. VAN HOUTTE's also sell good French bread, fresh shallots, French cooking-utensils, arranged in the hardware-store manner, soap from Marseilles, and a useful fluid called Vichy Supreme Purgative.

Stop at the UNION COFFEE CO., 160 St. Catherine St. E. —

again, that wonderful smell. The people here roast their own beans and have a greater selection of blends of beans than anywhere else in Montreal. A friendly establishment. In case you haven't had enough, here are a few additional baking shops.

The GENEVA PASTRY SHOP, 1861 St. Catherine St. W., makes a delicious *vacherin* as well as home-made chocolates.

You'll be relieved to know that one of Montreal's essential industries, bagel making, goes on twenty-four hours a day. You can personally supervise their manufacture at the BAGEL SHOP, INC., 263 St. Viateur, and watch the bagel man make 300 dozen bagels a day — that's how many they sell. All are boiled in honey and water. Hot bagels are usually available.

You will find excellent French bread at the BOULANGERIE PARISIENNE, 7285 Chabot, as well as at AU PAIN DORE, 6838 Marquette. Both stores distribute their bread all over the city. THE WILLIAM TELL BAKERY, 2055 Stanley, has wonderful rum cheesecake.

Finally, here are a couple of suggestions on Chinese specialties. The best place to buy your Chinese-style pork, barbecued or roasted, is at SUN SING LUNG, 72A LaGauchetière W., and for Chinese-style pastries it's FONG WONG, 1057 St. Lawrence — written up in *Time* magazine for the excellence of their moon and almond cookies and their honey noodle cakes.

If you are in Montreal on a nice sunny Saturday, don't forget that there are three outdoor markets in full operation in the spring-to-fall season on Atwater, Jean Talon and St. Lawrence streets.

Hull

Two excellent French pastry shops manage to keep alive in Hull. GEORGES PRADIER, 148 Eddy, and PATISSERIE FRANCAISE AU CROQUEMBOUCHE, 282 Laramée: Open Sunday from 10:30 a.m. but closed Monday and Tuesday, AU CROQUEMBOUCHE has a wonderful confection called *brioche à la russe*, as well as *croissants*, *brioches* and French pastry.

Phone and ask them to reserve; they run out quickly. (M. and Mme Com, mentioned in Chapter Two, are the proprietors.)

Wakefield
(north of Ottawa)
ORME'S BAKERY: home-style bread (you can see the old ovens), delicious raisin buns, and very good doughnuts. This shop is on the way to the ski hills and summer-vacation lakes. Buy the buns hot and eat them in the car. OGILVY'S DEPARTMENT STORE on Rideau St. in Ottawa now carries their bread.

ONTARIO

Ottawa
Ottawa has managed to keep her stomach where it should be — in the centre of her body: the Ottawa Market is within walking distance of the Parliament Buildings, just behind the largest department store in town. Other markets in Canada have been cut down, or put aside in some obscure corner of the city and left to die, like the former Main Street Market in Winnipeg, but the Ottawa Market ignores suburbia and satellite cities, and with supreme self-assurance creates a traffic engineer's nightmare on fine days, winter and summer. May it always be thus. Farmers from eastern Ontario and Quebec sell maple sugar, wild garlic, bedding plants, headcheese, blueberries, and dried wheat sheaves and bullrushes for decorating embassy hallways, depending on the season. Bargaining is permitted. No self-respecting diplomatic, political or government wife would choose the first bunch of leaf lettuce offered her from one of the outdoor stalls. Apart from the farmers' stalls which come into their own in the summer, the Ottawa Market has many indoor shops.

PETER DEVINE, at 41 York St., is not in the heart of the Market but close enough to qualify for membership. Devine's is an old-fashioned cracker-barrel store, par excel-

lence. Besides the local people who come in for chats with
Mr. Devine, diplomats wander through for pots of Greek
mountain honey and English blends of tea. Devine's fresh
turkeys have a reputation for being tastier than thawed
supermarket birds, and the sign above their block of cheddar cheese says, "Our cheese bites back." It is the only shop
in Ottawa to have had a window display of prunes three
months running.

The fruit and vegetable shops in the Market have quite
an exotic stock for a city the size of Ottawa. Fresh fennel,
snow peas, Ugli fruit,* and fresh ginger root have all been
seen on the counters of TOP BANANA. Within a stone's
throw are ZUNDERS and SHULMANS. Competition does help:
the condition and variety of the fruit and vegetables in
these three shops is much better than that of the supermarkets, while prices are equal and sometimes lower.

THE BEECHWOOD DELICATESSEN, 53 Beechwood, which
used to be Austrian, and still sells knockworsts and strudels,
is now owned by Mr. Fahed Khoury from the Lebanon. Mr.
Khoury and his wife offer their own brand of yoghurt, free
of chemicals; if one is a yoghurt glutton this should be kept
in mind. There are other temptations — tiny stuffed vine
leaves that would be perfect for cocktail *hors-d'oeuvres,* and
a most delicious salad called *taboulé. Taboulé* is made from
parsley, tomatoes, onions, and cooked bulgar wheat, all
chopped to an incredible fineness and seasoned with a little
lemon juice. Another unusual preparation that could also
be used as cocktail fare is *kebé,* finely ground lamb mixed
with onions, spiced with cinnamon and covered with a
wheat germ coating. For those of you who adore the salty,
pungent taste of goat cheese, Mr. Khoury has discovered a
goat and a Swiss farmer. This combination results in a very
fine cheese that is rolled into small balls, placed in plastic
containers and topped with a little oil for lengthy keeping.
All these specialities have an authenticity and home-made
flavour that is unusual in this era of frozen food and chemical additives.

KUO FUNG FOOD SUPPLIES, 254 Albert St., and FAIRWAY

TRADING COMPANY, on York St. between the Market and Sussex St., should satisfy the desires of anyone who is attempting to cook Chinese. Most of the dried and canned goods in these stores comes from Taiwan and Japan, but their winter melon, Chinese cabbage and bean sprouts — all fresh — must come from a nearer source. If you have a passion for black Chinese mushrooms, both stores have them by the sackful. Woks, Mongolian steamers,* chopsticks and fans are available, as well as soy sauces, rice flour, preserves and tea. Nearly all the items are on display shelves, so browsing is easy. THE FAIRWAY TRADING COMPANY gives away recipe sheets. If you want to cook chicken wings in oyster sauce or bamboo shoots, directions and ingredients are cheerfully supplied.

THE CHEESE SHOP, now at 200 Bank St., has the largest selection of European cheeses in the city as well as six kinds of Canadian cheddar. The fresh ricotta cheese, a curdsey cream cheese of Italian origin, has far more flavour and better texture than the smooth, tasteless American type. It is not chemically treated, so it does not stay too long in the cooler. One should eat it within a week of purchase — not a hard thing to do. Brazilian, African and Columbian coffee beans with strong and mild roastings are sold from their sacks and can be ground at the shop for you.

THE BRONSON BAKERY, 1076 Wellington St., specializes in German cakes, sausages and strudels. Especially good are the apple strudel and squares, since the apple filling in them is not a canned goo but freshly-cooked, sliced apples with a fine tart flavour. The custard cakes are made with fresh butter and cream — no trace of the floury or artificial aftertaste that is found in the custards made in supermarket bakeries. The people behind the counter are very patient while you make your choice of pastries and will describe the ingredients slowly and in detail.

BLACK FOREST CAFE, 1323 Wellington St.: Excellent German-style pastries.

KARDISH DELICATESSEN, 979 Wellington St.: Smoked meat, rye bread, good pickled herring — the best in town.

NATE'S DELICATESSEN, 316 Rideau St.: Smoked meat and fish, rye bread.

Perhaps places like these will make a dent in Canadians' tendency to settle for artificiality and inauthenticity in their experiments with different cuisines. Frozen egg rolls, processed cheese, and Dream Whip debase our taste in food. It is encouraging to see Chinese, Germans and Lebanese trying to expand the range of tastes and habits of the average Ottawan.

Kemptville
GRAHAME'S BAKERY, on Clothier St., sells bread that is baked in a brick oven with cedar twigs as fuel. The best time to arrive is 11:00 a.m. when the bread is just coming out of the oven. (No additives in the bread.) Their sweet rolls are famous.

Bells Corners
BALDERSON CHEESE FACTORY outlet: Cheddar cheese of all ages.

County of Leeds
FORFAR CHEESE FACTORY, on Highway 42 (one mile off the Smiths Falls-Kingston Highway; turn off at Crosby): Cheddar cheese; home-made pies as well.

Toronto
Toronto is an international food bazaar and the wares of its vendors are as diverse as lacquered duck Peking-style, Austrian *kugelhopfs*,* and pigeon peas and black eyes from the West Indies. There are shops that answer the demand for rich chocolates at $4 a pound, *petit fours* soaked in Grand Marnier (notwithstanding the price of imported liqueurs), artichoke salads, lobster cooked in twelve different ways, and a dish called Chicken Seagram — a dubious reminder of Canadian culture. It may not be Toronto the Good any more, but it certainly is Toronto the Rich. Many

shops cater to people who have neither the time nor the desire to cook, but who are willing to spend a large sum of money on a small cake. High-rent districts like Bloor St. have so-called ethnic pastry shops that attract the most well-heeled elements in Toronto, along with those New Canadians whose nostalgia for the Austro-Hungarian Empire is based on such gastronomic relics as *Doboschtorte** and feathery cheese strudel.

A. A. AMJARV'S, on the ground floor of the Colonnade, and THE CAKE MASTER, 116 Bloor St. W., are in this category. They face each other, forcing their doomed (calorically speaking) clients to make a choice between them. A. A. AMJARV'S siren voice offers apricot cheesecake, warm, spiced meat-pie, and ham *croissants,* as well as beautiful, buttery meringue cake starting at $4. For something more austere try their fresh fruit jellies at $2 a pound. THE CAKE MASTER has a little counter in the back of the store, and nothing gives a more sinful feeling than to sit there at 3:00 p.m. eating a cheese danish and then a "plain" cake with fresh cherries artfully spread through it. The people here have home-made yoghurt, their own butter and cheese spread, *croissants, kugelhopfs,* and poppy-seed confections of all kinds. Very expensive.

High living does not stop at the end of Bloor. PAUL'S FRENCH FOOD SHOP, 425 Spadina, is not your average cracker-barrel store — but if you decide to hang around you'll get more than a glimpse of how the upper half lives. A couple returning to Winnipeg were stocking up on PAUL'S famous veal and ham pie, rare roast beef and special *hors-d'oeuvres,* the better to face the Manitoba winter. Sophy, a charming lady who has been with PAUL'S for twenty-three years, inquired after the health of the parents of a young girl buying home-made Russian dressing. "Very well," she replied, "divorced, and both will re-marry next month." Next, a sleek blond gentleman with make-up anxiously asked, "Are my little Christmas cookies ready yet?" And amid the pink, whole-cooked shrimp, celery-root salad ($1 per half-pint), and rum-soaked *petit fours,* he was reassured by Sophy.

CHEZ CHARBON, 3336 Lonsdale Rd., is the same sort of shop, but M. Charbon, a Swiss, has only been in business for seven years. His kirsch tartelettes, *pâté de foie gras* ($4.40 a pound), and artichoke salad ($2 a pound), are some of the superior items. The highly decorated butter-cream French cakes start from $3.

LE PETIT GOURMET, 858 Millwood Rd. and 1064 Yonge St., is a slightly less-expensive version of these fancy French take-outs. The *croissants* are excellent, a bargain at two for a quarter, and the *pâté maison* is only $2 a pound. There is a tea room in the Yonge St. store.

PICKERING FARMS LTD., 852 Yonge St., a diverse in-town market, will offer you live and cooked lobster at a reasonable price, while offering you a chance to mingle with a more than usually interesting crowd of shoppers.

Shopping in Toronto's Kensington Market is good for the ego, especially if you're female and a stranger. Vitality is the principal characteristic of the Market. Everything is very much alive, from the poultry to the male-chauvinist vendors who flirt with any female under sixty. Sample conversation with a bald, toothless, vegetable man: "How fresh is the broccoli?" "Not as fresh as I'd like to be with you."

Mr. Daiter of DAITER'S SILVERTHORN DAIRY LTD., 64 Kensington Ave., force-fed us with his special lactic-bacteria buttermilk and cream cheese, which he unwrapped from cheese-cloth containers. They tasted infinitely better and fresher than any brand on the supermarket counters. He related the secret of his successful dairy plant to us, "Four hours work, four hours cleaning." His whole-milk cheese, cream cheese, and sour cream are the freshest and most authentic in Toronto.

Next door is the DUTCH DAIRIES, where you can buy imported cheeses at very low prices. There are specials, like Gruyère at $0.49 a pound and Edam at $0.45 a pound.

People come in and buy up the blocks of fresh butter and Mr. De Silva's own cheese spread. It is the only cheese shop in Canada which broadcasts tangos for the benefit of the passer-by.

You can buy sheep's heads, goat meat, unsalted pumpkin seeds, and medium *kasha* (see p. 107) at the ROYAL FOOD CENTRE, 199 Baldwin. Mr. Perlmutar of PERLMUTAR BAKERY, at 175 Baldwin, claims that he has the only Jewish bakery that sells onion bread with onions baked inside the loaf. Mrs. D. Rabovsky came 120 miles from Owen Sound for a supply of Perlmutar's bread.

Still in the Kensington Market, the ROMANIAN AND HUNGARIAN FOOD SPECIALTY AND PASTRY SHOP, 17 St. Andrew St., has delicious Turkish delight, bulk chocolate, and perfect baklava (containing pure honey only), all made by Helen, whose baking motto is "our clients are our masters". Stop also at GOLDLIST's, 188 Baldwin St., for fresh geese (with feathers for making down, if desired), and at PALLA's TROPICAL FOODS, 173 Baldwin, for West- and East-Indian food.

Once out of the Market, drive past the Risorgimento Billiards on College St. and you will find JOHNNY LOMBARDI's, 637 College, where whole parmesans, fresh ricotta, and machines for making your own pasta are available. This store is in the heart of the Italian district. Miss Lombardi has been there for twenty-three years, and will slice you some prosciutto from the whole ham. The SICILIAN ICE CREAM STORE is just one block past, at 712 College St. It's the only place in Toronto that makes cassatta with real rum and anisette, and ice-cream "truffles" with a surprise centre of glacéed fruit. Four portions of cassatta are $1.50, and truffles are a quarter each. You can eat there, while sipping an espresso.

DARRIGO, 900 St. Clair W., is an Italian market with an unequalled selection of fruits and vegetables. Fresh fennel, artichokes, rappini and zucchini abound, besides the more mundane things. There is an excellent selection of olives, some with red pepper sprinkled over them, and there are home-made Italian sausages. The place is very clean and spacious.

PASQUALE'S, over in the St. Lawrence Market on 145 King St. E., has over 120 varieties of cheeses, including a noisette (hazelnut) cheese and a liptauer cheese-spread that Kenny, their cheese specialist, created. He says that he will tell only eleven of the twelve ingredients of the liptauer spread. Their artichoke salad is reasonable at $1.20 a pound. There are also home-made pure pork sausages.

The most unusual fish store in Toronto is MISNER'S FISH MARKET, 1993 Yonge, owned by Mrs. Ellie Knight, a former dress designer whose creations cost $500 each. Mrs. Knight buys all her fish directly from primary sources. She says "fish in Toronto stay too long on wholesaler's slabs". She has been in business only a year and is the first fish market consistently to provide steamer clams, red and gray mullet, and soft-shell crabs to Toronto. Her rainbow trout are alive — they are killed upon purchase. MISNER'S is one of the few fish markets in Canada to follow this excellent practice. Mrs. Knight sells as much fish from Monday to Thursday as she does on the week-end because fresh stock is ready for her customers at all times. She also carries unusual fish, like fresh-water salmon and striped sea bass.

MORE BAKERIES

KING BAKERY, 932 the Queensway (Borough of Etobicoke): Good Italian pastries, especially the cheese and crusty dough, and *sfioglie*—clam-shaped pastry with dried fruits and ricotta cheese; Italian bread.

THE CHESTNUT PASTRY SHOP AND DELICATESSEN, 1394 Eglinton Ave. W. at Farleigh Cres.: Delicious home-baked Hungarian cakes and cookies.

PALLAS BAKERY, two locations: 680 Bloor St. W., east of Christie, 642 Danforth, west of Pape; home-made phylo* dough, glazed fruit.

YEREVAN BAKERY, 2030 Avenue Rd.: Armenian specialties, home-made yoghurt, salt-free bread, burrecks (cheese-filled pastries).

ODDS AND ENDS

Those who resent American economic take-overs must draw the line at BASKIN-ROBBINS 31 ICE CREAM store, 1018 Eglinton Ave. W. Their 31 flavours of ice-cream are richer and creamier than anywhere else in Toronto. The pints are all hand-packed and you can get free tastes. The Toronto favourite is Jamoca almond fudge, but I liked gooseberry sherbet. The fruit flavours are made with fresh fruit. A new branch at Yonge and Eglington.

GOLDY'S EGLINTON DAIRY AND APPETIZER DELICATESSEN, 938 Eglinton Ave. W., has green-pepper salad and smoked fishes, delicious salmon sliced off the whole side, and smoked whitefish and sturgeon. There is also marinated salmon and Daiter's fresh milk- and cream-cheeses. Open Sundays.

SPLENDID CHOCOLATES, 896 Eglinton Ave. W.: Mr. Liberman is proud of his dark chocolate. His pet peeve is peanuts — he uses the more aristocratic Brazils and cashews.

INDO-PAK TRADING CO., 111 Dupont St.: Indian spices, flours, pappadums, betelnuts, and specially ground curry powder.

OLD WORLD CHEESE SHOP, 809 Yonge St.: Wine-cured cheddar, and delicious cheese bread.

SIMON DE GROOT'S MEAT MARKET, 481 Church St.: Maritime atmosphere surrounds home-pickled meats and sausages *à la maison*.

ESTE MEAT PRODUCTS, 691 Mount Pleasant Rd.: Scandinavian specialties, including *Lut Fisk* (see p. 116) at Christmas. Closed Mondays.

The Town Mall, at 81 St. Clair Ave., is a brand new shopping centre with underground parking. You can find there THE CHEESE SHOP with 150 varieties of cheeses; LES CAVALIERS PASTRY SHOP, a pastry and lunch place owned by PAUL'S FRENCH FOOD; and THE FRUIT FAIR, selling fresh pepper cress and bunches of garlic and shallots, as well as a fine selection of fruits, vegetables and flowers. THE COFFEE BLENDER, also in the Mall, has beans from Columbia and other places, whole and ground, and black telechery whole pepper, as well as lots of Chinese and Indian tea.

Environs of Toronto

Follow Highway 400 from Toronto; turn off at Highway 88 and go east to Bradford. There are roadside vegetable stands along Highway 11 just south of the town. Proceed to Highway 9 and go east through Newmarket to Woodbine Avenue; drive south to Gormley. Head east to Ringwood for PHILLIPS GROCERY: Fresh honey, mild May apple butter, whitefish and salmon trout, home-made bread, cheesebread and rolls.

NORMAN FRETZ MEATS, R.R. 3, Claremont, sells delicious farmer's sausage.

Oshawa

FUNDY FISH MARKET, Simcoe St.: Good seafood — clams, oysters, shrimp, scallops and lobsters — much of it from the Bay of Fundy. The proprietor also sells other fish, including cod's roe. Well-heeled Torontonians have been seen buying their fish there.

MANITOBA

Winnipeg

The original settlers in Winnipeg were the Scotch, but speaking gastronomically, it is the Ukrainians, Jews, Hungarians and Italians who are more evident now. During the thirties, the PICARDY pastry shops supplied the Scotch population with their tea cakes, butter tarts and home-made boiled salad-dressing. Today that is just a memory, and the absence of these shops from the city is regretted by even those who haven't a drop of Anglo-Saxon blood in their veins. Scones, oat cakes and haggis have been replaced by perogies, knishes, and blood-and-buckwheat sausages. There is nothing wrong with the latter items, provided you know the best places to find them.

OASIS DELICATESSEN & FRUIT LTD., 906 Main St. (the name is odd — Winnipeg in January, at twenty-seven below, does not remind anyone of the Sahara Desert): The owners of the OASIS are Jewish; many of their products, such as excellent corned beef, chopped liver, and flaky dough knishes are high quality specialties for the large Jewish population in Winnipeg. Their knishes are superb (knishes are a crisp, round pastry filled with cottage cheese, meat or potato). The OASIS knish dough is stretched by experts in that special art, in the back of the shop. However, the OASIS has branched out beyond its Jewish clientele and serves the Icelandic, German and Ukrainian population of Winnipeg as well. The array of herrings in special cases is unequalled in the whole country: Holland milkers, Icelandic headless and Alaska fat herring are sold fresh or pickled (they do all their own pickling) in various national styles. The owners also sell cabbage rolls, a Ukrainian specialty, and smoked fish, such as whole sides of salmon and coonie (inconnu). While I was there, a Ukrainian lady living in the wilds of St. James had come all the way to the OASIS in north Winnipeg to buy eight boxes of buckwheat grains, or *kasha*. The Oasis has a large counter with stools where you can taste all the specialties.

THE M & S MEAT MARKET is just across the street from the OASIS at 915 Main St. Their great specialty is home-made sausages of all kinds. Hungarians, Germans and Ukrainians come there for the special headcheeses, blood-and-buckwheat sausages, wieners, and specially smoked boneless ham. They even supply fresh blood if you want to make your own blood sausages. I saw a full jar of blood being passed over the counter to a gentleman who is only satisfied with his own recipe. According to those who know, M & S are the cleanest sausage-makers in town. They also sell home-made lard and home-cured back bacon.

The people at THE PEROGY House, 412 Dufferin Ave. at

Salter, make all their own perogies. When you go in to buy a package, you can see the ladies rolling out the dough and adding the fillings. The machine age has not overtaken them. They also specialize in *holopchi* — cabbage rolls filled with rice, or buckwheat, or meat. The perogies are from $0.65 a dozen, and *holopchi* from $0.60 a dozen. Free delivery anywhere in the Metro area, minimum order $2.50.

Some of the best bread in Winnipeg comes from a Jewish bakery, GUNN'S, on 247 Selkirk (try their rye bread) and the PASTICCERIA GIOIA, or ITALIAN PASTRY SHOP, on 637 Corydon St. Both offer country-style bread with a crisp crust and an inside part which tastes of bread, not mush. It's a treat to go into the ITALIAN PASTRY SHOP and stare at the homemade marzipan candies — apricots complete with blemishes, cherries on a stem, and brown chestnuts. It also sells a small bread-dough pizza.

NEPTUNE'S FISHERIES LTD., 472 Dufferin: Fresh whitefish and pickerel, and frozen pickerel cheeks, a great Manitoba delicacy.

AUBY'S DELICATESSEN RESTAURANT, 1411 Main: Delicious coffee cakes, cinnamon buns and Danish pastries.

SASKATCHEWAN

Regina

Saskatchewan is not a consumer's paradise, so far as specialty food shops are concerned. Nevertheless, good bread, sausages and Ukrainian Easter eggs are available in Regina.

ITALIAN STAR CONFECTIONERY, 1611 Victoria Ave., carries cheese, Italian coffee beans, olives and a variety of pasta, as well as prosciutto ham.

HIRTH SAUSAGE COMPANY, 11th Ave. at Toronto St., specializes in German sausages, smoked meat, and cheeses.

THE UKRAINIAN CO-OPERATIVE ASSOCIATION, 1801 Winnipeg St., has very good bread, home-made Ukrainian sausages and Ukrainian Easter eggs. Occasionally it has pastries.

OLD FASHION FOODS, 511 Victoria Ave., sells food with no additives. The owners grind their own peanut butter and sell ice-cream wafers as they used to be.

Saskatoon

TRAEGER'S BAKERY, 510 33rd St., has excellent baking (three other locations). Try ROY'S GROCERY, 904 Victoria, for a wide range of goods for East-Indian cooking.

EUROPEAN MEAT PRODUCTS, 308 20th St. W., has sausages, cheeses, breads and various imported goods. The accent is Ukrainian. At FOREIGN IMPORTS AND DELICATESSEN LTD. in the Avalon Shopping Centre, you can also find a good selection of cheeses and sausages, as well as rye bread and German delicacies. OLD FASHION FOODS has a branch in Saskatoon, as it does in Prince Albert. At the ORIENTAL SHOP, 429 20th St. W., you can get imported Chinese groceries, herbs and spices, and exotic meats.

ALBERTA

Edmonton

Edmonton is in Alberta, and to those interested in food this means that the very best beef in Canada is as close as the nearest meat market. There is also a fairly large Chinese community and a sizeable Italian and German population. No one store in Edmonton is unique in Canada, but there are many unusual shops to visit.

THE QUEEN CITY MEAT SUPPLY LTD., 9909 101A Ave., has a fine display of Alberta beef. In fact, the store specializes in pickling prime ribs (an extravagant taste, but where else in Canada can it be indulged?). All pickling and sausage stuffing is done on the premises.

SCONA MEAT AND DELICATESSEN, 10001 82 Ave.: European-type sausages. The owners will process wild game.

STRATHCONA MEAT MARKET, 10105 82 Ave.: Although the STRATHCONA MEAT MARKET started out selling to the European community in Edmonton, Mr. Braun, the owner, says that fifty per cent of his customers are now native-born Canadians. He sells home-stuffed sausages of all kinds and meat loaves containing cheese, and others with mushrooms.

ADRIAN'S BAKERY, 10107 82 Ave. (two other locations), is just around the corner from the STRATHCONA MEAT MARKET. This area is the heart of the Austro-Hungarian Empire in Edmonton. You can buy good rolls, and *kugelhopfs* of different flavours. HOME BAKERY, at 10007 82 Ave., sells German pastries as well, and it's a stone's throw from the previously mentioned shops. Their specialties are sourdough rye bread (which may be bought in bulk for freezing, 10 pounds for $4) and an elaborate cake that looks like the bark of a tree.

Most Italian products may be bought between 109th and 108A Aves. Two grocers, SACCOMANNO BROTHERS on one corner and THE ITALIAN CENTRE Store on the other, will supply you with olives in bulk, and frozen, stretched strudel dough. The espresso-coffee place in between (I was unable to discover the name of the shop) will sell you Italian ice-cream in bulk. It's made in the shop.

If you want Chinese products, the MEI HEONG BARBECUE COMPANY, 10134 97 St., does a good job of supplying buried eggs*, "some with a sweet and some with a salt taste," fresh ginger, and lacquered duck to the Chinese community. There are fresh kumquats and dried duck at the ORIENTAL TRADING COMPANY, 9718 Jasper Ave.

The only Japanese shop in town is the JAPAN FOOD CENTRE, 6519 111 St., where Canadians buy rice crackers for cocktail munching, and vegetarians buy bean paste for protein intake.

THE PALACE OF SWEETS, 10122 Jasper Ave., makes all its own candies in the basement of its store. I saw Bob Giffen, the chief candy-maker, from Ireland, stirring the egg whites in a copper pot for the toasted coconut marshmallows, (Thursday, Friday and Saturday only). The owners use only fresh cream and butter in their candies; their velvet mints are famed as far as the Chateau Laurier Hotel dining-room in Ottawa. They sell 200 candy apples a day (a remarkable amount). Chocolates are hand-dipped.

THE JAVA SHOP, 10122 100A St.: Coffee beans from all over the world, tea and spices, also espresso coffee to drink there, and good home-made doughnuts.

THE SCANDIA BAKERY, in the Meadowlark Park Shopping Centre, makes the best Danish pastry in Edmonton, if not in all of Alberta. The price is $0.65 a roll. The tart shells here are of a fine quality.

THE HICKORY FARM STORE in the same shopping centre sells good cheese, and the people at the MEADOWLARK DELICATESSEN make their own sausages.

CAMELOT ICE CREAM SHOPPES, 11754 Jasper Ave. (and three other locations), sell ice-cream with flavours like pumpkin spice and swiss moka (mocha).

The Edmonton Market is open on Saturdays and is recommended for fresh vegetables, flowers and fish.

Calgary

Calgary has Italians, Chinese and Germans living within its walls, but its greatest foreign-born group is American. The supermarkets carry a lot of made-in-U.S.A. products, especially in the frozen-food line, that are not too common in the eastern part of Canada.

THE A.B.C. FOOD STORE, 1110 17 Ave. S.W., realizes Calgary's multi-ethnic potential and carries the delicacies of every man. Bulk olives, millet, poppy and sesame seeds satisfy the varied clientele. A lady who accompanied me to the shop was pleased to find fresh white turnips there. THE A.B.C. has the best selection of cheeses in Calgary. But do the elderly clientele really like the piped-in rock music (from a local FM radio station)?

THE WOODEN SHOE PASTRY SHOP, 819a 49 Ave. S.W. in the Britannia Shopping Centre, makes crunchy brandy-snaps with nuts and fresh apple-cake. The almond short-bread is rich and good.

Also try the FRENCH PASTRY SHOP, 126a 10 St. N.W.

THE CHALET PASTRY & CHOCOLATE SHOP, 1305 17 Ave. S.W., is owned by Mr. Zielke, who sells his potent liqueur chocolates for $4.25 a pound. His Easter bunnies are cheaper or dearer: they start at $0.50 but Mr. Zielke will provide one for $100 if you wish. He uses pure chocolate, never cocoa, and the butter-cream meringue cakes are flavoured with whiskey and wine.

BRIDGEMAN'S CHOCOLATE SHOP, 1217 1 St. S.W., is also recommended.

OLIVIER'S CANDY, 1005a 1 St. S.W., has something I've never seen in any other candy shop — clear-coloured candy figures, some in the shape of pipes, others in the form of teapots. You can buy a small assortment for $1. All the candies are home-made with pure cream and butter. I particularly like the molasses butter-drops.

BRITISH COLUMBIA

Vancouver

Vancouver has shops appealing to every nationality and every taste. It is a rich city, and the variety of food shops reflects its prosperity. Do you want Viennese-style pastry shops that sell slices of their baking on the premises, with a cup of coffee and whipping cream? Or how about some take-out Chinese lacquered duck, or Melton Mowbray pie, or gorgeous glazed fruits from an East that is more familiar to Vancouverites than mysterious Toronto? It's all here, by the sea. Strangely enough, Vancouver's greatest natural gastronomic product, fish, is not too well represented.

Fish markets do not abound in seaports in Canada. When I went to Fisherman's Wharf on Campbell St. there was no great display of salmon, crab or oysters, and I was told that the individual shopper is not particularly welcome there.

Vancouver people love pastries. The MOZART KONDI-TOREI, 1011 Robson St. (or *strasse,* as it is known because of

the number of German food shops on it), and GIZELLA
PASTRY, 775 Burrard St., cater to this taste. Both have little
restaurants and both serve a variety of European pastries.
GIZELLA's has an attractive old staircase. However, the finest
pastry shop, for my money, is the BON TON, at 874 Granville St. Mr. Notte, the owner and chef, uses egg whites to
make his cakes rise, not baking powder. He refuses to put
whipped-cream cakes on display (they must be ordered in
advance) because he won't add preservatives in the cream
to keep it stiff. Everything is made with fresh butter. The
nuts on the cakes are ground fresh by a man in the back and
the jams in the cakes are made by BON TON chefs out of
fresh berries. (I saw a cook lining a Black Forest cake with
the BON TON's own fresh cherry preserve.) Real, not artificial, rum is used in their chocolate-rum truffles ($3 a
pound) and other rum confections. There are twenty-eight
employees, and as Mr. Notte says "If they stay six months
they stay twenty years." The cakes start at $0.70 and the
beautiful meringue shells are $1.90 a dozen. A *St. Honoré*
or chocolate *mousse* may be ordered in advance for about
$5.50. Even the mincemeat tarts are made from the shop's
own mincemeat.

The most beautiful butcher shop in Canada is JAMES
INGLIS REID LIMITED, 559 Granville St. It was established
in the middle of the last century; long, marble counters and
elegantly displayed cuts of bacon make it the Tiffany's of
butcher shops. The owners advertise "Wiltshire and Ayrshire bacon, own cure" and sell haggis, black and white
puddings and fresh local lamb and veal. The meat is cut
with style and without fat. Bacon sells from $0.81 a pound
to $1.20; home-made sausages are $0.90 a pound. They also
make and sell Scotch scones, oat cakes, meat pies, and a
Paris bun that is full of currants and crystallized fruits. Try
the soda scones, toasted. They taste as if they were just
shipped from Glasgow.

GALLOWAY's, 1084 Robson St., sells the most gorgeous
glazed fruit in Canada. It is all sold in bulk. A Vancouver
lady told me "When you want to make fruit cake, buy the

dried and crystallized fruit there because it will cost you half of the supermarket price." On Saturday it's very busy, with Vancouverites frantically buying dried raisin clusters (stems included), glazed apricots and sugared Chinese ginger. Poppy and sesame seed are sold in bulk. The dates are exquisite. GALLOWAY's has been around for thirty years.

Thirty thousand Chinese live in Vancouver, the second-largest Chinese population in North America. Most of them may be found on Pender Street East Saturday afternoon doing their week-end shopping. LUN CHONG POULTRY will cut up fresh chickens, Chinese style, and give you the feet as well to enrich your soup. The vegetables in all the shops on Pender Street are of excellent quality — little, fresh spinach leaves, fresh water chestnuts, kumquats, and the biggest bean sprouts I've ever seen. WING HING CO. LTD. on 280 E. Pender Street is a kind of Chinese supermarket. It has a whole cooked pig hanging over the counter, its skin crusty and crackling, along with dried mushrooms, fresh bean curd, and 1000 kinds of noodles. If you want to snack, go to YIP HONG YUEN RESTAURANT and eat custard tarts and almond cookies baked on the premises, or go to the DOLLAR MEAT STORE for take-out Chinese lacquered ribs and duck, and barbecued sausages. All these shops are very close to one another, but some of the street numbers are not too readily visible.

DEAN'S ROAST CHICKEN, 848 Granville: English-style Melton Mowbray pie, deliciously light sausage-rolls (2 for $0.35), home-baked ham and chicken, apple fritters — all to take out. Reasonable prices and good food. Open Sunday.

SZASZ DELICATESSEN AND RESTAURANT, 2881 Granville St.: Central-European-style cooking — wonderful meringues and apple pastries, sausages, liptauer cheese, and breads of all kinds. Open Sunday.

MURCHIE'S TEA AND COFFEE STORES, two locations, 850 Park Royal and 1008 Robson St.: Enormous selection of teas and coffees from all over the world.

PURDY'S CHOCOLATES, 2853 Granville: The chocolates here are made from fresh butter and cream. The dusky chocolate creams are rewarding and fattening. Fresh lemons are squeezed for the flavour in the lemon creams. Excellent dark chocolate. PURDY's now sells ice-cream with fresh-fruit flavours and sixteen per cent butterfat.

OLIVIERI's RAVIOLI STORE, 1900 Commercial Dr.: The people here make their own pastry — ravioli, tortellini, gnocchi — and sell it packaged, fresh and frozen, at approximately $1 a pound.

THE OLD CHEESE SHOPPE, 1041 Robson St.: Vancouver's first cheese shop. The owners also import frozen French and cream desserts like *mandarin givrée*.

Two fish markets are ROYAL SEAFOODS, 868 Park Royal, W. Vancouver, and VILLAGE FISH AND OYSTER MARKET, 1482 Marine, W. Vancouver.

VENICE BAKERY, 1350 Main, North Vancouver: Good sourdough bread.

BROADWAY BAKERY, 3115 W. Broadway: Greek baking including baclava.

WOLLNER's BAKERY, 3735 West 10th: Very good *croissants* at $0.09 each, and challah, a twisted egg loaf.

LEE's CANDIES, 4361 West 10th.: This is a family candy business. Especially recommended are rocky road (nuts, marshmallow and chocolate) and the solid, flat mint-truffle.

AUSTRIAN BAKERY, 2660 Alma Rd.: Sourdough, French and raisin loaf.

FEINSCHMECKER's DELICATESSEN, 1080 Robson St.: Excellent home-made German meat and sausage products, cheeses and ready-made salads.

Victoria

Victoria has more millionaires per square inch than any other city in Canada — at least that is what the visitor is told on arriving. The combination of retired upper-income groups and the English "ethnic" flavour of Victoria results in elegant sweet shops like R. C. PURDY CHOCOLATES in the Empress Hotel (they are also in Vancouver), ROGERS' CHOCOLATES, 913 Government St. and LEES ENGLISH TOFFEE SHOP, 643 Yates St. Victoria is certainly the Candy Capital

of Canada. ROGERS' CHOCOLATES, an extremely dignified
shop, almost church-like, was established in 1885, and has
maintained its original décor. It is the founder of the Victoria cream, a huge, round chocolate filled with peach or
pineapple, or "Prince of Wales" rum cream. If soft centres
do not excite you, the chocolate-coated English almond-
toffee might cause a heart flutter. All chocolates and toffees
are hand-made in the shop. A pound of assorted chocolates
costs $3.25. The shop does a large mail-order business
throughout the United States and Canada. LEES ENGLISH
TOFFEE SHOP is the kind of candy store that you wish you'd
had around your corner when you were a child. The walls
of the shop are lined with 680 jars, filled with rock crystal,
horehound drops, toffees, mints and aniseed cough-drops.
Ninety per cent of the candies come from the "old country,"
but there is some chocolate from the colonies — Australia,
for instance. Mrs. Belle Felton, who has been selling at
LEES TOFFEE for twenty years, says they had been out of
butter brazils for the last two years, but, to their relief, a
shipment finally arrived. Ribbon candy, a delicacy for highly refined tastes, is difficult to find, so they make it themselves for those in Victoria who care. Another specialty is
Easter eggs, which they also make, of pure Cadbury chocolate. Their greatest customers are retired English, looking
for the pear drops of their youth, and Americans who buy
out the shop.

WILLE'S BAKERY, 537 Johnson St., was established in
1887 and still bakes bread in a brick oven, the only one in
British Columbia. The bread is marvellous. In fact, the
sourdough rye is certainly one of the finest single gastronomic items in the country. WILLE'S also has a crusty
French loaf, as good as anything in Montreal. A different
kind of bread is baked every day, including 100 per cent
whole wheat and pumpernickel. The baker is Gordon
Stewart Wille, great-grandson of the founder. Stacks of old
loaves are lined up against the wall; above them is the sign,
"Free Bird Bread, Take Away". Closed Sunday and Monday.

THE DUTCH BAKERY & COFFEE SHOP LIMITED, 718 Fort St., specializes in marzipan, puff pastry and pineapple kirsch slices, all beautifully decorated.

THE CHEESE 'N GIFT WORLD, 795 Fort, not only sells cheeses, but makes delicious scones and tea biscuits in a little oven just behind the counter. WILLIAMS MEAT MARKET, part of the same shop, is the only place in Victoria where you can buy Vancouver Island lamb and veal.

MORLEY CO. LIMITED, 552 Fisgard: Ingredients for Chinese cooking.

THE CAIRO IMPORT LTD., 1609 Douglas St., has been in business over fifty-five years and offers a variety of Indian chutneys. It claims that its "Madras Curry Powder and Curry Gravy" is world famous.

STEVENSON'S HOMEMADE CHOCOLATES AND CANDY, 1425 Douglas St. in Victoria, and 2521 Beacon Ave. in nearby Sidney: Home-made chocolates, fudge, and Victoria creams. The main store has been going for sixty-three years.

ADRIAN'S GOURMET DELICATESSEN, 1628 Hillside: Sausages, home-made salads, meat pies, sausage-rolls, Melton Mowbray pork pie.

JACOB'S LADDER, 595 Sooke Rd., RR 1, Sooke: Every variety of fresh herbs in pots.

Where to Eat if You're Fussy and Broke

IF YOU ENJOY only so-called elegant dining, this chapter is not for you. The obsequious waiters, the chateaubriands, the ambience of hushed mock-oak panelling and carefully antiqued "ancestor" paintings (created especially for the luxury-restaurant trade), have nothing in common with the eating places that I'm going to mention. But if the bill at these places is too high for your pocket-book, or if, from time to time, you froth at the mouth because of the fancy price you have to pay for interior decorating, then perhaps "my" hot-dog stands, fish and chip shops, roadside cafés and restaurants might interest you.

I've tried to find out about places to eat in Canada that cost under $2, or $3 at the very most. Naturally, some of these are only snack bars; you might only want to have a cup of coffee and a piece of pie. Others will serve you a full meal in a very unpretentious setting, perhaps strictly counter service. A good many do have tables, and some even have a liquor licence. What they all have in common is good food for the price. You will not go away feeling cheated, and you might even feel you've had something exceptional to eat. All these restaurants are excellent for families driving through the country who don't want to pay $5 a head, and are in a hurry. Young people wandering through the cities during the summer might want to splurge and buy themselves a good meal, and even those of you who are stationary might like to know where you can get something good to eat at a low price in your own home town.

It is, of course, an impossible task to cover every good little café in Canada. This is just a sampling of what may be found in various cities and towns. Most, I've been to personally, and a few have been vouched for by knowledgeable people who spend a lot of time and little money eating out. Again, I must stress that some of these places are hardly more than coffee counters, but they serve something — perhaps a very special pizza or good home-made cake — that makes the stopover worth-while.

NEWFOUNDLAND

The tourist in Newfoundland can travel many a mile before he finds other fish than cod. Newfoundlanders have always been poor, and perhaps because of this a perverse pride makes them go in for the food easiest come by. Mussels, clams, crabs abound in the sea; yet most Newfoundlanders prefer to eat canned luncheon meat rather than scrape the bottom of the ocean on their doorsteps. It's only been a few years since Newfoundland restaurateurs realized that lobster would have an appeal — even now it's not easily available or properly prepared. The true Newfoundland specialties are salt cod, rabbit and seal-flipper pies, and jigg's dinner, a sort of New England type boiled dinner with pork riblets, turnip tops, parsnips and cabbage.

St. John's
TOWNE AND COUNTRY, on Water St., closes at 6 p.m.† It is one of the few places in St. John's where you can taste some

† In this chapter hours of service for restaurants are given only if they are out of the ordinary — if, for example, a place closes in the evenings, as above, or between lunch and dinner. A few of the places in tourist regions are open only during the summer months.

genuine Newfoundland food at extremely reasonable prices. Although the TOWNE AND COUNTRY is basically an eat-and-run restaurant, it does have a licence. With the amount of salt cod they serve, it is a good idea to have a beer. The customers of the TOWNE AND COUNTRY are the girls who work in the shops across the way, fishermen who have strayed off their boats, and single male eaters in black who come in every day for the "special". The Friday special can be an excellent salt-cod dinner served with boiled potatoes and scrunchions, or jigg's dinner.

Many people from St. John's feel that the TOWNE AND COUNTRY cooks fish better than most of the more pretentious restaurants in the city. The salt-cod dinner costs $1.80 — a good soup and an unidentifiable dessert pudding come with it. The ambience does not make you want to have a second cup of coffee. Neither does the coffee!

CAPTAIN'S CABIN, in Bowering's Brothers Department Store, Water St. (founded 1811): Easily found because of all the signal flags in front. It's a cafeteria, and has several things that recommend it to the impoverished tourist. The view of the harbour is magnificent — one whole wall is a window. The buns and scones, along with some of the simpler pastries, are of a home-made or cottage style and quality. There is also the usual cafeteria-style meal available — often with a daily special of Newfoundland fish. Good coffee. Licensed.

THE PARKER HOUSE, 332 Duckworth St.: The doughnuts and coffee are excellent, and there is also an extremely tasty roll, shaped in the form of a snail. The pastries are made on the premises and have a much lighter texture than their counterparts elsewhere. They don't look different than the usual stuff, but they do taste better. Avoid the doughnuts with the yellow jelly blobs on them. Duckworth Street lawyers come here for their 10:30 coffee-break and, like the rest of their compatriots, they make politics, rather than law, the subject of the conversation. Counter service only.

CHES'S FISH AND CHIPS, 9 Freshwater Rd.: Do not be confused by the other Ches's at number 5. CHES'S at number 9 is the real CHES's where the best fish and chips in St. John's may be found. The view and atmosphere are suitable for this type of establishment: there is an excellent view of Dr. L. K. Chang's Freshwater Medical Clinic from the window. But you should be content with the fresh cod, the fried-to-order potatoes, and the light, crunchy batter. Chicken is also served. A few crumbs on the counter and the too-small paper cartons, which make your portion of chips spill over, do not detract from the quality of the food. No tea or coffee. Take-out service also.

Deer Lake
SHORTS HOTEL: "Great beef and kidney pie" and "great dessert pies". The Hotel is just off the Trans-Canada Highway.

Cornerbrook
THE GLYNMILL INN used to be the staff house of Bowaters Paper Company but it is now open to the public. Extremely attractive grounds, with a pond, and the meals are moderately priced. Hearsay has it that the salmon and lobster are well prepared. Licensed.

Grand Falls
CARMELITE HOTEL: For the professional traveller. Good home-made soup; impressive urinals — seven feet high (I did not test them myself). Licensed.

NOVA SCOTIA

Halifax
In the central part of Canada, deep-fried batter can be used as a substitute for a coat of armour, but the people in the Maritimes deep-fry a lot of fish, and the experience has taught them how to make a batter that is light and crisp. The best place in Halifax to eat fish and chips is CAMILLE's

FISH AND CHIPS, 2564 Barrington. It's near the MacDonald Bridge, up from the docks in the north end, near the sea and the warehouses. A deep-sea diver told me to go there for really fresh fish, and presumably he should know. CA-MILLE'S FISH AND CHIPS is clean and spacious with two rooms — one with a counter for those in a hurry. The décor is not forgotten. The walls are encrusted with mock sea-shells for a nautical touch. The other room is done in var-nished pine and has tables for more formal dining. The fish and chips ($0.35 a portion, with a dime extra for each extra piece of fish) are encased in a batter that is worthy of the Maritime culinary tradition of expert deep-frying.

If you want to splurge, order the clam chowder for $0.70. There are more clams in CAMILLE'S bowl than in those served by more expensive places in town and, to be trite, the chowder is a meal in itself. For the last of the big-time spenders there is the Mariner's plate for $2, with deep-fried shellfish. There is also something called "weiners alone," and "southern fried weiners and chips," for those who hate fish. CAMILLE'S is extremely pleasant to eat in and caters to a late-night crowd. Counter service, tables, jukebox.

WILLMAN'S FRIED FOODS LIMITED, 5644 Kane: Good fish and chips; take-out service only.

CHICKEN TANDOOR, 1655 Argyle St.: A cheap but excel-lent Indian restaurant where everything is freshly cooked by the owner and his wife. Their shrimp biryani is one of the best I have ever tasted anywhere in Canada. It is fla-oured with lemon and coconut. They also serve chicken Korma prepared with fruit and nuts, and chicken Madras, which is quite hot, but good. However, there is no chicken Tandoor because Haligonians won't wait for its lengthy preparation. Each dish is about $1.70. Open 11 a.m. to 2 p.m. and 5 p.m. to 9 p.m., seven days a week.

Digby

FUNDY RESTAURANT, 34 Water St.: Clam chowder, fried clams, and haddock, fresh, and cooked to order. A superb view of the Annapolis Basin from an addition built over the waterfront. Licensed.

Yarmouth
HARRIS' SEAFOOD RESTAURANT, Highway No. 1 just outside Yarmouth (in Dayton), and HARRIS' QUICK 'N TASTY, just across the road from the Restaurant, serve good fried scallops, clams, and haddock. The Restaurant is licensed but it is open only during the summer months.

Hubbards
SHATFORD'S Lobster Pound has picnic tables, home-made rolls and biscuits, and fresh-cooked lobster. Nine miles from Peggy's Cove.

PRINCE EDWARD ISLAND

Hope River
(near Cavendish)
ST. ANN'S PARISH LOBSTER SUPPERS: Open every evening except Sunday, from the last Monday in June to the first Saturday in September. A few years back, Father Gallant, the parish priest of ST. ANN'S, decided that the Church needed a little money and that tourists needed a place to eat. So, he opened a restaurant in the basement of the church, using the ladies of the parish as cooks, and the teenagers as waitresses and waiters. His lobster is served hot or cold, and is caught by the local fishermen. The home-made cole-slaw, potato salad, rolls and apple pie have been praised up and down the Island. ST. ANN'S is not only a tourist haven; neighbouring Islanders come here as well. The Father packs in about 700 people a night. For $4.50 you can get fresh lobster, hot buns and delicious apple pie, and the Prince Edward Island accents are accompanied by electric-organ music. There are red-checked table-cloths on the tables. Although over the $3 limit, the dinner is exceptional, and children eat for $2. Licensed.

Charlottetown
GENTLEMAN JIM STEAK HOUSE, K-Mart Plaza: Good steaks, and probably the best hamburgers on the Island. Take-out as well. Very good value for your money. Licensed.

Summerside

LINKLETTER MOTEL, 311 Market: Very general menu, and good food at reasonable prices. Fresh fish in season. Excellent breakfasts. Licensed.

TARTAN RESTAURANT, Water St. E.: Good fresh fish in season, and one of the best clam chowders to be found in the Maritimes. Friendly atmosphere and good service.

NEW BRUNSWICK

New Brunswick is fish country, and fried clam stands are as common here as hot dog stands in the West. Lobster and crab rolls are another popular item on the menu of the roadside café — the bun is like a hot dog bun but there is lobster or crab salad inside. When you drive through Moncton and any other part of New Brunswick that belongs to the Acadian culture, you will be surprised by signs that say *"Poutine Rapée* — to take out". Former Acadians now living in Vermont and Maine drive up every summer for their portion. Loosely speaking, it is a potato dumpling with bits of pork fat nestled in the very centre of the ball. It is very complicated to make — a lot of raw potatoes have to be grated — so people prefer to eat them out as a treat; hence, take-out *poutine rapée.*

Moncton

BORE VIEW SEA FOOD, 437 Main: A well-known gathering place for *aficionados* of *poutine rapée* and freshly fried fish. Most of the neighbourhood passes through the door carrying casseroles from their own kitchens to hold the dumplings. Once their pots are filled with *poutine,* they return to their waiting families. For those who wish to linger at one of the tables, there is an extremely good dinner of fried fresh smelts and chips for $0.80. The smelts are fresh and lightly fried; the chips are crispy and hot, and taste of the unfrozen potato. The chocolate milk shakes are

of a high quality too. Fried clams and a cold lobster plate
are on the menu, as well as the usual banalities. The service
is extremely friendly — the owners have been around a long
time. Even the staff has been there for years and years.
Décor is non-existent. Tables and counter service. Open
seven days a week.

HYNES RESTAURANT, 497 Mountain Rd. (on the truck
route): A classical Canadian "eatery" with booths and soda
fountain. The service is laconic but adequate. We were
assured by the manager of one of Moncton's main fish
stores, a purveyor to the restaurant, that HYNES always has
good fresh clams. For $1.45 HYNES offers a huge plateful
of crunchy, just-fried clams with chips and cole-slaw. It
also has fried scallops, shrimp- and lobster-salad, and
lobster in a toasted hot-dog bun for $1. Although there is
a good amount of lobster in the roll, the latter's Kleenex
texture does not add to the taste sensation. Individual
juke-box players in each booth.

Shediac
There are several good places in New Brunswick's vacation
spot for take-out or eat-inside seafood. Experts in this field
claim that GOULD'S has the best take-out fried clams, as
well as other delicacies. CHEZ LEO, two miles from the
Shediac bridge, has the best lobster rolls. At the LOBSTER
POT, you can buy a whole, cooked lobster that was alive
ten minutes before, and eat it warm in your car or on the
premises. AU ROI DU HOMARD has good lobster to take out
or eat inside, as well as crab and clams. Licensed.

Sussex
Sussex ice-cream is available at the SUSSEX CHEESE AND
BUTTER COMPANY, 644 Main.

Saint John
THE COFFEE CORNER, in the City Market on Charlotte St.,
has no formal menu but Mr. and Mrs. Isaac Brown make
their own soups and pies, and serve delicious lobster rolls.

The fish chowder is exceptional. Lobster rolls are $0.95.

REVERSING FALLS restaurant has a fine view of the gorge and excellent lobster rolls.

New River Beach
(about 30 miles from St. John)

THE GULL AND HERRING: Very good, and very fresh, seafood. The prices are reasonable. Gordon Fairweather, M.P. for Fundy-Royal, likes the lobster stew and takes guests there. The atmosphere is authentic: real cork and real nets from the beach.

Evendale
(thirty-seven miles north from St. John on the old road to Fredericton — the drive is lovely)

EVELEIGH HOTEL, on the St. John River, specializes in home-style cooking, even gingerbread. In the summer, fresh sweetpeas are on every table. Licensed.

Alma
THE FUNDY DINING ROOM, inside the gate of Fundy Park, serves good seafood. Open from May 15 to October 1. Licensed.

Bathurst
DANNY'S LIMITED: Pan-fried mackerel at $1.60 and boiled lobster for $3.25. Good sandwiches and apple pie. Licensed.

QUEBEC

Matepedia
RESTIGOUCHE HOTEL: It is possible to get a good and reasonable meal of fresh fish, including salmon, cod and sole. Excellent home-made desserts. Prices range from $1.25 for cod to $3.75 for filet mignon. The dining-room is pleasantly old-fashioned. Licensed.

Quebec City

People in this city don't like to snack. They like to sit down
with a carafe of wine, a bowl of soup, and a dish of meat
or fish and have a leisurely meal. To do this cheaply and
well is not easy, even in Quebec City. However, lunches
can be cheap. To avoid the government restaurant tax,
which starts at $1.25, many places have a set lunch at $1.24,
but at dinner-time it's a different story.

CHANTAUTEUIL, 1001 St. Jean, will serve you a full-course
meal for under $2 until the end of the afternoon. The
menu du jour changes every day, and the choices are written on a blackboard. I had soup, a decent portion of rare
roast beef and some French pastry for $1.90 — and then
mounted up the price with a carafe of imported wine for
$1.10. The restaurant also serves pizza at $0.80, and hot
cheese on toast with ham at $1.25. If you want to meet the
élite of Quebec, that is, the bureaucrats and future bureaucrats — the students of Laval — this is the place to come,
especially in summer when the terrace is in full use. Open
11 a.m. to 3 a.m. Reservations useless. Licensed.

CAFE DE L'EUROPE: Reasonably-priced continental food.
Licensed.

Montreal

Montreal is the restaurant city of Canada. There are almost
350 restaurants described by Helen Rochester in her guide
to Montreal restaurants, *Dining Out in Montreal.* Because
so many eating places have been written about in this city,
I have concentrated on the less documented towns in
Canada. I have one observation to make about Montreal.
It's easy to find a good lunch at practically any recommended restaurant for under $3 — but in the evening it's a
different story. Generally, the prices soar, the table d'hôte
goes off, and value for money stops. Why don't more
restaurants continue their lunch-time practices at dinner?

Here are some restaurants that represent the broad spec-
trum of different styles of cuisine in Montreal and that are
as reasonably priced at dinner as at lunch.

For French cooking, the onion soup at La Crepe Bretonne, 2080 Mountain St., is excellent, and if you stick to that and a glass of wine you will have a good lunch. Some people love their *crêpes*, but I am not an addict. Licensed.

Le Colibri, on 1485 Mansfield, is tiny, and as cheap as you can get for nicely cooked, simple French cuisine in Montreal. Their *sole meunière* is well worth ordering. Licensed.

Lutece, 630 Maisonneuve is good for onion soup and *coq au vin*. Reasonable prices. Set lunches are about $2. Table d'hôte about $2.25 to $3.75. Licensed.

At the Creperie Bretonne, 933 Rachel St. E., just off the northwest corner of Lafontaine Park, you can have a meal of very tender *coquilles St. Jacques* (scallops) and homemade *gâteau Breton,* which should keep you barely under the $3 range. Both dishes are the best of their kind in Montreal. Their *crêpes* are less interesting. Licensed.

Le Bistro, on Mountain St., offers good sandwiches on skinny, crusty French bread, almost like the Parisian kind. Licensed. Also, for French cooking, I can suggest L'Escargot, at the top of the Place Ville Marie Tower. It has a huge variety of snails, done in different sauces. If you order a plate of snails and a glass of wine, your bill will be under $3.

It is possible to eat Canadian-American style for under $3.50 at Joe's Steak House, 1459 Metcalfe St., and be satisfied. You are offered huge amounts of cole-slaw and pickles, which are not as good as the steaks. Nevertheless, its convenient location and quick service, as well as the steaks broiled over an open grill, make it very popular among those who don't like to throw away too much money on a chunk of meat. Licensed.

Standard Canadian food: One of the first barbecue houses in Montreal, and still one of the best for chicken, is Laurier Bar B-Q, 381 Laurier W. Try their desserts; I liked especially the mocha cakes, although some prefer the chocolate custard pie. Take-outs as well.

The province of Quebec used to guard, as male preserves, taverns that served beer on tap, and inexpensive meals. Now the law has changed and tavern-owners who have the gumption may allow women on their premises. Those who have done so report a fifty per cent increase in clientele. Such a one is the BRASSERIE CRAIG, on the corner of Place d'Armes, a sort of picnic-style place — you buy cheese, *pâté* and bread and make your own sandwiches; the draught beer is $0.35; apple cider is also served. Apparently, TAVERNE LA GRANGE A SERAPHIM, 1223 Amherst, is going to stop being male chauvinist and will soon allow women to eat its *tourtière* and pork and beans.

For French-Canadian cuisine, LE GOBELET, 8393 St. Laurent, serves draught beer, pork and beans, and, more unusually, duck and beans. Since women have been allowed in, this former tavern has added *canard à l'orange* to its menu. The furniture is traditionally French Canadian. Closed Sunday.

BENS DELICATESSEN, 990 Blvd. Maisonneuve W., is known to everyone in Montreal. It provides kosher-style meals for crowds of people, and the service is geared to get you out as fast as possible. Order the pea soup and corned beef at 2 a.m. when the real Montrealers are having their bedtime snack. BENS' popularity owes much to its location. However, if you're a true corned beef enthusiast you will have to go to the MONTREAL HEBREW DELICATESSEN, 3895 St. Lawrence Blvd., for the best smoked meat in Montreal; the people here smoke their own tongues, beef and turkeys. They have a reassuring sign, "no additives in our steaks". Another delicatessen, PUMPERNIK'S, 5131 Décarie Blvd., caters to a more middle-class clientele. It has table-cloths, delicious pastries, sandwiches, snacks and full meals. Licensed.

The SNOWDON DELI, 5265 Décarie serves high-quality smoked-meat sandwiches, smoked whitefish and salmon, and chopped liver fine enough to please the most difficult of customers.

CHEZ VITO, 5412 Côte des Neiges, is the place where the students and professors from the University of Montreal go for a cheap and decent Italian-style meal. You can get spaghetti for two, with a half-bottle of Chianti, for about $5. The pizza is very good. Open till 2 a.m. You can also eat good Italian food quite cheaply at the OSTERIA DEL PANZONI, 2070 Metcalfe St. The style of cooking here is much more subtle than the usual slapdash spaghetti-and-meatball variety. Licensed.

The PIZZERIA DANTE, 6828 St. Lawrence, serves moderately-priced daily specials and a fine *osso buco* (see p. 83 for my recipe for it).

The SUN SUN CAFE, 1023 Clark, serves as good a Chinese meal as you'll find in the city, and its prices range from $1.75 to $2.50 per dish. The batter on shrimps and chicken is light, the vegetables hot and crisp, and everything prepared to order. Licensed.

Here are three other highly recommended and reasonable Chinese restaurants: TEAN HONG, on the corner of LaGauchetière and Clark (1025 Clark), has an excellent chop suey, and won ton soup. The steamed fish with ginger is equally good. THE SHANGHAI, on Bleury and Dorchester (1129 Bleury), has first-class stuffed pancakes and crystallized apples, while the PEKING, 103 St. Catherine E., serves Peking duck. It also offers one of the cheapest mandarin banquets in Montreal, if you order in advance.

If you're interested in middle-European food, the COFFEE MILL ESPRESSO, 2046 Mountain St., serves goulashes, stuffed peppers, home-made soups and dumplings. You can fill up the children on table d'hôte menu, which runs all day and ranges in price from $1.24 to $2.25. The restaurant has a large selection of rich pastries and, of course, espresso coffees. The clientele is always interesting — Hungarian coffee-house intellectuals, ladies taking a quick coffee and pastry after a hard day's shopping at Holt Renfrew, and salesgirls. You will never go hungry there.

THE STABLE GALLERY, just behind the Montreal Museum of Fine Arts, offers a sort of middle-European style of cooking including strudel and chicken — all home-made.

Here are a few places that don't fit into any special category:

DORA'S DINING ROOM, 1423 Bleury, serves gefilte fish, pickled pike, and traditional Jewish dishes for as little as $1.25. Very reasonable home-style cooking.

The LIME LIGHT COFFEE HOUSE, 1451 Pierce St., serves nourishing, and vaguely English-style, meals, for under $2.50. Ham with raisin sauce, home-made soup and gingerbread, and good baclava are some of the specialties. A selection of teas and coffees is available.

The *cognoscenti* claim the best hamburgers are from MR. STEER, 486-A St. Catherine. The best submarine sandwiches are made by a branch of MIKE'S SUBMARINE, at 1813 St. Catherine.

I should also mention, for French-Canadian style cooking, AU PETIT POUCET, in Val David, north of Montreal. For about $1.50 you can eat delicious home-sugar-cured ham, and genuine pork and beans, Quebec-style. It's a must if you are in this skiing area. The view of the Laurentians is excellent from the dining-room.

ONTARIO

Ottawa
Some people think Ottawa is the worst place in Canada for eating out, whether it's the high priced steak houses or the inexpensive little beaneries. Wherever you go, the food is never cheap enough or good enough. The reasons for this are unfathomable. Perhaps it has something to do with the many civil servants living in this town — they don't like making a fuss, even in a restaurant.

CAFE COLONNADE, 280 Metcalfe, according to popular opinion, and my own, makes the best pizza in Ottawa. The dough is cooked through and is very crisp — this makes all the difference. One of the dining-rooms has tables with table-cloths, and the other, booths. Pizza to take out. Licensed. Open Sunday to Wednesday till 1 a.m.; Thursday to Saturday till 2 a.m.

NATE'S DELICATESSEN AND STEAK HOUSE, 316 Rideau St.: You can have a bowl of home-made bean and barley soup, a corned-beef sandwich, and garlicky cole-slaw until 3 a.m. NATE'S is everyone's hang-out, from federal cabinet ministers and reporters from *Le Droit* (Ottawa's French-language newspaper, whose offices are across the street), to the average Ottawa family, who want a reasonable meal without going bankrupt. Steaks are $3.25. The walls are decorated with pictures of Bill Davis, John Turner (looking a bit dyspeptic, not a good advertisement for the restaurant), an unidentified torch singer, and a lion. Beer on tap, as well as other alcoholic beverages.

KARDISH DELICATESSEN, 979 Wellington St., lacks atmosphere but has the best delicatessen food in Ottawa.

CAFE 99, 99 Metcalfe St.: An authentic soda-fountain café, small and clean. All the sandwiches are freshly made, the soups home-made, and the fish and chips first class. Those who frequent CAFE 99 like the western, and the bacon, lettuce and tomato, sandwiches — and the friendly service. In the summer, the business-girl lunch atmosphere changes, and wandering youth takes over (about six booths and a counter).

LUCERNE CHICKEN BAR-B-QUE, 303 Bank St.: Excellent barbecued chicken, perhaps the best in Ottawa, at very reasonable prices. Licensed.

NEW STAR RESTAURANT, 496 Rideau St., is certainly one of the cheaper places in Ottawa, and it serves authentic Chinese food. There are dumplings for Sunday lunch and very good fried shrimp and beef with snow peas. Prices are between $1.50 and $3.00 a dish.

MOORSIDE TEA ROOM, Kingsmere in the Gatineau Park, twenty minutes drive from Ottawa: Mackenzie King's old summer place turned into a small restaurant with fresh flowers, fireplace, and table-cloths. You can have good scones, pumpkin spice pie and tea, while overlooking various displaced hunks of ruins from old Ottawa buildings. Good for kids, grandmothers and visitors. Open only in summer.

Toronto

Toronto has more restaurant guides and critics than any other city in Canada, but this is not to say that the food is necessarily the best. Among the cheaper eating places, small ethnic restaurants and hamburger drive-ins predominate. The best of the latter, according to people in the know, is P & S CHARCOAL HAMBURGERS, 804 Sheppard Ave. E.

Here are some of the simple places (other than drive-ins) that hold their own, within the limited price range of the restaurants in this article.

The MEAT AND POTATOES, 338 Huron St., has large portions, and small prices for much better than average food. The "Incredible Hamburger" was thick, juicy, and rare in the middle, as requested. Its garnish of tomato, cucumber, cheese and onion, on a kaiser roll, gave it added allure. Home-made French onion soup is very popular, and the curried chicken, while not straight out of the Punjab, was more than edible. For dessert there was a very impressive carrot cake, rich and unusual. Twelve different kinds of teas. The décor is attractive — white walls, black trim and barnyard siding. Lots of seats. There is even a folk singer and a player piano. Sometimes the service is slow.

There are two reasonable French restaurants. MOUNT PLEASANT LUNCH, 604 Mount Pleasant Rd., has been taken over by an ex-maître d' from Mr. Tony's (one of the ritzier restaurants in Toronto) and he has done a good job. He serves extremely good veal cutlets with vegetables and potato puffs for only $1.50. The entrées include steak, $1.95, sole and omelettes for $1.35. All entrées come with home-made soup, dessert, and coffee, tea or milk. One dozen escargots cost $1 and they're as good as the best in Toronto. Open 11:30 a.m. to 2:30 p.m. for lunch, 5 to 10 p.m. Sunday to Thursday for dinner, and 5 to 11 p.m. on Friday and Saturday. The other French-style place L'OMELETTE, has two locations, 197 College St. and 48 Wellington St. E.; these are among the cheaper, and most popular, French restaurants in Toronto. Naturally, everyone eats omelette here. The price can be higher than $3. Licensed.

RICHARD'S FISH AND CHIPS, 769 Mount Pleasant Rd.: A map of Scotland on the wall proclaims the nationality of the owners of this excellent fish and chip shop. Mr. and Mrs. Godwin have been in Canada just six years and have recently taken over RICHARD'S FISH AND CHIPS. The fried fish and the shrimps are light and crunchy, and you can pick out your own soft drinks from the cooler. Fried halibut and chips $0.70; fried shrimps and chips $1.60. Closed Sunday. Take-out and booths.

MERCURY RESTAURANT, 189 Bay: Best coffee in town say the cabbies and the police. Wholesome meals large enough to fill a working man at reasonable prices.

CSARDA TAVERN, 720 Bay: Good middle-European food; moderate prices; gypsy music.

THE GOULASH POT, 727 Yonge St., serves cabbage rolls and sauerkraut, and extremely good goulash. Festoons of artificial fruits and vegetables hang from the walls. Two people can eat there for about $3.75 and the service is quite good.

DON QUIJOTE, 300 College St., still serves well prepared tortillas for around $1.25 despite its new and fancy surroundings. The shrimps sautéed in garlic and butter also have an authentic taste — and are surprisingly cheap. The prices go up in the evening. Licensed.

ETHEREA NATURAL FOODS, 341 Bloor St. W.: Even though you may be indifferent to health foods, you'll find that the cooking here is excellent. Their sandwiches are well filled, soup is a quarter, and you can get a whole meal for $1. People are pleasantly surprised by this place.

Here are two of the best pizza places: NEW YORK PIZZA HOUSE, 620 Yonge — a whole fourteen-inch pizza was eaten by two people, not even a bit of crust was left! The crust is very thin, and very crisp. It's one of the best pizzas in

Toronto. No delivery. Also excellent is the MONTE CARLO RESTAURANT AND TAVERN, 1028 Eglinton W.

For good snacks and delicatessen food try UNITY GRILL, 708 Queen W. (home-made soup); SWITZER'S DELICATESSEN AND CATERING, 322 Spadina Ave.; COLEMAN'S RESTAURANT AND DELICATESSEN, 3085 Bathurst; the TEL AVIV RESTAUR- ANT, 440 Spadina Ave. and 3520 Bathurst (for blintzes); The CREST GRILL, formerly CRESCENT GRILL, 466½ Spadina Ave. (for wonderful bacon and eggs).

Good, standard Canadian cooking can be found at the SHIP INN RESTAURANT, Marine Museum, Canadian Na- tional Exhibition Grounds. The fruit pies are better than most, and the rest of the food has been called "homey". Licensed.

There are several very good Oriental restaurants. Go to the INDIAN RICE FACTORY, 490 Dupont, for excellent and reasonable Indian food. The SAI WOO, 123a Dundas St. is, in my opinion, the best Chinese restaurant in the city. The individual dishes are under $3, and some are much cheaper than that. Everything is beautifully cooked, and the kitchen is lavish with snow peas and Chinese black mushrooms. SAI WOO also has fresh periwinkles. There are delicious custard tarts for lunch.

Two bars with food are DOOLEY's, 49 Wellington St., west of Bay — the fish and chips have been praised; and BASSEL'S TAVERN, 389 Yonge St. — a good kaiser sandwich with a beer costs about $1 at lunch.

Chaffey's Locks
(near Kingston)
THE OPINICON: Good home-style food in a charming, old- fashioned hotel. A little above the $3 limit but you get four courses. Limited space for non-hotel guests.

Deep River
(Highway 62, about a mile north of Combermere)
THE CONTINENTAL INN: Home-made bread, pastries, European-style cooking. Licensed.

Port Hope
TURCK's RESTAURANT, 63 Walton St.: Reasonably priced food including a rib-eye steak for under $3. Ample portions. Clean surroundings and friendly service.

Orillia
PAUL WEBER DRIVE-IN, Highway 11 five miles north of Orillia: The charcoal-broiled hamburgers and hot dogs are the best in the area. Picnic tables under the trees, for your convenience.

London
EATON's MAYFAIR CAFETERIA, fourth floor, Wellington Mall: The pies and soups are better than most, and the cost is reasonable.

SMALESPACE, 453 Clarence: A health-food restaurant that serves a good bowl of chili or stew for $0.75. It also has home-made cobblers and bread puddings that come warm from the oven. The selection of coffees and teas is probably the best in London.

SAY CHEESE, 375 Talbot: Home-made soups and sandwiches.

Windsor
STEVE & EDDY's FISH AND CHIPS, 462 University Ave. W.: Their deep-fried haddock and home-fried chips have been satisfying Windsor people for forty-eight years. You get a large portion for $1. No pre-cooking. Closed Sunday and Monday.

Temiscaming
MARG's RESTAURANT: Marg serves excellent, fresh, deep-fried walleyed pike. Her soups, pies and butter tarts are home-made. Open seven days a week.

Niagara-On-The-Lake
BRASSBOUND's GALLERY, 13 Queen St.: Good for snacks like sandwiches, omelettes, soups. Open from noon to 1 a.m. daily.

Petersburg

THE BLUE MOON HOTEL, four miles west of Kitchener on route to Stratford: In The Cellars dining-rooms you can get a cheap German-style meal, as well as imported and draught beer served in wonderful goblets. The dining-rooms are elegant, compared to many of the others described in this article. They serve large portions of pigs' tails, pork hocks, spare-ribs and steaks. The soup was good, also the home-made mustard. Desserts are home-made but sometimes a bit stale. Closed Sunday. Open from noon to 2 p.m. and from 5 to 8 p.m. Licensed.

Kitchener

PENNSYLVANIA KITCHEN, 34 King St. W.: An attractive cafeteria-style restaurant which specializes in Waterloo County Pennsylvania-Dutch food. Although the prices are relatively high for cafeteria meals — from $1.85 to $2.25 for a main course — the portions are enormous, and the quality of the food is excellent. The day I was there the choice consisted of pork hocks, dressed spare-ribs, dressed chicken, cabbage rolls, and a delicious eisbein sausage made with caraway seed. The man behind the counters also puts huge dollops of scalloped potatoes, sauerkraut and a first-class bean salad on your plate. I noticed the restaurant because a boy wearing a sandwich-board advertisement for it was sauntering down the main streets of Kitchener. I was glad to see this thirties tradition still being kept up.

Hamilton

AERO RESTAURANT AND TAVERN, 650 Barton St. E.: A favourite of Judy LaMarsh's for Chinese food. Especially recommended is Chow Sai Foon, a mix of Chinese vermicelli, shrimp, barbecued pork, egg and onion. Special banquets may be ordered in advance (they are said to be quite remarkable) .

The BLACK FOREST INN, at 255 King St. E., serves German-style meals at reasonable prices. The great specialty is pork schnitzels. Open seven days a week. Licensed.

Burlington

TIEN KUE INN, 1106 Plains Road E.: Although this is not as cheap as many of the other places in this list, it is worth stopping here because of the wide and unusual selection of dishes in a region not noted for its restaurants. Choose from the specialties of the house, including several dishes with pickerel, as well as shrimps and Peking duck. The specialties run about $3.50 and up, while the less interesting-sounding dishes are cheaper.

Paris

THE TRADING POST RESTAURANT, Junction Highways 2 and 5: Home-made soups and pies. The table d'hôte runs between $3 and $4. There are children's plates and a special lunch menu. Open from June 1 to August 31.

Terrace Bay

TERRACE BAY HOTEL AND RESTAURANT, Highway 17: The fresh lake-trout is excellent and the service agreeable. The hotel and restaurant, overlooking Lake Superior, belong to Kimberley-Clark Pulp and Paper Company.

Kenora

KENRICIA HOTEL: This is the place for a dish of fresh wall-eyed pike. Licensed.

MANITOBA

Winnipeg

Kosher-style cooking in Montreal and Toronto is cursed by modernity and has become an industry instead of a culinary art. Blintzes come from blintz factories. No longer do Jewish grandmothers bang the blintz skins out from their special six-inch frying pans. Instead, they are shipped out frozen, packed in foilwrap containers, to ignorant third-generation communities who don't know a good blintz from a bad one. A blintz may be filled with cheese, meat, *kasha,* even chopped lung and onion, but it must have one essential quality to be in the first rank — unlike the humans who eat them, blintzes should be thin-skinned. I don't care if the blintz is filled with caviar and cognac, if the skin or crêpe-like dough around it is thick, throw it away.

SIMON'S KOSHER STYLE RESTAURANT, 1332 Main St., is not prepossessing. Its décor consists of arborite tables (not too many) and a counter with a mirror. But all the food is made in the kitchen and the people there have mastered the art of the thin-skinned blintz. (Purists must be warned that they are not triangular in shape but rolled in sausage-like fashion.) Apart from their excellent blintzes, SIMON'S offers home-made pea soup and roast chicken or beef short-ribs garnished with peas and carrots, potatoes and *kasha* all for under $2. The helpings are ample, and the soup thick and rich. The *knishes* are made from stretched dough, a virtuoso technique that can only be practised on a large table in a hot kitchen. SIMON'S has an extremely light hand with *pyrohy,* still another dough-wrapped morsel eaten by people of Slavic background, be they Jews, Ukrainians, Poles, or Russians. I have been assured by a Polish count that SIMON'S *kishke* (stuffed cow-intestine) is unequalled in Winnipeg. Closed Mondays and for three weeks in the summer.

There are two other good delicatessens with home-made kosher cooking and excellent Winnipeg corned beef: OASIS DELICATESSEN, 906 Main St., has top-quality knishes, corned-beef sandwiches, and herring — pickled, plain and in salads. Counter and take-out service. OSCAR'S DELICATESSEN STORE, on 1236 Main St., is a very old establishment. Some people claim that they still make the best corned-beef sandwiches in the city.

KELEKIS RESTAURANT, 1100 Main: The best chips in the whole of western Canada. Unfrozen, shoe-string, crunchy and delicious. Good hot dogs too. Tables, counter service and take-out window.

PONY CORRAL, 1919 Pembina, in Fort Garry: Modern, very good, spacious, family coffee shop. The pies are home-made and famous in Winnipeg — pecan, strawberry and chocolate cream.

THE WHITE HOUSE, 443 Selkirk Ave.: Immortalized by *Maclean's* magazine because of their spare-ribs and cole-slaw. The spare-ribs are lean, the sauce piquant, and the cole-slaw garlicky. The décor is, as *Maclean's* said, "early arborite". Licensed.

THE SALISBURY HOUSE: A major chain of restaurants in western Canada, was started in Winnipeg at least forty years ago and still serves excellent soup, chili, and graham wafer pies, all specialties of the house. Some SALISBURY HOUSES are fresher and cleaner than others but the food is consistent. Most of them are small; many, but not all, are drive-ins, and most are open all hours of the day and night. This is a Canadian-owned chain and it has maintained some peculiar character of its own. At a number of their places, you can count on meeting a cross-section of students and the after-the-movie crowd looking for a good cup of coffee.

THE HILTON RESTAURANT, 812 Main St.: A large restaur-ant with booths and tables. An ordinary menu with some very good Ukrainian specialties and fresh-fish dishes. Ex-cellent home-made borsch for a quarter, delicious fried whitefish for $1.99, and first-rate *holopchi* for $1.50. The menu also features home-made head cheese for $1.40 and boiled spare-ribs and sauerkraut at $1.60. The steak is not recommended, and I was not impressed with the home-made apple pie. Generally speaking though, this is a place to have a good meal at very reasonable prices. The dining-room in the back (for family dining) is open only on Sundays. THE HILTON is an excellent place to go if you want to sample well-prepared Ukrainian-style food at a low price. Licensed.

THE HUNGARIAN VILLAGE RESTAURANT, 174 Isabel, is part snack bar, part restaurant, with a minimum number of tables. In the evening the snacks are put to rest and the owner barbecues pheasant and rabbit for $2. Soup, salad, home-fried potatoes and dessert are included in the price.

Lockport

SKINNER'S DRIVE INN, a half-hour's drive, due north from Winnipeg: The hot dogs are a must, extra long, the bun filled with onions and pickles. This drive-in has been around for at least forty years.

SASKATCHEWAN

Saskatoon

THE 70's SOUP AND SANDWICH SHOP, 215 23rd St. E.: Home-made soup for $0.19, crackers are one cent more. It's a cafeteria — bright, clean and full of hungry youngsters.

THE NATIONAL CHOP SUEY, on 325 Avenue C South, probably has the most authentic Chinese food in town. One of its devotees, a cabinet minister, especially likes the pineapple chicken and egg rolls.

Saskatoon has something that, so far as I know, is unique in Canada — a drive-in serving Ukrainian food. It's the O & O DRIVE INN, 1202 20th St.

The KALPANA RESTAURANT, 22nd St. and Ave. P, has Ceylonese food, while the DEL RESTAURANT, 120 2nd Ave. N., serves Mexican-style food. Also, try the VENICE PIZZA SPAGHETTI HOUSE for pizza "like you get in Milan". For take-out seafood there's TOPS SEA FOOD at 906 Victoria Ave.

Moose Jaw

If you can, stop at CLUB 71, 71 High W., and sample the home-made pies and coffee. They are reputed to be excellent.

Regina

It's possibe to get a good steak at BOB'S STEAK RANCH, 100 Albert St., for a reasonable price. The steaks are under $4.

LITTLE BAVARIA, in the Northgate Shopping Centre, serves German-style sauerkraut and wienerschnitzel. The prices are within the $1.50 to $3.50 range. Licensed.

VINCE'S PIZZA PLACE, 1849 Broad St., has good pizza for Regina, a city not noted for its Italian restaurants.

ALBERTA

Edmonton

Edmonton does not have the reputation of being Mecca for the epicure. Even Edmontonians shrug their shoulders when asked about restaurants in their town. Nevertheless, the CORNER HOUSE, in the Empire Building on the corner of Jasper and 101st, is a cafeteria with some style. Usually when I eat in a cafeteria, I am reminded of penitentiaries and prisoners shuffling back and forth with trays of steam-oven food — only we're allowed knives (but not sharp ones). But the CORNER HOUSE cafeteria is light and bright, with red and yellow chairs and delft-blue patterned wall-paper. You can have a hunk of prime ribs of Alberta beef sliced right off the bone for $1.60 — and fresh vegetables as well. Another interesting item is the whole hot ham on the bone carved in front of you for $1. The pies are made on the premises and the boisenberry is delicious, tart, and juicy; the crust is way above standard beanery quality. Despite the cheapness of the prices and the serve-yourself style of dining, the lunchers are not impoverished students but prosperous businessmen, lawyers, and even judges. If you object to the sight of Edmonton's *crème de la crème* tripping around with trays like jailbirds, come around 5:30 p.m., when your sense of decorum will be less affected. Open 8 a.m. to 7 p.m. Monday through Saturday.

From the best-of-its-kind Canadian cafeteria-style restaurant, we go to the GASTHAUS STRATHCONA, 10105 82 Ave., which gives a fair sample of the cuisine of Edmonton's large German community at prices that are as appealing as those

of the Corner House. The Gasthaus is owned by Strathcona Meat Market, which specializes in making delicious
smoked meats, salamis, and sausages. Many of their specialties, like smoked pork, liver and blood sausages, are served
by the Gasthaus for under $2, with a large side order of
sauerkraut and fried potatoes. You can also have a huge
dish of roast veal or pork, and something called sour kidneys, which is not a disease but kidneys cooked in a meat
sauce with a touch of vinegar. The restaurant is far from
being fancy, but the tables have cloths and the fresh young
girl who did the serving looked as though she'd stepped out
of the Austrian Alps, even though she wasn't wearing the
yodelling costume that seems obligatory in so many Austro-
German-style schnitzel houses. Closed at 8:00 every night.

Buffalo Bill's Steak Village, 11307 Kingsway Ave.
(near the airport): Good steaks at reasonable prices. Children like it because of the Wild West décor. The rib-eye
steak is extremely tender for $2.19. If you don't want cheese
on your hamburger, say so in advance. The cook here
specializes in making birthday cakes for children's parties.

Astoria Restaurant, 10231 98th St.: Excellent beef
borsch and sauerkraut; soup for $0.30. Perogy served burn-
ing hot. Generous portions of eight, some potato-filled and
topped with crumbled bacon, others filled with cheese.
Thursday is the day for cabbage rolls. Breaded whitefish is
$1.25. The people here make their own pies. Take-out
service as well. Ambience of dolls and eastern European
handicrafts.

Calgary

Several places in Calgary fit the bill of serving something
special for a low price. Pizza has a tendency to be the same
all over, but a little restaurant in Calgary makes a pizza that
is different and delicious. It's different because of the really
crisp crust, and the unusual combinations of ingredients
on top. The Pizza and Spaghetti House, on 728 17 Ave.
SW, includes fresh tomato and shrimps as toppings, and
even a Hawaiian-style pizza (I could do without a pine-

apple pizza, mind you). They also have the usual an-
chovy, green pepper and mushroom variety. Monday
through Thursday from 11 a.m. to 3 a.m., Friday and
Saturday, 11 a.m. to 4 a.m., Sunday from noon to 1 a.m.
Free delivery.

THE WHITE SPOT RESTAURANT AND STEAK HOUSES (don't
confuse them with the ones in Vancouver) serve good
steaks, salad and garlic bread for $2.25. It's only fitting that
the meat capital of Canada should have a series of restaurants like this. The one at 1101 4 St. S.W. is open twenty-
four hours a day. Take-out steaks.

The "Rimrock Room" in THE PALLISER HOTEL, is a very
informal dining-room where you can get a cup of coffee and
a piece of very good pie without having to order a main
course. The apple pie is made with fresh apples; some like
the lime chiffon and chocolate cream. The Rimrock Room
offers a $1.60 lunch that includes a large bowl of clam
chowder, home-made bread and a beverage. The broth is
very rich, but they could put a few more whole clams in it.
Licensed.

PETER'S DRIVE INN, 303 16 Ave. N.E., has the best hamburgers in Calgary.

DON'S DELICATESSEN, 114 8 Ave. S.E.: Hot corned beef,
hot barbecued beef on a bun, and all sorts of combination
sandwiches, under $2. The intelligentsia of Calgary seems
to gather there. Open seven days a week. Licensed.

Jasper
MARMOT BASIN SKI CHALET: The cafeteria has good pastries.

BRITISH COLUMBIA

Vancouver
The standards of the average restaurant in Vancouver are
high, the prices are not exorbitant and there is quality in
the food offered. But first-class restaurants do not exist here

— as they do in Quebec City and Montreal. There should be more fish restaurants in Vancouver with all those salmon, halibut and crabs swimming so close by. One of the cheaper places I found, devoted to cooking fish, was a weird and wonderful place called the ONLY CAFE, on 20 East Hastings Street. The ONLY has been around for sixty years and the original décor has been maintained: it is perhaps the worst-looking eatery I've seen, especially at 11:00 o'clock at night when some of the rubby-dubs from the skid-row neighbourhood are to be seen hunched over the counter shovelling in pepper-pot soup. The window is full of frozen carcasses of fish, and inside the restaurant, behind the counter, a small but fearless Chinese chef seems to be climbing in and out of steaming vats of oil. It is not necessary to dress up for the ONLY; I wore a cocktail dress and my companion wore an ankle-length red cloak and her new blonde wig, and we stopped all conversation when we walked in. After it was established that we were not famous go-go dancers, the clientele relaxed, and my hippie neighbour gave me a forkful of tasty, fried B.C. oysters; a lady of about seventy-five on my left, with no teeth, said the best thing to eat was the sole. She was right. The fried sole was the most delicious fish I have ever had in Vancouver, and the salmon was beautifully cooked. You might have trouble getting your order across, since the waiter has his own ideas on what you should eat. The most expensive food is crab at $2.10, but most dishes cost between $1.10 and $2. Helpings are large, and the accompanying fried potatoes are fresh and crisp. There are no toilets, and table napkins were not available the night I was there. Open from 10:00 a.m. to 11:30 p.m. Closed Sunday and certain religious holidays. The waiter wasn't sure what church the boss belonged to so he couldn't say exactly when the holidays would come up. No liquor.

THE MARINE VIEW COFFEE SHOP, on Campbell Ave. on Fisherman's Wharf, is another unpretentious and cheap fish-place. It has very good fresh salmon, halibut in season, and a view of the sea and ships.

TOMAHAWK BARBECUE, 1550 Philip Ave., North Vancouver, has some fame because a national magazine said it serves one of the best hamburgers in the country. Certainly there are a lot of things inside the bun, like bacon, weiners, cheese, mayonnaise, but I would like the actual hamburger to be a bit thicker. What attracts me to the TOMAHAWK are the Yukon-style bacon and eggs — the back-bacon fans over the hash brown potatoes like a deck of cards spread out by a Las Vegas croupier. People return again and again, just to look at, and then eat, the most stylish bacon and eggs in Canada. A vaguely Indian-style atmosphere permeates the restaurant; when I was there, a very large Indian chief with a bangled doeskinned suit, and a feathered headband extending far down his back, was sitting next to me at the counter drinking coffee. He was, in fact, not from the Indian reserve nearby, but from somewhere north in the British Isles. Counters and tables, pleasant atmosphere, crowded on Sundays. No alcohol. Open from 8 a.m., except on Sundays when everyone sleeps in an hour.

SZASZ DELICATESSEN AND RESTAURANT, 2881 Granville St.: Many well-prepared Hungarian- and Austrian-style dishes for reasonable prices. Among them are paprika chicken with dumplings, SZASZ's famous pizza buci, and desserts like *Doboschtorte,* strudels, Hungarian pancakes and a justly renowned French custard for $0.40.

THE WHITE SPOTS in Vancouver are one of the oldest chain restaurants in the city. They are famous for clam chowder, fruit pies, and their fried chicken — "chicken pickens" — which has a much better batter than Colonel Sanders'. Some people with long memories think they have slipped in quality since General Foods took over their network of drive-in and/or sit-down restaurants. There are also WHITE SPOTS in Victoria and Nanaimo.

Two inexpensive and good Chinese restaurants are ON ON TEA GARDEN, 214 Keefer St., and JADE PALACE, 252 East Pender St.

TROLL's at Horseshoe Bay in West Vancouver is highly recommended for fresh fish.

New Westminster

KING NEPTUNE RESTAURANT, 800 Front St.: Smorgasbord Friday, Saturday and Sunday, starting at 4:30 p.m. Oyster stew for $2.50. View of the docks.

Victoria

Appropriately enough, one of the best, if not the best, fish and chip shop in Canada is in Victoria. THE OLD BRITISH FISH AND CHIPS SHOP, 1316 Broad St., dates back to 1917, and the lady who does the frying may not have been there quite fifty-five years, but nearly. The waitress is English and calls customers "love" (for the American tourists?); the tea is made with leaves that mess the bottom of the pot; and the fresh cod is covered with a crisp, light batter that goes perfectly with the chunky, English-cut fried chips. A friend of mine has a special routine when he comes to Victoria. He runs on the roof of the YMCA for twenty-two minutes, then stops at THE OLD BRITISH FISH AND CHIPS SHOP for some "to go" (taking lots of serviettes with him; otherwise the malt vinegar will seep through the bag into his hand), and then walks to Bastion Square to eat and watch the other tourists.

THE COCK PHEASANT, 5285 W. Saanich en route to Buchart's Gardens, is well known for its delicious English teas with home-made scones and jams. Closed each year from December till Good Friday; open every day except Monday, from noon to 8 p.m.

THE EMPRESS HOTEL serves tea with crumpets in the lobby.

At Point-no-Point, on the most southerly point of Vancouver Island, there's a wonderful tea-house right out on the rocks where you can enjoy the view and watch the sun set in the most westerly location in all of Canada. The owner, a Boston school-teacher, serves a good tea, with home-made baking. It is always crowded in the summer.

The restaurant in the ART GALLERY OF GREATER VICTORIA also has good teas.

Prince Rupert

SMILE'S, on the wharf, has excellent seafood, including well prepared salmon, halibut, sole, abalone, oysters and prawns, and scallops. The pie is home-made, and there is a good view of the harbour (snack bar in front, small dining-room behind). Licensed.

En route from Jasper to Prince George on the British Columbia side of the Yellowhead Pass, forty miles from McBride, is TETE JAUNE CACHE LODGE, a small coffee-shop-cum-restaurant run by Mr. G. M. Van Essen, a Dutchman who has decorated it with Indonesian antiques. All of the bread, rolls and pastries are baked by his cook right on the premises.

McBride

The hamburger drive-in next to the McBride Hotel has a wonderful selection of burgers, including oyster burgers for $0.75, and fourteen flavours of milkshakes.

Riske Creek

CHILCOTIN LODGE: Home-made bread, fresh baked-salmon.

NORTHWEST TERRITORIES

Yellowknife

THE YELLOWKNIFE INN, 50th Ave. and 50th St., has an excellent coffee shop which, if you ask, serves fresh trout and Arctic char at very reasonable prices. The service is fast and friendly. Open from early morning until midnight. There's also a licensed dining room in this hotel, but it is slightly more expensive and is open only for lunch and dinner.

A Bad-tempered
Inquiry into
Canadian Restaurants

WHENEVER I THINK back to that lunch . . . the memory of it alone seems almost enough to sustain life. The next course was *truite au porto* which, the headwaiter told me, had been prepared by M. Point himself; brook trout boiled in water to which vinegar, pepper, salt and bay leaf had been added, and then skinned, split in half, and filled with a ragout of truffles, mushrooms and vegetables. With it came a sauce made of butter, cream and port wine. It was a masterpiece.†

The meal usually led off with an eerie gumbo identified as pumpkin soup, puce in colour and dysenteric in effect. This was followed by a crisp morsel of the fish called selangor for want of a more scathing term, reminiscent in texture of a Daniel Green comfy slipper fried in deep fat. The roast was a pale, resilient scintilla of mutton that turned the tines of the fork, garnished with a spoonful of greenish boiled string and a dab of penicillin posing as a potato. For dessert there was . . . a glutinous blob of sago swimming in skimmed milk

† From *Blue Trout and Black Truffles* by Joseph Wechsberg (New York: Alfred A. Knopf Inc., 1953).

and caramel syrup, so indescribably saccharine that it produced a singing in the ears and screams of anguish from the
bridgework . . . . the diner stiffened slowly in his chair, his features settling into the ghastly smile known as the risus sar-
donicus. . . .†

Rarely, eating in Canadian restaurants, do we have the sub-
lime experience of Mr. Wechsberg or confront, course by
course, the horrors of S. J. Perelman's dinner. It has never
been necessary, in my Canadian adventures, to clutch at my
throat and then call for a food inspector — but on the other
hand, I've never eaten a meal superb enough to merit
Wechsberg's ecstatic description.

In eating, as in many other areas, Canadian do not specialize in extremes. Yet we know what it is to eat both well
and poorly in restaurants throughout this country.

What we lack are reasonably-priced restaurants offering
the fresh produce of the land prepared and served with the
right combination of skill and simplicity. Too many
restaurants in Canada spend enormous sums of money on
hardware — and forget that they are supposed to feed
people as well. How many restaurateurs can afford to sink
$100,000 into interior decoration and also pay a decent
wage to their chef and their waiting staff?

Even if a chef is well paid, a good one will not work in a
gastronomic vacuum. Like good artists, they are inspired by
the materials they work with. Jean Pierre Chaum came to
Canada after a stringent chef's aprenticeship in Lyon,
Geneva and Paris, but returned to France disgusted. He
worked as a *sous-chef* in LA SAULAIE, near Montreal, and in
Toronto's SUTTON PLACE (neither restaurant is exactly
your average beanery). M. Chaum complained about the
pervasive use of frozen meat and fish, and vegetables that
were too bland and too big. Above all, he objected to the
emphasis on the control of food costs in even the most expensive restaurants in Canada.

† From *Westward Ha* by S. J. Perelman (New York: Simon & Shuster, 1948).

Portion control and second-quality ingredients are anathema to good cooking. If expenses have to be cut, the saving should be on the table settings, the interior decoration and the size of the restaurant itself. Size is most important in a restaurant. Supervision is easier with a restaurant of 20 tables than with one of 200. It's often the case in our country that as soon as a restaurant becomes successful on 20 tables, the owner wants to expand. And usually that's death to the quality of the food. Unless the restaurateur can be sure that his increased number of personnel will be just as reliable, and his own supervision just as effective as before, his restaurant will never be as good as it was. Prices will go up and quality will deteriorate in 100 different areas. A good restaurant-owner should never over-extend himself. Small menus, simple surroundings, and the owner's constant personal attention are the keys to good and profitable restaurants.

But owning even a small restaurant, with all its attendant headaches, demands a special kind of devotion — if the place is to be a success — and few are prepared to give it. For many, the only solution is dependence on the family unit — mamma doing the cooking and relatives waiting on the tables. As I mentioned earlier, the Hungarians, the Chinese, Italians, Greeks and Germans seem to have the energy, know-how and motivation to manage these little "family places" where the price of the meal doesn't make you feel that you'd better wait for a special occasion — like the celebration of sweepstake winnings.

A tradition of more elaborate French cooking does exist in the province of Quebec. It's there that one still can find an expensive meal that is perhaps *worth* the price, as well as medium-priced ones that are still satisfactory. Toronto and Vancouver have a great many excellent "ethnic" restaurants — Chinese, German, Greek, Italian and Hungarian, but the classical French cuisine still escapes the grasp. A word on Italian restaurants; too many of them rely heavily on tomato sauce, and few of them make really light pasta; this is especially true in the West and in Ottawa. The worst restaurant city in Canada is my home town, Ottawa — it specializes in high prices, unimaginative menus, and poorly prepared food. Winnipeg, Edmonton, Calgary and Halifax are much better restaurant-towns of similar or smaller size.

For most of Canadian history, great dining meant eating in a hotel run by the railways. In every major city of Canada the CPR or CNR hotel was invariably the best place to eat and the dining cars of the trains extended the same opportunity. This is what Pierre Berton says of the good old days of CPR dining:

> As the decades rolled on Canadian railway dining became known the world over, for it was without doubt superior to any other. The mounds of crackling crisp Canadian bacon, the evenly grilled Calgary sirloins, the plump, pink spring lamb chops, the succulent goldeyes with their melting pat of parsley butter, the juicy lake fish, slightly charred, the Oka and cheddar cheeses and the hot seasonal blueberry pies — all these came to be associated almost exclusively with our transcontinental train service. It is perhaps not too much to say that, if there is a distinctly Canadian style of cuisine, it is this; and not too surprising that, in an artificial nation bound together by bands of steel, it should spring directly from our dining cars.†

It's a good thing Pierre Berton marked that down for posterity: now the Canadian dining car is a sordid short-order mobile snack bar specializing in pre-cooked fodder for the trapped passengers.

Today, CN and CP feed Canadians with expensive but tasteless meals in a good many of their hotel dining-rooms, coffee shops and cocktail bars throughout Canada. The one that I am most familiar with is the Chateau Laurier in Ottawa. Because of the Hotel's prime location beside the Parliament buildings, it has a very busy bar-cum-lunch place, the COQ AND LION, which charges some of the highest prices anywhere for drinks and sandwiches. What do you think of $4 for a Bloody Mary, a slice of ham between some

† From *The Centennial Food Guide* by Pierre and Janet Berton (Toronto: McClelland & Stewart, 1966).

bread (often stale), a cup of coffee and slow service? Almost invariably, in town after town in Canada, the great railway hotels offer costly, insipid, pretentious, unimaginative food in over-elaborate and often flashy "international style" surroundings. I could name a few exceptions but the list would be very short.

In addition to the railway hotels, there are many other ostentatious, expense-account extravaganzas on my black-list. The dining-rooms operated by other major hotel chains — the Holiday Inns and a number of others — are truly unmemorable, but again, charge the customer a good amount of money for the privilege of dining there. A new trick is the restaurant that revolves, a favourite of some hotels. The huge sum of money you pay out in these places must be for the electricity, not the food and service.

Hotel dining-rooms very often have a fancy fold-out menu with long descriptions, gold embossed, of the food, telling everything except the truth (more than likely the veget-ables are canned and the steaks have been hanging in the deep freeze). Mock-obsequious headwaiters hide their ignorance by putting down the customer, and the dinner bill is high enough to make Howard Hughes blench. These are flashy showoff restaurants that have everything but a civilized meal at civilized prices.

The big hotel restaurants are fond of the convention people, who are a kind of captive prey when they are there, but with the conference crowd it's a case of here today and gone to Wawanesa tomorrow. Restaurants that cater pri-marily to a shifting clientele are open to the temptation of charging high prices for non-quality, because no one will be around the next day to complain.

A restaurant is worth its salt when the cost accounting is balanced by a personal and genuine interest in the food served, when chefs, not computers or management experts, decide menu choice (imagination is still a prerogative of the human species), and when the clientele comes back for another meal.

Having made all the above charges, I must now admit

that Canadian restaurant owners have reason to resent people like me who complain about their bad food and worse service: The difficulties arising from the high cost of skilled labour — if such a thing still exists — and sky-rocketing rents are shared by restaurant owners all over the world. Canada has no monopoly on bad restaurants.

The Colony Club in New York, a favourite rendezvous of Jackie Onassis (and whoever elso *Vogue* Magazine deems worthy of note), closed down — good labour was impossible to find. Even Paul Bocuse, a temple of gastronomy near Lyon, in France (rating three stars in the *Guide Michelin*), claims it loses monew constantly. B. Bocuse says, "My restaurant is an expensive hobby." Perhaps it is his related activities, such as wine-exporting, that make his restaurant financially possible. And despite the fact that restaurants in London are supposed to be better than ever, I tramped many a mile to avoid over-cooked, over-sauced dishes with high-faluting names and prices to match — and service which was the essence of that particular British blend of condescension and ineptitude. Raymond Sokolov, food critic who succeeded Craig Claiborne of *The New York Times*, called the every-day fare of the Connaught Grill, which has a first-class reputation in London, "high mundane".

I ate recently at Le Francais, one of the ten restaurants in London awarded a "laurel wreath" by the usually reliable British *Good Food Guide*. Although the first course was excellent (a fish *pâté*), the complicated *pièce de résistance*, a stuffed, boned little bird, was tough enough to have resisted the edge of Saladin's sword. We complained; the headwaiter was apologetic and announced that the chef agreed with our criticisms and would cook no more birds that evening. Well and good, except for the sight of uncomplaining Englishmen struggling with their tough, stuffed, boned birds, still being brought from the kitchen two hours later as we finished our coffee and cognac.

Since the law courts are bedeviled by medical experts with contrary opinions on why the victim died, it is amusing, but not surprising, to read about knowledgeable people's disagreements on restaurants. For example, *The Good Food Guide's* judgements are brought to account by Raymond Sokolov. Parkes restaurant in London, long praised by Londoners, is also given a laurel wreath by *The Good Food Guide*, but Mr. Sokolov ate there on a busman's holiday and later wrote "The chic variety is best represented by a detestable place called Parkes that has to be seen to be believed . . . Everything is heavy . . . most things are repulsive."

Putting aside the conflicts of the critics, the truth of the matter is that the difficult standards of French cuisine, on which the best hotel restaurants fifty years ago based the precepts of their cooking, are practically impossible to maintain. In France where Escoffier was born and trained and where cooking and restaurants are an integral part of civilization, the trend is away from the elaborate in every aspect of the restaurant trade. Simplicity of surroundings and small menu choice are being stressed. Bistro-type restaurants with rough furniture, cotton table-cloths and earthenware plates have replaced *fin de siècle* chandeliers, damask, and porcelain service plates. Unless the owner of the conventional luxury-style restaurant happens to be a wizard of finance as well as a genius in the kitchen, these simpler places are the popular and profitable restaurants of the future all over the world.

The comments that I make on restaurants in the pages that follow are not objective appraisals of the best places to eat in Canada. They are highy biased, impressionistic descriptions of what it's like to eat well in our country.† I'm positive there are many other restaurants just as good as those I discuss in this chapter but I happened to have had a good time and a delicious meal or two in these places, and I want to share my experiences.

† If you want a restaurant guide, see the latest edition of *Where to Eat in Canada* by Anne Hardy and Sondra Gotlieb, or the many city guides that ars published in Montreal, Toronto and Vancouver (mentioned in the appendix at the back of this book). Also, take a look at my account in this book of cheap but good eateries across Canada.

The only common denominator in the restaurants that follow is the excellence in their own special field of cuisine: The SAI WOO in Toronto is unprepossessing, with no liquor license, but it excels in Chinese cooking; LA SAPINIERE in Val David, Quebec has one of the biggest wine cellars in Canada; the MARSHLANDS INN in New Brunswick makes no pretence of fancy Parisian cooking but serves excellent local food; and CHEZ BARDET in Montreal prides itself on its French sauces. Each place reflects the cultural environment in which it is located, as well as, at times, its geographical situation. The places I'm going to mention are, I think, typical of the best sort of eating and cooking one gets in their regions. You may not agree with my choices but it doesn't matter . . . this is not a list of the best three, five or ten restaurants in Canada but an account of my own agreeable restaurant experiences. By way of contrast, I will also touch on a few less agreeable experiences.

In my descriptions of what's authentic and good in Canadian restaurants, I start with French Canada, in particular, Quebec, because our oldest and most sophisticated cooking traditions are there and I end with the Maritimes, where you can find very simple but very pleasing restaurant-cooking. In between, Ontario, the West, and British Columbia are discussed. In this highly selective account, equal weight is not given to all good restaurants. I deal at some length with a few because they are illustrative of a certain type of solid, consistent, not-too-expensive restaurant which needs to be encouraged in Canada. I hope we can see more of them.

Montreal and Quebec City are our meccas for classical French cooking. Toronto restaurants may charge high prices and even write their menus in French, but they cannot match the quality and quantity of restaurants in these two cities. Most French restaurants, anywhere in Canada, are expensive, but if I decide to spend $15 to $20 on a meal, I would rather do it in Montreal or Quebec, where there are more good restaurants per capita than anywhere else in our country.

Montrealers and Quebecers are more knowledgeable about their food than their counterparts in Toronto, and they expect more from their restaurants. In Montreal, if you order something simple yet classical, like poached or grilled fish, it is less likely to be overcooked or over-sauced. Restaurants in Montreal are not superb, but no restaurant in North America merits that adjective. They are a bit lazy — their menus lack adventure and imagination. Any restaurant that offers something other than steak done in several different sauces, orange duck, or stuffed *crêpes* is a rare establishment. All too often their new or imaginative dishes are not all that successful. Even so, Montreal restaurants are generally superior to those of Toronto.

CHEZ BARDET, 591 Henri Bourassa East, is considered by many to be the finest restaurant in Montreal. The service, the freshly prepared food and the wine cellar are second to none, but the price of a meal is high, as high as you'll pay in this city known for its expense-account restaurants.

Yet BARDET's menu is not all that exciting when you look at it with a cold eye. The main courses offer chicken, veal, and steak done in cheese, cream or wine sauces, a rack of lamb, and a different daily special. I liked the unusual and freshly-made tiny puff potatoes that accompanied my steak *à la Clermont*. But there were no real surprises. Perhaps that's just as well; resources — animal, vegetable and human — should never be strained beyond their limits. The single most delicious dish I've eaten at this restaurant is the *coquilles St-Jacques Nantaise*. The scallops come in their traditional shell bordered by a purée of potato and baked in a fish and wine sauce. Succulent. If you want to be more certain than anywhere else in Montreal of getting every item on the menu cooked to order in the classical style, along with impeccable service (M. Bardet is always present, watching his waiters), go to BARDET. There is no establishment anywhere in Montreal that can match it for consistency and traditional good cooking, but the price is high for gastronomic security.

THE ST-AMABLE, 188 rue St-Amable, is another restaurant that aims high and often succeeds. However, I don't think its standards are met as consistently as CHEZ BARDET's. The restaurant is in a restored eighteenth-century building on Place Cartier in old Montreal. Everything is decorated in old-Canadian or nineteenth-century-French style. But the tables are crowded, so there is not enough room for the waiters to serve in the grand style that is typical of M. Bardet's. Nevertheless, dishes like *tournedos opéra* (filet mignon in a pastry shell with a filling of mushrooms, foie gras and truffles in a port wine sauce) and *la sole soufflée armorique* (sole stuffed with lobster- and truffle-mousse, poached in a blend of white wine, butter and shallots, and garnished with lobster sauce) are *chef d'oeuvres*. The menu is ambitious and the chef, Pierre Garcin, is equal to his tasks. You will pay a fistful of money at THE ST-AMABLE in the evening, but lunches are extremely reasonable, and better prepared than in many places that have less interesting décor and less efficient service. The last time I was there I ate a *ratatouille*, grilled lamb chop, and a piece of the *Toscan Maison,* a liqueur-soaked Italian cake ($1 on the evening menu), all for $2.35. Not a bad price for a first-class Montreal restaurant.

CHEZ SON PERE, 5316 Park Avenue, has moved from St. Laurent Blvd. and so have the prices, upwards, but it is still less expensive than BARDET and THE ST-AMABLE. This is the sort of restaurant that Montrealers have relied upon for careful cooking for over forty years. There are no surprises and no disappointments. The owner-chef is François Bouyeux, one of the best known of his profession in the city. It is comfortable to go to CHEZ SON PERE and know that the fish will be perfectly done and that the vegetables and salad will be without fault. I had poached fresh Pacific salmon with hollandaise — it tasted better than the salmon I ate in Vancouver at THE CANNERY, a restaurant that faces the sea. The secret is the cooking — the salmon was not overcooked as it was in British Columbia. For dessert, order the *Pavé Harlequin,* a very good chocolate mousse enclosed in a cake.

Montrealers can be fickle when it comes to restaurants. They like the new, fashionable spots. When I was last there, I was told to go to CHEZ GEORGES — "that's where all the new divorcées dine" — and LES HALLES, another new restaurant that a half-dozen people, all unknown to one another, said was "it," as far as good and fashionable eating places were concerned (if such a thing can ever be equated). LES HALLES offers beefsteak for $3.25 and a plate of *terrines* and *galantines* for as little as $1.20. These prices are less expensive than those of the usual first-class restaurants in Montreal, but you pay for what you get: the three-dollar beefsteak was a three-dollar beefsteak and the *terrines* were greasy. The restaurant is crowded with *le tout Montreal*. Reservations are a necessity.

Quebec City restaurants are as good as, if not better than, those of Montreal for French food. The quality of the food, the service — and the prices — have remained more stable here than anywhere else. There are a number of restaurants that offer excellent, if somewhat similar, menus. CHEZ GUIDO, the AMBASSADEUR and the MONSEIGNEUR are all owned by the same person — he clearly knows what it is to run good restaurants. The scampi and veal dishes (especially the *escaloppe de veau au morilles*) are exceptionally well prepared; the pastries are rich and full of flavour, whether of coffee or of liqueur — worth eating even on a full stomach.

The CONTINENTAL also comes into this category; it's a restaurant that knows what it's doing. The crab, the mushrooms *à la Grecque*, and the rum cake are all first class. An establishment that is not quite as fancy but which serves fine meat is LA CHAUMIERE, 22 rue Couillard. Its specialty, *la pièce de boeuf gastronome* grilled with a hint of mustard and garlic, was perhaps the best prepared piece of meat I have had in eastern Canada.

All these restaurants offer good food and excellent service for less money than those in Montreal. New restaurants keep opening up all the time in this city. Considering the small population, the interest in food in this region is phenomenal.

The hobgoblin of every restaurant in the world is consistency. Your local café's onion soup and goulash may be a commendable Thursday lunch but by Friday the cheese in the soup tastes like chewing gum and the goulash looks like something your dog eats. Many restaurant kitchens in this country are shifting and unstable — you can never be sure of getting the same meal, service and cooking twice in a row. A good restaurant must have the same standards on Monday as it does on Saturday. And this depends on the competence and attitude of the owner, chef, headwaiter and manager.

North of Montreal there is a hotel restaurant noted for consistent good food and fine service, LA SAPINIERE in Val David in the Laurentians in Quebec. The choice of dishes ranges from boiled beef (*bouilli de Québec*) and maple-cured ham to beef Wellington and *canard à l'orange* on the table d'hôte; and although I am not an admirer of the *flambé* technique, I admire the way the waiters there flurry about to flambé steaks and *brochettes* of beef for those who eat *à la carte*.

It is the table d'hôte menu at LA SAPINIERE that I find most interesting to eat. There is a choice of twelve or thirteen main courses, all carefully prepared, and served by adept and cheerful waiters. The chef, Marcel Kretz, has been at LA SAPINIERE for twelve years; the manager, Phillipe Belleteste, for five years, and they both have had intensive training in France and Switzerland, There are restaurants that attempt more superb and complicated individual dishes but few are capable of maintaining the day-to-day level of LA SAPINIERE. Attention to details is really the key to the success of this restaurant. The headwaiter chided a new waiter for taking away the bread before the cheese was served, and all of the waiters anxiously worry if you leave something on the plate. The indifference you meet in many restaurants does not exist at LA SAPINIERE.

Twelve per cent service is automatically added on to the bill so the excellent *esprit de corps* of the waiters is not due to a hunger for tips. They actually seem to enjoy their job. When I asked M. Belleteste about this he said that they have special training sessions, twice a week, and he always tells them that good will and a desire to please is more important than putting the dessert spoon in the right position.

Perhaps the most gratifying aspect of La Sapiniere is the use of fresh vegetables and local ingredients. Fresh artichokes, cauliflower, beans, spinach, braised celery and zucchini are all part of their regular table d'hôte. I noticed that M. Kretz's repertoire even includes (during the season) an asparagus soup made from fresh asparagus — something that I've seen nowhere else in Canada. He also prides himself on serving Canadian lamb that has never been frozen, and oysters, mussels, scallops, sole, mackerel, halibut, pickerel and salmon that arrive at La Sapiniere directly from their sources. He smokes his own salmon and ham and makes all his own *terrines* and *pâtés*. There is one that has truffles and a crust that makes the heart stop for a moment. Here's the recipe:

Pâté en Croûte

1) Put through the mincer 3 times:
   2 pounds veal (shoulder or shank)
   2 pounds fat port or "sausage meat"
   1 pound pork liver.
2) Put through the mincer (large holes) once only:
   8 ounces veal
   8 ounces fat pork or flank
   8 ounces pork liver
3) Cut into 1/2-inch squares 2 pounds chicken livers.
4) Brown slightly 2 ounces chopped French shallots.
5) a) put aside 1 or 2 truffles, chopped (can be left out if found to be too expensive and replaced by 2 cups of finely chopped fresh mushrooms) ;
   b) 1/2 cup shelled and peeled pistachio nuts (to peel them, blanch them for a few minutes).

6) Spices to be used:
    1 pinch of each:
      bay leaf (ground)
      thyme
      cinnamon
      nutmeg
      white pepper
      rosemary
      basil
      allspice
      cloves
      savory
    (This mixture is called "mixed spices for *pâtés*" and can be used in several other kinds of *pâtés*.)

7) 2 glasses dry white wine
    1 glass Madeira wine
    2 ounces brandy
    salt to taste
    2 teaspoons icing sugar helps (helps to keep the *pâté* pink)

8) Once all these ingredients are ready, mix well — with the mixer or by hand.

PATE PASTRY

2 pounds flour
4 ounces egg yolks
5 ounces butter
5 ounces shortening
12 1/2 ounces (fluid) water
1 teaspoon salt

Mix water, egg yolks, salt, flour. Add butter and shortening; proceed as with pie pastry. Let stand in the refrigerator overnight.

The next day roll out the pastry 1/4 inch thick. Use a special *pâté en croûte* mould or any mould with only sides (no bottom). Line the mould, reserving some pastry for the cover. Fill up. Seal well. Make two small holes on the top (to let out the steam while baking). Baste with egg yolk. Bake at 375° for about one hour and a half. Let cool. The next day fill up the two holes with aspic. This is a basic recipe for a medium sized pâté.

Although M. Kretz is a Swiss, trained in France, he does not despise regional dishes. In fact, he has made a specialty of Quebec cooking. His *tourtière* is thick and juicy with a very light crust, and it is accompanied by his home-made relish or "marinade". Desserts include *maple mousse* and *tarte au sucre,* as well as Black Forest cake and French pastries.

It is the dependability of the ensemble that is worth noting as you proceed from course to course. The fish is not overcooked, the grilled *brochette* is done to order, and the vinaigrette sauce with the artichoke contains finely chopped shallots. (M. Kretz cultivates his own herb garden.) This sense of care, the contempt for portion control (there are lots of oysters in the oyster soup), the freshness of the bread, the intense taste of a light soup, the desire to please on the part of the waiters — all these things distinguish LA SAPINIERE from many other restaurants. Perfection is not theirs, however. A friend who ate there recently complained that the *boeuf tartare* was tasteless and discoloured, and their truffled *terrine* is not on the menu often enough.

The wines in Quebec restaurants are always expensive. Restaurateurs are obliged to pay a special tax to the Quebec Liquor Board over and beyond the tax already included in the price of the wines as listed in the Liquor Commission. Nevertheless, the cellar at LA SAPINIERE is huge by Canadian standards, with 200 bottles of imported wines, or rather 198 (there are two Canadian wines on the list). Reading through the list is an education — the growth classification is described (I can't recall seeing that on a wine list before — *premier, deuxième, cinquième cru* etc.), the year, the wine, and the name of the shipper, as well as the price. The prices, by the way, are not as exorbitant as they might be, given the choice and quality of the wines. Among the vast selection I noticed champagnes of vintage years, a white Châteauneuf-du-Pape, and most unusual in Quebec, a Château Gloria, an up-and-coming red bordeaux of a bourgeois *cru* that is considered by some experts to merit a growth classification. To finish off a splendid meal there are some great sauternes, like Château d'Yquem and Château Rayne Vigneau, a favourite of wine connoisseur and writer Alec Waugh.

For me, eating in Toronto means eating Indian or Chinese, or eating in one of the city's many other ethnic restaurants — simple places without expensive menus and airs of high cuisine. It does not mean French-style, although there are certainly many — far too many — places that claim they cook in the French tradition.

One of the dining-rooms in the THREE SMALL ROOMS comes into this latter category. Their cuisine is a nebulous international, rather than French, and their prices are astronomic — $8 to $9 for fresh dover sole. Some of my anger with the place, it must be confessed, stems from the way the staff appears to treat single women diners. One week night at about 7.45 I attempted to enter the restaurant. The room was one-third filled, yet I was stopped and told to wait "so we can see if any tables are free." After I was seated, the headwaiter asked me if I was staying at the Windsor Arms Hotel, of which the THREE SMALL ROOMS is a part. Being too easily intimidated, I said yes. Then he asked me my name! I felt as if I needed a special permit to eat there. After a further delay of five minutes (presumably he was checking up on me with the reception clerk), a menu was finally handed to me. The shabby treatment that single female diners sometimes receive in restaurants like this one is as a valid a cause for complaint as badly cooked dishes and exorbitant prices.

The best thing about THREE SMALL ROOMS, gastronomically, is their desserts, grilled meat and vegetables in that order. However, the jumbo prawns I ordered needed a saw rather than a knife, and the tomato sauce on them was crude and uninteresting even at $6.75 *à la carte*.

On the other hand, I recently had a memorable eating experience in Toronto — at the SAI WOO (praised in my chapter on cheaper restaurants). A banquet organized by Bill Wen, the owner, was supposed to simulate "The Cuisine of Emperors and Kings and the best of President

Nixon's Peking Banquet as given by Premier Chou-En-Lai".

The place was packed. Two floors were taken up by Sai Woo regulars — one half fantasizing themselves as Pat and Dick, and the other as Chou-En-Lai or the Dowager Empress. (although SAI WOO is not exactly the Summer Palace).

The best way to describe the meal is to set out the menu as it was printed, with a few of my own comments.

"Dai Gut — Tangerine"
I peeled and ate it.

"Soong Dong Daahn Tong — Six Flowers Soup"
Water chestnuts, white fruit, black mushrooms, bamboo shoots, peas, eggs blended with chicken stock.

This soup contained *fresh*, not canned, water chestnuts. They have a sweet, full taste that the canned variety cannot emulate.

"Chien Mei — Chinese Hors D'Oeuvres"
Red cooked barbecued pork, wafers of abalone, ancient eggs with pickled scallions, spiced pork tripe, barbecued livers, soya beef and red fried octopus.

The wafers of abalone were rubbery but interesting, and the ancient eggs were black with a flavour that is an acquired taste, which I have not yet acquired. A friend of mine, an Occidental who lived in Hong Kong for several years, says he'd walk a thousand miles for one of them.

"Buk Ging Opp — Festival Peking Duck"
The President's favourite in Peking.

The skin was served first with side dishes of fresh coriander and thinly sliced scallions. The crisp skin married perfectly with the fresh herbs. Then came the meat, boneless and tender; a third dish arrived, the bones artfully formed into the shape of a duck, with the backbone acting as the head. The waiters bring the bones out to prove to the guest that no part of the duck is left in the kitchen. I could have gnawed quite happily on the bones for the rest of the evening but I had nine more courses to go.

"Yeh Gee Guy — Coconut Chicken"
Braised boneless chicken with fresh coconut in "a supreme sauce of Hainan Islands".

It was piping hot and the sauce was sweet, a contrast in texture, taste and temperature to the Peking Duck. Fresh coconut does make a difference.

"Yee Chee Tong — Three Shred Shark Fins in Chicken Broth. Famous in Kwangtzse"
The fins are aged for at least a year, then immersed in hot water for 12 hours. You do not eat the shark fins — only the vermicelli-like filaments which are separated from the fins. These fins were imported dried and whole especially for the Sai Woo. "Few can afford this luxury dish," the menu states. I enjoyed it, filaments and all, but I don't know if I'd want to be an Empress just for the soup.

"Hangchow Siu Yee — Whole Pickerel with Wood Melon"
The fish is served with head and tail, in a vinegar and cane-sugar sauce in ginger. The chef at Sai Woo is an expert at deep frying. He plunged the whole fish in boiling oil and it rose up brown and beautiful. Wood melon tasted like sweet pickles.

At this point Long John scotch was poured into our glasses instead of Liebfraumilch — to keep us going through the long night.

"Jar Yuk Yuen — Pearl Balls"
Spheres of meat and water chestnuts served on a bed of crisp marsh yams.

This, for me, was the highlight of the meal. The little meat balls had an ineffable, spicy taste; the yams had been made into a paste and then fried, forming lacy pancakes. How did the chef manage to keep them so crisp and hot for so many people?

"Doong Gu Pa Toi Om — Hearts of Mustard Greens"
From Shanghai, hearts of mustard greens sautéed with whole black mushrooms and garnished with smoked Chinese sausage as served in Peking.

I had never before had a Chinese dish that had enough black mushrooms in it. This one did and I could not eat them all.

"*Guong Boh Haah Ding* — Bright Precious Prawns"
Szechuan style, with hot pimento peppers.

Stomach distended, chopsticks wavering, I stared at the chopped prawns and peppers and finally had a mouthful. Their hotness cleaned the mouth and the lightness of the dish did not fill me up any more. It was a perfect way to finish off the meal.

But it was not exactly the finish.

"*Yang Chow Chow Fahn* — Yangchow Fried Rice"
"The Supreme of Fried Rice," according to the chef, with Chinese sausage, shrimp, barbecued pork, lettuce and bean sprouts.

Fried rice is fried rice. I let that one pass by without one regret.

"*Hueng Yeun Woo* — Almond Junket"
Miniature spheres of ground almonds and rice served with lichee and cherries.

It was not a junket, but little balls of almonds floating around in a sweet, rice-water bath. A little too sweet and gooey for me.

Pastries
They looked good, but for safety reasons (fear of stomach explosion) they did not pass through my lips.

Tea from Fukien
The spout of the tea-pot must not be pointed at any of the guests because that means that the host wishes to eliminate that person.

The meal was remarkable, given the variety of dishes served and the number of people eating them. Shee Hong Chin, the chef, is a master of organization as well as of cooking. His son, who was sitting at my table during the meal, is working during his summer holidays as a short-order cook making hamburgers for Occidentals. So it goes.

When it comes to eating in western Canada, I invariably follow one rule — it's always best, wherever you are, to eat the food of the region. It is foolhardy to ask for green lasagna in the Orkney Islands or oatmeal porridge in Naples.

There are many western restaurants — Winnipeg is glutted with them — devoted to an expense-account clientele; they offer "International Cuisine" on huge scrolls with as much ornamentation and annotation as the eighth-century Book of Kells. They offer you French lobster *cardinale,* Spanish *gazpacho,* chicken *Kiev* and Swiss *fondue.* Avoid these restaurants like the plague. Their real specialty is pretension. No good restaurant in New York, Montreal or Paris would attempt such diversity of cuisines. Why a restaurant should promise the impossible is one of the mysteries of the trade in this country.

If you want a good meal in western Canada, eat what is best in the west — beef, cooked in the simplest manner possible. The best steak house in the west is, in my opinion, HY's STEAK HOUSE in Calgary at 316 4 Avenue S.W. People might argue that steak houses should have more on their menu than steak, but I say beware. Why order Cornish hen "almondine" in a place that prepares steaks ninety-nine per cent of the time? Would you go to a brain surgeon to have a hysterectomy? If you go to a steak house, order steak. Avoid the latest culinary aberration — "surf and turf" — a chunk of sirloin and a frozen lobster tail. (The word "turf" is unfortunate in itself because of its horsey connotation.) Eating lobster is one kind of experience and eating steak is another — both need different preparation. The only possible pleasure one might get out of eating them together is the thrill of ordering the most expensive dish on the menu.

HY's is not without its own form of pretentious Spanish-hacienda décor. The motif includes a lot of iron grillwork and a sort of Latin patio walk. Inside, everything is heavy and dark, supposedly the desired decorative effect for rich men discussing oil deals. Many restaurants throughout

Canada (but especially in the West) have decided that pseudo-Spanish or mock-Tudor is the only possible environment for "elegant dining". Is there a fear, among the owners, that a lighter and simpler décor would attract women ordering chicken salads? I wish they would trade the andirons and brass warming pans for fresh vegetables. Canned, watery potato balls and mushy "baby" carrots are no substitute for a nice plate of hash browns, prepared to order, and fresh green beans.

When I went to HY'S, I was alone and as I've already pointed out, a solitary female diner does not always get the very best out of waiters at some restaurants. But despite this, and the fact that I am a difficult person to deal with in restaurants (I send things back, complain about salad dressings and, in general, am bad news for busy waiters), the service was perfect. HY'S waiters, showing no sign of discontent, made the oil and vinegar salad-dressing three times for me before I was satisfied. The waiters at many of the HY'S restaurants seem to be taller and broader of shoulder than those in eastern restaurants. They look like the second string of the Calgary Stampeders doing a bit of moonlighting. It's not an unpleasant sensation for a female to be waited on by virile looking waiters.

I also like the lavishness of the bread basket at HY'S — as much as you want of good hot cheese- or garlic-bread. And of course the steaks. They are perfect, cooked to order and full of flavour and juice (not like some I've had elsewhere, which might come rare, as ordered, but dry as a bone). The baked stuffed potato was as good as any I've eaten at any steak house. The pastry is ordered from an excellent bakery in Calgary, the WOODEN SHOE, and the little cakes taste of butter and real meringue.

Eating at HY'S in Calgary is a very satisfactory if conservative experience. Conservative, in this case, is not a perjorative description — it means tried and true, better safe than sorry. And that's what HY'S is all about. There are other Hy's restaurants in the West, including locations in Winnipeg and Vancouver. The establishment in Van-

couver is even more restricted in its menu choice. HY's
PRIME RIB, at 1177 W. Hastings Street, has a fine view of
the Vancouver harbour, and two choices on the menu,
roast beef and rib steak. But as the name suggests, it's really
the roast beef that people come for. At the PRIME RIB it is
perfectly prepared and carved to specifications at the table,
depending on whether you like thin English slicing or the
thicker American style. And there are even good vegetables,
creamed fresh spinach and an excellent salad freshly tossed
for you — not prepared hours before and left in a refrigerator where the greens become so cold that no taste remains.

This sort of restaurant, in my opinion, is far superior to
places that try to cook everything and wind up providing
nothing really good to eat. A general rule of thumb seems to
be, the smaller the menu the better the individual dishes,
but of course, as with every rule, there are some glaring exceptions. I've eaten at a restaurant in Toronto, TROY's, a
place with a great reputation for French-style cuisine, where
the menu choice was small and where I found each of the
few dishes poorly prepared. I was told proudly that the chef
had never been to cooking school. Heavy sauces drowned
delicate meats like baby lamb, and the sweetbreads were
broiled into hard little marbles. However, other people
have had better luck at TROY's. Mine was an off-night perhaps.

Dining well in restaurants in British Columbia means
three things: eating beef (see my comment about HY's
PRIME RIB), eating Chinese food in one of the city's vast
array of Chinese places (see "Where to Eat if You're Fussy
and Broke"), and fish, both the ocean and fresh-water
variety. Surprisingly, good fresh fish is not always easy to
come by in Vancouver restaurants. If you like a simple fish
meal with a glass of wine and you want to be safe, I would
recommend TROLL's at Horseshoe Bay in West Vancouver
(a half-hour from Vancouver). This is a family-run place
that prides itself on the freshness of the fish (most of the
seven or eight menu choices are caught the morning of

the day they are served). TROLL'S is inexpensive, and consistent in quality. The fresh sole, done in a remarkably light egg batter, is $2.50; their fish and chips are cheaper, and excellent. I also recommend the steamed sturgeon. This is a restaurant with a view of a ferry wharf, busy bay and peaceful mountains.

Is it possible for the tourist in the Maritimes to have an eating experience that is based upon regional cooking traditions and ingredients? The Atlantic provinces have their share of hamburger stands and greasy diners that specialize in that delectable concoction, the hot turkey sandwich. But there are restaurants that still serve the home-made bread and pies, the fresh fish and chowders, and local berries and vegetables described in nostalgic accounts of Nova Scotia and New Brunswick childhoods.

Go to Sackville, New Brunswick, just across the Nova Scotia border, near Amherst. Sackville is the home of Mount Allison University, as well as some of those Victorian houses, wooden frame, fancied with turrets and hand-wrought iron gates, that grace the towns and villages of the Maritimes. Nevertheless, the imperative reason for making a detour to Sackville, if you are 100 miles out of the way, is to eat a meal and spend a night at MARSHLAND'S INN. It is probably the only place in Canada where cocoa and cookies are passed around before bed-time, where a silver dinner bell on the table brings out the maid, and where local ingredients are prepared according to family recipes.

You must sleep over at the Inn. There are only ten bedrooms open to the public so reserve well in advance. Everything from the food to the furniture, from the household staff to the old-fashioned plants and bucket-shaped bath tubs, takes you back fifty Maritime years. There are hotels in Europe and New England where the furniture is signed, every piece of china on the sideboard is rare Meissen or Ming, and the condescension of the owners insufferable. These are museums where you look from a distance, whisper at dinner, tip-toe to bed — and cancel your next night's reservation. But the MARSHLAND'S INN has an easy informal air, despite the family Spode and the four-poster beds. The furniture belonged to the owners' grandparents and it's good, strong Edwardian stuff that sensible Maritime merchants with large families bought to last, and not just to prettify the parlours.

The silver is displayed on the sideboard, but there are, thankfully, no little cards underneath it describing its preciousness. None of the surroundings are so exquisite that you feel oafish. Everything has charm; the slightly sagging armchair and the antimacassar set awry on the sofa bring comfort to the guests.

In 1935 the family grindstone business declined and Mr. and Mrs. H.W. Read, instead of selling their father's big, nineteenth-century frame house and going to New York, decided to stay in Sackville and entertain paying guests. Mrs. Read did the cooking with the help of some young local girls and Mr. Read took care of the business end. Mrs. Read senior is not alive today but some of the same young girls, now somewhat older, continue on in the MARSHLAND'S kitchen with Mrs. Read's recipes for baked scallops and lemon sherbet. Mr. Read, well past eighty, still acts as host and takes the guests into the dining-room, while his son and daughter-in-law, Mr. and Mrs. H.C. Read, look after the restaurant and Inn.

Everyone dines off the family silver and china, no bill is presented in the dining-room, and unless the weather is hot, the living-room fire is always lit, even in the morning before breakfast. The Reads live in their home and treat the people staying there as invited, rather than paying, guests.

The food is good plain Maritime cooking. Home-made rolls (the best I've eaten in Canada), excellent chowder, fresh fish, well and simply prepared, roast goose, mashed turnips, snow pudding and fresh fruit pies are all house specialties. (Roast turkey is also on the menu but given the choice between goose and turkey, most people choose goose.) The Reads grow their own vegetables in the summer and make their preserves from the berries in the garden. Mr. and Mrs. Read go to Advocate, a small town near Sackville, for their foxberries. A local specialty, the Tantramar mushroom (darker, tastier and larger than the kind sold in most stores), is picked by the husband of one of the cooks so that the MARSHLAND'S INN always has a supply, canned, or fresh in season. And the turnips — made with sugar, butter and mashed potato (a very Maritime combination) — are superb. Regular customers from Moncton phone Mrs. Read to find out if the turnips are on the menu that day. The callers will then drive thirty miles for their dinner. Even the baked New Brunswick potato does not have that mealy, old taste that is the rule rather than the exception in practically every restaurant in Canada. The scallops are baked with milk and bread; this doesn't sound imaginative, but the result surprises. Stale bread cubes are buttered and placed on top of the scallops, then broiled; the scallops remain tender in their bath of milk.

Breakfast is old-fashioned oatmeal porridge, slow cooked, special hot-cakes made from wheat flour, crisp and melting in one mouthful and, of course, eggs. The eggs are laid by MARSHLAND'S hens (every spring Mr. and Mrs. Read buy a hundred or so) — the yolks are huge. Breakfast juice is freshly squeezed and the marmalade is home-made like the toast and muffins. What more can I say except that every bedroom is supplied with a can of bicarbonate of soda.

None of the dishes at the MARSHLAND'S INN resembles the fancy high-priced pseudo-international cooking that so many establishments in Canada like to push on their customers. The Inn is not pretentious — it's just realistic. New Brunswick grows good turnips and potatoes, so the Reads serve them to their guests. Small tender Atlantic shrimps make up their shrimp cocktail, not the large rubbery American Gulf shrimp which are so prevalent in Canada, even in the Maritimes. The recipes they use are simple and good, not beyond the experience of the local housewives who come in and do the cooking. More Canadian restaurants should think about the gastronomic philosophy of the

MARSHLAND'S INN. Local ingredients are used as much as possible and regional styles of cooking are stressed, not suppressed by foreign invasions of chicken Hawaiian-style, South African Lobster Tail, and Danish Trout desecrated by a few almonds.

Here is the Inn's recipe for Cloverleaf Dinner Rolls:

Cloverleaf Dinner Rolls

2 tbsp. dry yeast dissolved in 1 cup lukewarm water in which 1 tbsp. sugar has dissolved.

Put 6 cups hot water into very large bowl. Add scant 1/2 cup shortening, 2 tbsp. salt and 2 tbsp. sugar. When mixture has cooled to lukewarm, stir in dissolved yeast mixture. Then beat in 6 cups Robin Hood flour and enough more flour to make the dough stiff enough to knead on a floured board. Knead well, then place in a greased bowl and cover with a clean dry dish towel. Let rise in a warm place until doubled in bulk. Punch down lightly with a kneading motion, and form dough into rolls. Let rise until doubled. Cook 15 minutes or more at 400°.

The MARSHLAND'S reflects the best of Maritime cooking; you will be hard put to find another such place driving through the region. But other eating experiences that do occur are worthy of note, and occasionally painful to remember.

YORK'S restaurant in Andover, New Brunswick, on old Highway 2 on the St. John River, is as far removed from pretension, flaming foods and flim flam as a place can be without catering to a mining camp. It's a motel with little white cabins facing the railway tracks and a ditch behind. The restaurant building is not prepossessing, the extension is a sort of glassed-in porch which has settled unevenly into the ground. We stayed the night in a rather primitive cabin: shower, toilet, two large beds with a partition in between, for $8.50. It was 6 p.m. when we drove up and cars were parked in front; people were already streaming in for fresh banana bread, lobsters and home-made pie.

Unfortunately the New Brunswick government will not allow YORK's a liquor license (although the restaurant has been established for over thirty years). They want the place "fixed up" and the owner figures it would cost him $100,000 to do so. The toilets are in a separate building, next to the restaurant. Is this also objectionable to the New Brunswick government?

Why is it all right for people to eat dinner in such simple surroundings but not all right for them to consume alcohol while eating there? Is the well-being of people who order wine and beer more important than that of people who drink pop? The physical requirements for restaurants everywhere in Canada are less if no alcohol is served, even if the same amount of people are packed into the building. There is a lack of logic in laws that insist on vast sums of money spent on fire doors, bathrooms and interior decoration only for those who drink spirits while they eat. In a funny kind of way, the laws treat abstainers as less important citizens.

The bathrooms at YORK's restaurant are very clean. We drank our own rye whiskey from the motel toothbrush glasses (the rye was bought two minutes before the 5 p.m. closing at the "Government store"), sitting outside on lawn chairs someone had placed directly in front of the bathrooms. One of the waitresses spent the length of our cocktail hour, back to us, on her knees, scrubbing the john like fury. Her activity was gratifying but the view was not ideally scenic.

The restaurant's interior is done in knotty pine and the decorations include a stuffed deer-head (or is it a moose?), a grandfather clock that says Coca Cola, and a soft-drink cooler machine (the sign of a good place — pop in bottles is better than pop made from syrup concentrate) and a picture of MacDonald Tobacco's Scotch lass on the wall.

A young waiter came up to us immediately, although the place was crowded with United Church ministers,

French-Canadian families, American tourists and trencher-
men of all kinds. In a sing-song voice he told us what there
was to eat (there is no written menu): roast duck, lobster,
scallops, fried chicken, smoked pork and Alaska king crab
(which is cheaper than the local queen crab). After we had
ordered he first brought us home-made white bread and
then banana bread with the soup. When we had finished
the soup, he placed an enormous corn fritter covered with
hot maple syrup in front of us; it comes unasked for, with
every order.

The fritter is not what dieticians would recommend, or
Escoffier would suggest, as a light *entrée*, but it was crunchy,
so we ate it. We ate our duck and lobster too, and the waiter
came by again and asked us if we wanted to taste anything
else on the menu, free for nothing, as we used to say when
we were children. A portion of pork chop, fried chicken,
and a whole side of lobster were placed before us, so we ate
them too. Everyone else in the room seemed to be getting
these second helpings — it is amazing how much people will
stuff into themselves if they are not paying for it. For dessert we had home-made mincemeat pie and banana cream
pie, appropriately running out of the crust onto the plate. I
hate cream pies that never let go. There were seconds, of
course. Total price for the dinner — $5.50. Total price for a
lobster dinner —$7.50.

Somehow we rolled ourselves out of the restaurant and
staggered into a little graveyard which was not too far from
YORK's restaurant. We felt like dying. Instinct must have
led us to the tombstones.

From
Château Mouton Rothschild
to Loganberry Wine

UNLESS YOU ARE rich, it's hard for you, as a Canadian, to
be knowledgeable about wines. Even then, you do not have
the opportunity of tasting as many wines, good, bad and
mediocre, as an American or an Englishman. The variety of
wines for sale in our liquor commissions is small compared to that in other countries, despite the tremendous
advances made within the last decade. I feel frustrated when
I read wine columns in the British newspapers, or price
lists advertised by wine stores in *The New York Times*. In
Canada, rigid controls on the importation of alcohol, the
cost of all imported wines, and ham-handed merchandising
techniques make the wine-lover's life extraordinarily difficult.

I am a lover of wine but I never tasted it during my
youth. In Manitoba, where the pall of temperance hung
over the land, no kindly rich uncle gave me my first glass of
beaujolais. At home, where one bottle of sherry lasted eight
months in the liquor cabinet, wine was considered a dan-
gerous frivolity. And the provincial government didn't
allow alcohol of any kind in restaurants.

It was the same throughout the West; so, when people did get hold of a bottle, they drank as if their lives depended on it. The night clubs strung out along the Pembina Highway in Manitoba used to provide "set ups" of glasses, ice and ginger ale. Teen-age boys brought cheap rye "hidden" in brown paper bags. The rye, of course, had to be finished on the premises. God help the boys if the police found a half bottle of whiskey in the car — even if the driver was sober. It was wiser to drink yourself blind and leave the empties at the night club.

No one drank wine.

During the late forties and early fifties there was an excellent restaurant in Winnipeg, owned by an Italian still under the delusion that an aspect of civilized life was drinking wine with your food. Fresh from Torino, his culture shock was profound when the RCMP jailed him for resisting barbarism by serving wine with food. He was ruined, financially and spiritually; the rigid attitudes of the Anglo-Saxon culture broke his Mediterranean spirit and Winnipeg lost a fine place to eat.

That was my drinking heritage when I left Winnipeg in 1955 and sailed for Europe on an Italian boat. On board, a rich gentleman in his mid-sixties bought me my first champagne cocktail and then ordered a bottle of Château Cheval Blanc, 1947, to accompany my spaghetti. I was rather taken with the champagne cocktail but detested the wine — it tasted musty, strange, and sour. He drank most of it. He was silly to have offered one of the world's great wines to a young savage.

I then spent a year in Oxford — and that is where the greatest wine tragedy of my life occurred, again because of my ignorance. The senior common room of my husband's college had a remarkable wine list, and all the wines in it were available to me. If the spirit had taken me, I might have drunk some more Château Cheval Blanc ('47) and Château Lafite-Rothschild ('43) for the equivalent of $2 a bottle; or a slightly lower-classed growth like Château Palmer ('47) at $1.25. But I didn't. I didn't taste one bottle of any of the wines in the Wadham Senior Common Room — instead I drank warm beer, and Pimms with cucumber in it. When I look at that 1955 wine list today before I buy Spanish Yago at my local outlet, my regret is bitter. Time is not a healer of heartaches of that sort.

Today, it's impossible to find the cheapest, most raw blends of unclassified bordeaux for $1.25 in the outlets of the Liquor Control Board of Ontario (the LCBO). A 1967 Château Lafite-Rothschild costs about $22 at the LCBO, and 1967 is not the best year for wines. (With all vintage wines, the price varies according to the quality of each of the vintage years.)

I moved to Geneva after Oxford and remembered that musty taste of the Cheval Blanc. In Switzerland, it is, of course, possible to buy wines of all kinds in restaurants and shops, although Château Cheval Blanc was harder to find and expensive to buy. The old gentleman had tried to push me down the slippery path too suddenly, but the seeds of desire had been sown on the boat despite my poor showing at Oxford. A second glass of Cheval Blanc was offered in Geneva and it carried me all the way down the hill. It was during my years there that I became a lover of wine.

One of the most glorious moments in my life happened about seven years ago in New York City. An American businessman asked a visiting group of Canadian professors for lunch, as well as a rag-taggle of wives who were hanging about — I was in the latter category. Our host had just recovered from a serious operation, was in the process of being eased from his job, and, after many happy years with a much younger mistress, had returned to his wife, for lack of anything better. The only thing that made any sense at all to him was drinking fine wine. Despite his contempt for his guests, his ill health, and his homely wife, he opened three bottles of an apricot-coloured German wine made from specially selected dried or overripe grapes called, in German, *trockenbeerenauslese*. The vintage, if I recall correctly, was 1951. *Trockenbeerenauslese* are partially covered with mould and shriveled by the sun, and only one drop of syrup can be extracted from them. These grapes are pressed separately from the regular grapes and the wine made from them is very rich and sweet. This is a dessert wine. It is not available from any of the liquor commission outlets in Canada. If it were, the price would be incredible because it is one of the rarest and most expensive wines in the world. We drank the three bottles with a hot cherry *soufflé* made by the businessman's wife. He cheered up, and I was in a drinker's paradise. Normally, I dislike sweet wines, but this nectar was unforgettably rich and fruity.

It is hardly possible that an experience like this will ever occur to anyone living in Canada. Our liquor commissions have improved immeasurably in the last two decades, but their selection of wines is still poor, and the exorbitant mark-ups reveal a lack of professionalism and business acumen that only private enterprise could cure. Worse than that, our laws and merchandising techniques are motivated by a hidden morality.

For better or worse, we accept the fact that wines and spirits must be heavily taxed. But why do we have to go to government-owned and bureaucratically-managed depots for our imported wines and spirits? Privately-owned stores in New York state and other states of the United States are allowed to sell wines and spirits. They compete with one another and use some imagination in importing wines. After all, they have to compete to survive. The result: lower prices and better service. Why do Americans have more freedom of choice in this area than we do?

Our fear of letting the private sector take over the merchandising of spirits seems to be based on the assumption that Canadians will run amuck once they can buy booze on every corner. It reminds me of my elderly neighbours' attitude during the dry era of Air Canada. When I argued for the serving of alcohol on Canadian airplanes (the airlines of most countries had instigated the practice long before), the husband said, "What do you mean? The passengers will get drunk and attack the pilot."

This moralistic belief in the necessity of having big

brother control the sale of spirits in our country really implies a lack of confidence in the maturity of Canadians. It is doubly ludicrous *vis à vis* the non-Anglo-Saxon element in Canada. The Italian-, German-, Hungarian- and Greek-Canadians — remember, half of Toronto is non-Anglo-Saxon — come from civilizations where drinking wine is an inherent part of everyday life. Modest cafés in their home countries offer wine at reasonable prices to the working people of the neighbourhood. In Canada, most of the restaurant and café trade is of non-Anglo-Saxon origin; immigrants have brought their special skills and applied them in these businesses for the benefit of all. Yet the liquor licensing boards in many provinces seem to be made up of people whose backgrounds are steeped in an Anglo-Saxon morality which includes a less than relaxed attitude about the consumption of alcohol; the result — many of these places cannot get liquor licenses.

We have come a long way since the nineteen-fifties, but there are more than vestigial remains of temperance thinking. Why can't a restaurant or café, providing it complies with the usual fire and health laws, automatically serve wine? Why must it go through the process of a waiting period and have to employ professional legal services to get a liquor license? And why is it that our laws favour the prosperous? Only the "better restaurants," that is, the higher-priced ones, seem to get wine and liquor licenses. We, the taxpayers, have to pay for all the inconveniences attached to our archaic alcoholic traditions.

Everything about the sale of wine through the liquor commissions in this country reeks of indifference and amateurism. Most of the wine catalogues, except for those of Quebec and Newfoundland, do not signify what year the wine was made. It is important to know the year of the harvest or vintage of imported wines since the quality and price vary accordingly, and, of course, the younger the wine, the cheaper it normally is. Yet most liquor outlets don't bother with anything except a small *v* for vintage beside the wine, and many don't even bother with that.

Unless the wine is displayed openly on shelves, and this is still not the general practice in Canada, you'll never know if you've been overcharged for a bad year until the wine is presented to you after payment.

All enlightened wine stores in the United States and England offer cases of young wine at reasonable prices for keeping — an excellent merchandising practice. It may be kept in *their* cellars (at minimal or no cost to you), or in your own, until you decide that it is mature enough for drinking. Often, the merchant will advise you when it should be opened. This kind of buying saves you from paying top prices later for the same wine in its matured state. Most British and American merchants list the same wine of several different years at different prices. No such service is offered at any of our Canadian liquor outlets. If our commissions run out of one year, they just substitute the wine of a later vintage. There never appears to be a lowering of prices if the wine is of a later year or inferior vintage.

One or two other points about the poor service at our liquor commissions: How are the wines stored? Wine should be kept at a controlled, cool temperature. But how often is an expensive, chateau-bottled wine brought out from a nice warm spot near the radiator? And the clerks don't seem to have much respect for the bottles they handle: the sediment in the wine is shaken through the bottles as they bang them down on the counter like bowling pins.

Prices in the liquor outlets are exorbitant by any standards. Although state tax is paid by wine merchants in such places as New York, and Washington, DC, the wines available there cost far less than those at the Ontario and Quebec liquor commissions. British Columbia, Nova Scotia, and Saskatchewan are just as expensive as Quebec and Ontario; until recently, Alberta marked its wines up the least. George Bain, wine columnist for the *Globe and Mail*, gives the following figures as one of many examples of what he calls the "hornswoggling" and "bilking and fleecing" of the public: a red bordeaux, Château Ducru-Beaucaillou, 1967, costing $49 a case in New York ($4.08 a bottle), costs

$100.40 a case ($9.20 a bottle) from the Ontario Liquor commission. The price comparison between the Canadian and us outlets was made at the same time — November 1971. Ontario's prices, at least, are sure to have risen since then.

In Quebec, the province with the most wine drinkers and the greatest selection of wines, the commission charges about $1.90 for a Préfontaine wine. In Paris, the same wine sells for $0.40 a litre (ten ounces more than we get in the Quebec bottle); Quebec buys the wine for $0.60 a litre — the mark up is not insignificant.

It is important to note that Alberta and Manitoba are the only provinces that do not put a higher mark-up on imported wines than on domestic wines. Canadian wines are favoured financially by all the other provincial liquor outlets. These higher mark-ups, according to Mr. Bain, "are plain and simply tariffs, which no province has the constitutional right to apply to foreign trade."

I don't know why Canadian wines are taxed less, since, in my opinion, the Canadian wine industry has not distinguished itself in the excellence of its product. The wine has a very high acidity. Andrew Pellar of Andres (Canada) Ltd. says, "Canadian grapes are known to contain more acid than European varieties. If you imagined that drinking a great deal of some Canadian wines gives you a headache, you are probably right." Since I do not care for Canadian wines I have not included them in this chapter. Too much patriotism can be the "last refuge of a scoundrel" — to use Samuel Johnson's phrase — and in this case can give you a headache as well.

Wines from the Bordeaux region of France are generally lighter but not less flavourful than those of the Burgundy region.† Red bordeaux is called claret in English. Far more varieties of bordeaux wines exist than of burgundies, and bordeaux is more abundant. That is why burgundies are usually more expensive. The wines from the Côtes-du-

---

† In the wine listings that follow in this chapter, Bordeaux and Burgundy, when given as regional headings, are understood to include only wines from those regions of France, not bordeaux- or burgundy-types.

Rhône in France are not considered as fine as the best burgundies and bordeaux, but they definitely hold their own among the choice of the burgundies and bordeaux in our liquor stores. The Côtes-du-Rhône are full-bodied and keep well but not, of course, as well as the bordeaux.

In 1855 a committee of wine brokers from Bordeaux divided many of the vineyards in the Médoc area into five classes. The system is numerical; the top grade, for example, is *premier cru*, which translates literally as "first growth," but really means vineyard of the top class. Any bottle of wine listed among the five growths is of a fine quality and gets a high market price. There is a lower listing called *cru bourgeois*, or bourgeois growth, which is below the fifth rank, but of an honourable classification.

George Bain gives this simple explanation of Burgundy wines: "The pyramid in Burgundy is constructed like this: At the base, the (relatively) large quantity of wine entitled to be called simply, Burgundy; next, wine of the two Côtes, the Côte de Nuits and the Côte de Beaune, and, at a half-step above, the same with the addition of the word, 'villages'; wines of the communes, such as Gevrey-Chambertin, Vosne-Romanée, or, in the Côte de Beaune, Pommard and Volnay; finally, at the top, the individually named vineyards."

Most provincial liquor boards in Canada will import wines of your selection if you write to a shipper in Europe yourself for a list of their wines. Send your selection to the liquor board and it will import the wine for you. Many people feel they can choose a better wine for the price than the liquor commissions. Often a group of people will get together to do this, since the minimum order must be a case lot, twelve bottles. Theoretically, no extra charge is added by the liquor commission for the service, but of course you must pay the same amount of money that would be charged at the retail liquor outlets for your choice of wine, had it been part of their regular offering. In my experience, ordering in this manner winds up being very expensive — perhaps prohibitively so.

It is difficult to write about the best buys in our liquor

commissions because the catalogues are always out of date. All the provincial governments put out fancy booklets with such added features as Blood Alcohol Charts, and pictures of provincial beauty spots on the covers. Because of their elaborate make-up, these books are revised only once a year, if that. But their stock is always changing and, of course, prices go up. Perhaps if the price list in these books was mimeographed every month, instead of printed once a year, the customer would be better informed and the cost to the taxpayers would be less.

The biggest wine lists in the country belong to Quebec and Ontario, with Quebec having the edge on Ontario by a big margin. The current Quebec catalogue dates back to 1970 and is a terribly disorganized book. Fortunately for me, I live in Ottawa and am able to check out the wines at the excellent new self-service wine store in Hull. The set-up here is in sharp contrast to the highly confused way in which liquor outlets are usually organized in Quebec — you see nothing and you have nothing to write on.

In the pages that follow, there are some discrepancies in the descriptions given for the same wine from province to province. This is because I have copied the precise description of the wine from the catalogue of each provincial liquor board. Here then, in my opinion, are some of the better imported wines in each province that sell for under $3 — and some higher-priced ones that are worth buying for keeping in your cellar. (Since this is basically a food book, I include only table wines in my selection.) But don't be too surprised if some of my suggestions are not available when you want them. Everything changes quickly and every price goes up in the liquor commissions of our country — and up and up and up.

QUEBEC

Quebec not only has the best selection of cheap wines in Canada; it also has a good choice of Armagnac, Marc de

Bourgogne and Calvados non-sweet "digestifs," to be drunk
after dinner, like brandy. The quality of the Marc is especially high for the price — $8.15. Buy it instead of the Cour-
voisier or Rémy Martin cognac. The only way I can
describe the taste is fruity but with intense brandy-like
overtones — well worth trying. It is distilled from the pulp
or *marc* that remains after the grapes have been pressed
for wine and the juice has run off. By the way, an unusual
and rather snob aperitif for sale is Pineau des Charentes,
which may be procured for $3.60. It has a rather astringent
taste.

The greatest selection of wines, cheap and expensive, in
the Quebec liquor outlets is, of course, French. Since
French wines are just as good as, and usually better than,
the wines of other nations, I've concentrated on them.

Quebec sells inexpensive red and white imported wines
(as well as domestic) in gallon jugs. I wish all our liquor
outlets would do this: it means a considerable saving for
the customer. One gallon, or 160 ounces, of Malbec bor-
deaux-type† rouge, a rough but drinkable wine, is $6.10.
There are over six bottles in every jug and one bottle of the
same wine costs $1.25, so you pay less than $1.00 a bottle if
you buy in quantity.

A little more expensive, but still cheap and good by
Canadian standards, are the following brands of wine sold
by the gallon. Remember that you get more for your money
if you buy by the gallon, but usually it is possible to buy a
single bottle of the wine as well.

RED

Ben Afnam — Algerian, bordeaux-type	$8.60
Bordeaux††	$7.60
(Slightly better quality than the Malbec)	
St. Emilion	$9.90
(A more robust bordeaux)	

†It is called bordeaux, but it really is Spanish in origin.
††In the listings in this chapter, the regional designations are by country of
origin (*e.g.* German or Hungarian) except for French wines, which are
listed as from Bordeaux, Burgundy, Côtes-du-Rhône, etc.

WHITE

Grand Supérieur — a bordeaux	$9.00
Entre-Deux-Mers — also a bordeaux	$8.75
(Light and drinkable, but not in stock when I asked for it. They said they were trying to get some more.)	

The remainder of the Quebec selections mentioned here are available only in single bottles.

RED *(under $3.00)*

Vins Divers
from France

Simplet	$1.75
(As the table says, a simple wine that pleases)	
Corbières	$1.65
Fitou	$1.85
Préfontaines	$1.90

Bordeaux

Domaine de l'Ile Margaux 1966	$2.10
(A low price for an excellent year)	
Mont de Monts	$2.10
La Tour Pavillon 1967	$2.85
(A Médoc worth trying)	

Côtes-du-Rhône

Margnat Monopole	$1.50
(An excellent wine for the price — full bodied)	
Côteau de Languedoc	$1.80
Tavel rosé	$2.75
(For many, the best rosé in France)	

Burgundy

Beaujolais Puits d'Amour 1969	$2.35
Beaujolais Pisse-Dru 1969	$2.50
(Quite good and the name is a conversation piece)	

RED   (over $3.00)

Bordeaux

Château Meyney 1964	$5.00

(Chateau-bottled, a bourgeois *cru* ranked just after the classified growths, for keeping)

Château Gruaud-Larose 1965	$5.40

(Chateau-bottled, second-growth wine that is priced low in the Quebec Liquor Board, for keeping)

Château Grand-Pontet 1964 — a St. Emilion	$5.50

(Also for keeping, chateau-bottled)

WHITE   (under $3.00)

French (various regions)

Blanc de Blancs — "Canard Blanc"	$1.70

(Very light)

Muscadet, Sèvre and Maine — Loire	$2.35

(Tart, good with shellfish)

Blanc de Mer — Loire	$2.20
Sancerre 1970 — Loire	$2.75

(A beautiful wine for the price)

Clos Ste-Odile — Alsatian	$2.90

WHITE   (over $3.00 but very good value and
exceptional in taste)

French (various regions)

Pouilly Fumé or Blanc Fumé de

Pouilly 1970 — from the Loire	$3.30

(Fruity with a deep, flowery after-taste)

Pouilly Fuissé — a burgundy	$4.00 — $4.50

(A good selection of this fine wine in the Quebec Liquor Board)

Two Swiss white wines that are interesting and most enjoyable when drunk chilled on a warm sunny day are

Fendant Etolie du Valais	$1.60 (half-bottle)
(A light, slightly bubbly wine; only in half-bottles when I checked the stores)	
Neuchatel 1969 Goutte d'Or	$3.05
(A light, slightly bubbly wine; travels well)	

ONTARIO

Ontario has the second largest selection of wines in Canada. The prices of LCBO wines are generally higher than those of Quebec and there is not the same large choice of drinkable wines under $3. Inexplicably, no imported wine is sold in gallon jugs in Ontario. The selection of German white wines is the most extensive in Canada but they are expensive. The LCBO bottles its own Spanish sherry and the result is a reasonably priced (around $2.10) and a very tolerable aperitif.

RED *(under $3.00)*

Bordeaux
Bordeaux Supérieur	$2.45
Roc Rouge	$2.45
St. Emilion 1967	$2.95
(LCBO used to have a 1966, a better year, for $2.85)	

Burgundy
Mommessin Export	$2.20
Beaujolais Puits d'Amour 1967	$2.75

Portuguese
Dao Red	$2.00

Italian
Valpolicella 1969 (Folonari)	$2.30
Bardolino (Folonari)	$2.85

Spanish
Yago $1.80
(One of the cheapest imported red
wines for sale)

RED   *(over $3.00, but worth tasting
if you want to splurge)*

Côtes-du-Rhône
Crozes Hermitage 1969 $3.95

Bordeaux
Château Roquevieille 1966 $3.65
(An excellent year)

Burgundy
Beaune Domaine de Saux 1966 $5.95

WHITE   *(under $3.00)*

Italian
Frascati (Patrizia) 1969 $1.80
South African
Paarl Riesling $2.10
Yugoslav
Traminac $2.05
(Now temporarily off the LCBO list;
this popular wine has a fruity but acid
taste.)

Bordeaux
Blanc de Blancs $2.30
(Dry, light, and always drinkable –
costs $1.70 in Quebec)
Entre-Deux-Mers 26 oz. $2.30
(Always drinkable – costs $8.75 a
gallon in Quebec)
L'Ancre Verte $2.10
(Always drinkable)
Mouton-Cadet $2.55
(Always drinkable)

WHITE *(over $3.00, but again,*
good value if you want to splurge)

German
Rudesheimer Rosengarten Spätlese —
a Rhine wine $3.40
(A spätlese wine signifies high qual-
ity, made from slightly riper, later
grapes, and with no artificial sweetening. Full bodied.)

Burgundy
Puligny-Montrachet $5.35
($4.25 in Quebec)

MANITOBA

At one time Manitoba was a prohibition province. Now it
has some of the most relaxed liquor laws in Canada. Anyone over eighteen years of age can drink without his parents. Minors may drink with their parents in a licensed
dining spot; sports fans have the right to guzzle beer at race
tracks and games; and the blue-collar worker, if he drinks,
can have one-ounce shots in a carpeted "beverage room"
and pay from twenty to fifty cents less than in cocktail
lounges and cabarets.

The wines listed in Manitoba used to be cheaper than
those of Ontario, but in May 1972 the liquor control board
raised the prices of wines considerably.

RED *(under $3.00)*

Bordeaux
Bergerac Dordogne $2.00
(An excellent wine for the price)
Corbières Vin Rouge $1.80
Mouton-Cadet $2.55

Hungarian
Egri Bikaver $2.00

Spanish
Yago $1.60

Italian
Valpolicella (Folonari) $2.50

WHITE   *(under $3.00)*

Bordeaux
Cordier Château Tanesse (v) $2.50

Burgundy
Mommessin Mâcon $2.50

German
Liebfraumilch (Schmitt's) $2.75

WHITE   *(over $3.00)*

Burgundy
Pouilly Fuissé (v) '69 (B&G) $3.45

SASKATCHEWAN

All the wines are very expensive in this province, and there is hardly any choice at all. There isn't even a little *v* for vintage year.

RED

Valpolicella (Folonari) $2.20

WHITE

Bordeaux
Graves (Eschenauer) $2.60

South African
Paarl Riesling $2.25

German
Liebfraumilch (Guntrum) $2.80
Liebfraumilch (Schmitt's) $2.80

ALBERTA

The prices of imported wines in Alberta are cheaper than those of Ontario and some other provinces. There is a relatively high proportion of sauternes, or sweet white wines, on the Alberta list.

RED   (under $3.00)

French (various regions)
Bergerac (v) $1.70
Côtes-du-Rhône (v) $1.85
St. Julien — a bordeaux $2.30
Mouton-Cadet — a bordeaux $2.50

Italian
Bardolino $1.75
Chianti Classico Brolio (Ricasoli) (v) $1.80

Spanish
Yago (Rioja Santiago Tinto) $1.50

Portuguese
Dao Terras Altas $1.65
(Considered by some to be better than the Spanish Yago)

The best buy in red wine over $3.00 is
Château Pontet Canet (v) $5.90

WHITE   *(under $3.00)*

German

Moselmaid $2.15

Italian

Orvieto (Ruffino) $1.75

Bordeaux

Graves $1.85

WHITE   *(over $3.00)*

Italian

Asti Spumante $3.40
(An excellent sparkling wine that is much cheaper
than champagne; $4.55 in Ontario)

Burgundy

Pouilly Fuissé (v) $5.10

The Alberta liquor commission has a small selection of high quality wines and a few liquors that are printed on a special list, other than their catalogue. For example, they offer a fine burgundy, Chambertin Clos de Bèze for $10.90. This, of course, is high, but Ontario offers the equivalent in quality Chambertin for $16.75. The store manager of your local liquor outlet should have a printed sheet with the list of higher-priced wines.

BRITISH COLUMBIA

The British Columbia government taxes its own provincial wines the least, while imported wines are heavily taxed. Canadian wines of non-British-Columbian origin are somewhere in between. The wine list, given the wealth and population of the province, is the worst in Canada. The choice is sparse, and the catalogue itself is very disorganized. White wines are listed with reds, and French Chambolle-Musigny, a fine rich red burgundy, is placed in the same listing as Crabbie's Green Ginger wine from Scotland. In this particular listing of "specialty items," it is impossible for the novice to tell if he is ordering a red or white wine, never mind the vintage. The names of the shippers are not marked in the catalogue. I am told that a new list for British Columbia is about to appear. It can only be an improvement.

RED *(under $3.00)*

Portuguese
Dao $1.95

Spanish
Yago (Tinto) $1.65

Chile
Pinot Red $2.15

A good red wine over $3.00 is *Chambolle-Musigny*, a fine burgundy, $7.75.

WHITE *(under $3.00)*

South African
Paarl Riesling $1.85

Bordeaux
Blanc de Blancs (Calvet) $1.85
Graves Supérieur $2.10

WHITE *(over $3.00)*

Burgundy
Meursault $4.95
(Very reasonable; it is $7.50 in Ontario. I hope B C has a large stock.)

NOVA SCOTIA

The wines are expensive. As in all the Atlantic provinces, there is a large selection of rums. Halifax has a self-service "Specialty Store" on 1445 Hollis where the wines I've listed are sold. Did you know that it is illegal in Nova Scotia to give wines or spirits away as gifts? Figure out the reasoning behind that one.

RED   *(under $3.00)*

Italian
Valpolicella (Lamberti) $1.95

Bordeaux
St. Emilion $2.70
La Tour Pavillion $3.00

Burgundy
Mommessin Export $2.15

If you can go over $3.00, try the *Château du Taillan*, especially if it's chateau-bottled. No year is listed.

WHITE   *(under $3.00)*

French
Entre-Deux-Mers $1.90
Muscadet $2.35

South Africa
Paarl Riesling $1.95

NEW BRUNSWICK

Lots of rum, little imported wine, all very expensive.

RED

Spanish
Yago $2.00

French (various regions)
Préfontaines $2.25
Médoc $2.75
Vin d'honneur (Margnat) $2.40

WHITE

Préfontaines $2.25

PRINCE EDWARD ISLAND

Again, more rum than anything else. The imported wine selection is practically non-existent.

RED

Spanish
Yago $2.00

Bordeaux
Médoc (B & G) $2.90

WHITE

Bordeaux (B & G) $2.45

NEWFOUNDLAND

This little province puts many of the bigger ones to shame. The Newfoundland Liquor Commission (NLC) selection of wines is far more extensive that that of rich British Columbia, and the catalogue is organized in a sophisticated, readable manner. Remarkably enough, it describes the vintage year and suggests certain wines for keeping. The NLC is the only liquor commission in Canada to do this.

Newfoundland has a huge selection of rums, including the famous Screech, bottled by the Newfoundland Liquor Commission. However, the *cognoscenti* go after a rum called London Dock, which costs $7.75 for 26-3/4 ounces.

Another Newfoundland curiosity is Newman's Port ($3.25). Newman's has been sending large quantities of port from Portugal to mature in Newfoundland, a practice that dates back 300 years. In 1679, a vessel laden with port from Oporto was chased by pirates from the Bay of Biscay. She finally went to St. John's and then continued on her way to London. Upon arrival, it was discovered that the port had changed; it was mellower and had a fine bouquet. The laying-up time in Newfoundland had improved the wine; so, the practice has been continued to this day.

The wines in Newfoundland are not inexpensive and many of the more interesting wines are over $3.00.

RED   (under $3.00)

Bordeaux
St. Emilion $2.90

Burgundy
Mâcon (Bouchard Aîné) $2.20

Spanish
Yago $2.00

WHITE   (under $3.00)

Bordeaux
Graves (Cruse) $2.20

South African
Paarl Riesling $2.20

There is a large selection of good wines for keeping for over $3.00. All are French.

RED

Bordeaux
Château St. Pierre Sevaistre $5.90
St. Julien 1966
Château Ducru Beaucaillou $7.75
St. Julien 1962

Burgundy
Nuits St. Georges Les Roncières 1964 $6.10

WHITE

Meursault Clos de Mazeray 1967, a burgundy $4.60
(1/2 bottle for $2.35)

All this concern about wine is rather ridiculous when you
think that each Canadian drinks only an average of nine-
tenths of a gallon of wine annually. In France and in Italy
the annual per capita consumption in the 1960's was over
thirty gallons.

The wine many Canadians prefer is not even made from
grapes. Prairie farmers, miners' wives and northerners
drink wines made from apples, loganberries and blueberries, usually sold in gallon jugs. Honey wine has a large
following of Canadian women, who like its sweetness and
colour. Loganberries grow only in Vancouver Island, on
the Saanich peninsula at the southern end, where conditions
are ideal. For many years the only wine sold in British
Columbia was made from the loganberry.

Moncton has a winery (Normandie) that was basically set up for blueberry wine. The berries were picked by Indians. The wine is still sold in New Brunswick and P E I liquor outlets. There is also a wine called Catawba, one of the cheapest sold in Canada. One member of the Ontario Legislature once referred to it as "block and tackle" because "you drink a bottle, run a block and are prepared to tackle anyone".

Table wine, that is, a grape wine served with meals, was not a big seller until the nineteen-forties; in 1946, it accounted for less than one-half of one per cent of the wines sold in Ontario annually. Twenty-two years later, in 1968, thirty-two per cent of all wine sold was table wine.

The radical change in the drinking habits of Canadians is partly due to travel and prosperity, but especially to the new immigrants from southern wine-drinking countries. Previously, Canadians came from northern countries where beer and strong spirits were popular. Now, Toronto has more Italians than Florence.

FOR NON-WINE-DRINKERS

Beer, of course, is the best of all authentic Canadian drinks. Try the local beers, especially in the Maritimes. They are cheaper and just as good as Molson's and Carling's. I am particularly fond of Canadian ales. These are somewhat heavier and more alcoholic than lagers and are widely respected, not just in Canada, but abroad. On special national occasions Canadian companies sometimes produce an extra stock with a higher alcoholic content than regular beer. For example, Labatt's made one for the Canadian centennial celebrations in 1967. I prefer native Canadian lagers and ales to those English pub beers that are now being made and sold here under Canadian licence. They have a clearer, cleaner and less complicated taste than their English rivals.

Another excellent Canadian drink is rye whiskey. Good choices are Seagram's Crown Royal and V.O., and Hiram Walker's Canadian Club. Crown Royal deserves its inter-

national reputation: its mellow flavour makes a very satisfying after-dinner drink that offers an alternative to brandy.
There is also a Canadian liqueur made from native whis-
kies — Tiedy's Canadian Liqueur. It is marketed in the
United States.

Remember when you're travelling, it's rum in the East,
rye whiskey in the West and wine in Quebec. Well . . . not
only wine in Quebec. Apple cider, twenty per cent proof
spirits, went on sale legally in Quebec last year in grocery
stores. The new cider industry has been having trouble ful-
filling the demand for its product. The sales figures have
surpassed ten million dollars in the first year and the producers expect to double their sales in 1972.

Conclusion
— an All-Canadian Menu

I suppose after six chapters about Canadian food, a Canadian menu is in order. I've had many different and "typical" Canadian meals described to me. One of the more intriguing ones was prepared and consumed at a Quebec fishing club. The diners whiled away most of the afternoon and evening eating partridge *pâté*, wild ducks with grapes, trout cooked in cream, and spiced caribou haunches. Ten courses were consumed; most had been prepared by the diners. Between each course they revived themselves with a *trou Normand*, what you might loosely call in English a snort of Calvados. Since many French Canadians' ancestors came from Normandy, 300 years back, sticklers for authenticity will be relieved to hear that the diners observed this custom of knocking back ten glasses of apple brandy throughout the meal. From a sociological and historical point of view the whole dinner would have been ruined for the serious student if the diners had drunk Mexican tequila.

Another dinner flaunting Canadian recipes and ingredients was recently served to an international gourmet association, the *Chaine de Rotisseurs*. The chefs of the Ritz Carleton and Chateau Champlain in Montreal impressed the foreign visitors with fresh periwinkles, and minced balls of seal and whale meat. My menu has no game — I leave that to the woodsmen — and no whale or seal meat, since only hotel chefs can find a supply of that. Here, though, is an all-Canadian dinner based on ingredients and recipes in *The Gourmet's Canada*.

Hors-d'oeuvres
British Columbia Gravlax
(marinated salmon with dill)
Smoked Arctic Char from Labrador
with a garnish of Atlantic Shrimp
Fresh Ontario Caviar

White Rolls (served hot in the style of The Marshlands Inn,
New Brunswick)

Soup
Saskatchewan Beet Borsch

Main Course
Veau dans le Chaudron from Quebec (loin of veal cooked
in Canadian beer or cider with red cabbage)
Wild Rice from Manitoba with Celery and Mushrooms
Local Corn on the Cob, or Asparagus (if in season)

Dessert
Mennonite Carrot Cake
or
Layered Maple Pie

Selected Cheeses
Aged Ontario Cheddar
Quebec Oka
Fromage Ile d'Orléans

Honeyed nuts made with Prairie Buckwheat Honey

Coffee

As an accompaniment to the meal, I would recommend a French white burgundy, such as Meursault, followed by a chateau-bottled bordeaux, perhaps Chateau Gruaud-Larose. (A good year to select for both wines is 1966, if you can get it.) If you wish to be thoroughly patriotic and drink Canadian, I would suggest that you drink a Canadian beer or ale throughout the meal and have a straight rye whiskey with the honeyed nuts and coffee. You'll need it: anyone who can get through everything on this menu should be in line for an Order of Canada medal.

Appendix

A bibliography of Canadian cook-books

I have profited especially by three Canadian cook-books: Madame Benoit's *Canadiana Cookbook* covers the country from coast to coast. Its recipes are written with gastronomic knowledge as well as historical accuracy. Madame Benoit has done tremendous service to this aspect of our heritage. Savella Stechishin has written an exhaustive book about Ukrainian food — *Traditional Ukrainian Cookery*. Her recipes come mainly from Ukrainian-Canadians living on the Prairies. She, too, combines historical accuracy with a cook's experience; she knows that short cuts are not always the way to better cooking. Edna Staebler has written an amusing recipe book about Mennonite country cooking in Ontario — *Food that Really Schmecks*. Her notes are not as scholarly as Mrs. Stechishin's but they are nevertheless a contribution to the culinary cause.

In addition, countless small community efforts and church- and benevolent-society publications have broadened my knowledge of cooking in this country. I hope they increase and multiply.

I am setting out below all the various cook-books and collections of recipes that I have had occasion to use in preparing this book, as well as those that I have in my library. This is not intended to be a complete list of Canadian cook-books or of literature on the gastronomic arts of Canada — far from it. I have made no attempt to list everything ever written in Canada — just those things I have personally come across. By way of exception, the list does include, for the information of the reader, a very small number of local recipe collections which I have not consulted directly but which are cited by other Canadian authors. These local collections will generally be available only by writing to the association or group involved.

The vast majority of books in the bibliography have been published in Canada. The others also deal with Canadian food, in whole or in part, but they have been published elsewhere. General cook-books and encyclopedias that deal with international-style cooking or classical French cooking are not included in the list; nor are reference books to the fish, meats, vegetables and grains of Canada, although I have, of course, consulted many such sources. Canadian recipe-collections put together by small local associations, church groups, etc. are sometimes undated and are often privately published. In these cases it is not possible to give complete bibliographic data. However, as much information as is available is given below. Such collections are often brought out annually for the duration of their existence; for example, the Winnipeg Hadassah's recipe collections have been published annually for almost half a century. Unfortunately, I can't guarantee in each case that the collection I refer to is the latest edition, but I have attempted to cite the most recent. The list begins with books that deal with Canadian cooking in general, and then goes on to books, booklets, etc. relating to cooking in each province.

Canadian cook-books — general

Aitken, Kate. *Kate Aitken's Canadian Cook Book.* Toronto: William Collins Sons and Co. Ltd., 1950.

Benoit, Jehane. *The Canadiana Cookbook,* a complete heritage of Canadian cooking. Toronto: Pagurian Press Ltd., 1970.

Benoit, Jehane. *Encyclopedia of Canadian Cuisine.* Toronto: Canadian Homes Magazine, second printing 1963.

Berton, Janet and Pierre. *The Centennial Food Guide,* A Century of Good Eating. Toronto, Montreal: The Canadian Centennial Library (McClelland & Stewart and Weekend magazine), 1966.

Brown, Dale. *American Cooking: The Northwest.* New York: Time-Life Books, 1970.

Canada. Department of Agriculture. *Food — à la canadienne.* Ottawa: The Queen's Printer, 1967.

The Canadian Home Economics Association. *The Laura Secord Canadian Cook Book.* Montreal: McClelland & Stewart Ltd., 1966, fifth printing 1971.

Leonard, Jonathan Norton. *American Cooking: New England,* with supplementary chapters on the cooking of Eastern Canada. New York: Time-Life Books, 1970.

— *The Best of Three Worlds,* a bilingual book of rare recipes & entertaining menus from French Canada, English Canada and

France. Toronto: "Les amis de la maison francaise," Roth-
mans of Pall Mall Canada Ltd.

Canadian cook-books — Newfoundland

— *C.L.A. Cook Book,* compiled and contributed by the Mem-
bers of the Columbus Ladies' Association, St. John's Nfld.
— *Newfoundlanders' Favourite Recipes,* a collection of recipes
from Newfoundland & Labrador, compiled by the Friendship
Unit of the United Church Women of the First United
Church, Mount Pearl, Nfld.

Canadian cook-books — Prince Edward Island

— *The Art of Cooking in Souris,* Souris Curling Club, Souris,
P.E.I.
— *Cook Book,* the annual edition of the Prince Edward Island
Guardian-Evening Patriot's cook-book supplement, Char-
lottetown, P.E.I.

Canadian cook-books — Nova Scotia

The Halifax Jaycettes. *Tastes of Nova Scotia.* Dartmouth,
printed by Munroe-Woods Litho Limited, 1969, second edition
1970.

Lunenberg Hospital Society Ladies Auxiliary. *Dutch Oven,* a
collection of recipes published in Lunenburg on its two hundredth anniversary, 1953 (cited in *The Canadiana Cookbook,*
p. 94).

Marie Nightingale. *Out of Old Nova Scotia Kitchens,* a collection of traditional recipes of Nova Scotia and the stories of the
people who cooked them. New York: Charles Scribner's Sons,
1971.

Women's Institute of Nova Scotia, Blue Mountain Women's
Institute. *Our favourite Recipes.* Blue Mountain, N.S.

Zinck, Hilda M. *Green Shutters Cook Book.* Lunenburg: Pro-
gress Enterprise Co. Ltd., 1959, (second edition).

Zion United Church, Zion Guild. *Perkins' Hearth,* a collection
of recipes published in Liverpool, N.S. on its two hundredth
anniversary, 1959 (cited in *The Canadiana Cookbook,* p. 94).

Canadian cook-books —New Brunswick

The New Brunswick Home Economists' Association. *New Brunswick Recipes.*

Volunteer Fire Department, Kingston Peninsula, N.B. *"Our Favorites" Cook Book.*

Canadian cook-books — Quebec

Asselin, E. Donald. *A French-Canadian Cookbook.* Edmonton: M.G. Hurtig Ltd., 1968, second printing 1971.

Batist, Bessie W. *A Treasury for my Daughter,* a reference book of Jewish Festivals with menus and recipes; recipe section edited by Sarah Ein, Anne Warshaw & Mary Davids. Montreal: The Ethel Epstein Ein Chapter of Hadassah, 1950.

Bouchard, Cecile Roland. Le Pinereau, *L'Art culinaire au Saguenay — lac Saint-Jean,* collections recettes typiques. Ottawa: Leméac, 1971.

Clark, Morton G. *French-American Cooking from New Orleans to Quebec.* New York: Funk & Wagnalls, 1967.

Lapointe, Suzanne. *Fondues et Flambées de Maman Lapointe.* Montreal: Les Editions de L'homme, 1970.

Marécat, Claire. *Le Poisson dans la Cuisine Québécoise.* Montreal: Les Editions La Presse, 1972.

Saumart, Ingrid et Cousineau, Louise. *Recettes pour chômeurs et grévistes.* Les Editions Québécoises, 1971.

Shoub, Lilian, editor and compiler. "Wonders of the Palate," a collection of favorite recipes, contributed by Members & Friends of the National Council of Jewish Women of Canada. Montreal section, 1966.

Vineberg, Trina. *Family Heirlooms,* a collection of treasured recipes. Toronto, Montreal: McClelland & Stewart Ltd., 1965.

Canadian cook-books — Ontario

Cartwright, Susan and Edmonds, Alan. *Capital Cookery,* Hundreds of recipes from the kitchens of Canadian Prime Ministers revealed for the very first time. Toronto: Pagurian Press Ltd., 1970.

— *The Canadian Home Cook Book.* Compiled by Ladies of Toronto & Chief Cities and Towns in Canada. Toronto: Hunter Rose & Co., 1877, reprinted by Coles Publishing Company, 1971.

Clarke, Anne. *The Dominion Cook Book,* containing recipes in all the departments, including sickroom cooking, 1898. Toronto: George I. McLeod Limited, 1898.

Denison, G.E.S. *The Canadian Family Cookbook* by Prominent Canadian Ladies. Toronto, 1914.

Gregory, Annie R. *Canada's Favourite Cook Book.* 1907.

— *Mrs. Clarke's Cookery Book.* Toronto: Grip Publishing, 1883.

Staebler, Edna. *Food that Really Schmecks,* Mennonite Country Cooking. Toronto: Ryerson Press-McGraw-Hill Company of Canada Ltd., 1968.

Staebler, Edna. *Sauerkraut and Enterprise.* Toronto: McClelland & Stewart Ltd., 1966, reprinted 1970.

Canadian cook-books — the Prairies & British Columbia

— *Canadian Mennonite Cookbook,* formerly *Altona Women's Institute Cookbook,* 1965. Altona, Manitoba: D. W. Friesen & Sons Ltd., fourteenth printing 1971.

— *Centennial Cook Book.* Ukrainian & Modern Favorites dedicated to the Pioneers by the Ukrainian Women's Association of Canada, O Pchilka Branch, 1967, North Battleford, Sask.

— *Galley Slaves' Guide,* recipes compiled by the Ladies Sailing Group, West Vancouver Yacht Club. West Vancouver: J. J. Douglas Ltd., 1972.

Goplen, Henrietta. *Saskatchewan Sportsman's Gourmet Guide.* Saskatoon: The Western Producer, 1968.

Lewis, Gwen, compiler. *Buckskin Cookery,* a collection of recipes from old-timers & natives of British Columbia. EMP Press, 1961.

— *The Mennonite Treasury of Recipes,* favourite recipes for large groups & families, contributed by all Canadian Mennonites, Steinbach, Manitoba.

— *Music in your Menus,* compiled and published by the Women's Committee, Winnipeg Symphony Orchestra, Winnipeg, first edition 1964.

— *Prairie Pantry Cook Book* (cited in *The Canadiana Cookbook,* p. 144).

— *Recipes by Lehava,* cook-book of Lehava Chapter Pioneer Women's Organization, Winnipeg, fourth edition 1969-70.

Regina Chapter of Hadassah. *Cook Book,* Regina.

Saskatchewan Golden Jubilee Committee. *Saskatchewan Homemakers' Kitchens,* published by Saskatchewan Homemakers' Club for their Golden Jubilee in 1955 (cited in *The Canadiana Cookbook,* p. 156).

— *Stampede Barbecue Cookbook* of the Calgary Rotary Club (cited in *The Centennial Food Guide,* p. 88).

Stechishin, Savella. *Traditional Ukrainian Cookery.* Winnipeg: Trident Press Ltd., 1971.

Wilson, Muriel. *Colonist Cookbook of Victoria* (cited in *The Canadiana Cookbook,* p. 182).

Winnipeg Hadassah. *Shoppers' Guide & Cook Book.* Winnipeg, 1970.

Winnipeg Hadassah, Wizo Bazaar. *Souvenir Book,* May 17, 1972.

Canadian cook-books — wild foods:
Northern and other remote areas

Angier, Bradford. *Wilderness Cookery,* 1961, Harrisburg, Pa.: Stackpole Books, 1970.

Berglund, Berndt and Bolsby, Clare E. *The Edible Wild;* a complete cookbook and guide to Edible Wild Plants in Canada. Toronto: Pagurian Press Ltd., 1971.

Boorman, Sylvia. *Wild Plums in Brandy,* a cookery book of wild foods in Canada, Toronto: McGraw-Hill of Canada Ltd., 1962.

Carver, Lawton. *The Compact Book of Fish & Game Cookery,* New York: Gramercy Publishing Co., 1966.

Dore, William G., *Wild Rice,* Canada Department of Agriculture, Ottawa: Queen's Printer, 1969.

Ellis, Eleanor A., *Northern Cookbook,* issued under authority of the Minister of Indian Affairs and Northern Development, Ottawa: Queen's Printer 1967, reprinted 1968.

Gaertner, Erika E., *Harvest without Planting,* Eating & Nibbling off the Land. Chalk River, Ontario: Erika E. Gaertner, 1967, third impression 1969.

Gibbons, Euell, *Stalking the Wild Asparagus.* New York: David McKay Company Inc., 1962.

Leclerc, Claire L., *120 recettes aux champignons du Québec,* Québec: Editions Garneau, 1971.

Canada. Minister of Northern Affairs & National Resources. *Remarkable Recipes for Sweet-Grass Buffalo.* Ottawa: Queen's Printer, 1961.

Guides to Canadian Restaurants

Brown, Jeremy & Adilman, Sid. *Dining Out in Toronto,* a complete and critical guide to Toronto's best restaurants, and a manual for practically everything else worth knowing about the city. Don Mills, Ontario: Greywood Publishing Ltd., 1971.

Divinsky, N. J. *Guide to Good Food in Metro Vancouver,* an intellectual gastronomic piece of gossipy fellowship, 1971.

Hardy, Anne & Gotlieb, Sondra. *Where to Eat in Canada,* 1971/72. Ottawa: Oberon Press, 1972.

Rochester, Helen. *Dining Out in Montreal.* Montreal: The *Montreal Star,* 1971.

Wasserman, Jack. *Vancouver on 5,000 Calories a Day,* a guide to dining out. Vancouver: November House, 1971.

A regional list of recipes in The Gourmet's Canada

Tarte à la Ferlouche (sugar pie)   66
Tortière with Tomato   51
Veau dans le Chaudron (veal and cabbage)   53

Ontario

Carrot Nut Raisin Spice Cake   72
Caviar — Classic Style   98
Deep Blueberry Pie   90
Edna Staebler's Funnel Cakes   73
Garlic Turnips   88
Lemon or Avgolemeno Sauce for Ontario Lamb or Chicken   84
My Mother-in-law's Caviar Recipe   98
Osso Buco (veal shanks)   83
Perfect Cheddar Cheese Soufflé   80
Sour Cream Icing   73
Steak and Kidney Pie   81
White Bread and Rolls (Old Ontario style)   76
Yorkshire Pudding (or Popovers)   81

The Prairies

Blintzes   103
Honeyed Nuts   105
Kasha and Mushrooms   108
Kreplach or Perogy Dough   106
My Mother's Chocolate Icing   105
Mrs. Bell's Scones   102
Muffins and Saskatoons   128
Ordinary Beet Borsch with or without Russell or Kvas   112
Pure Beet Borsch made from Kvas   111
Rose Petal Preserves   110
Russian Butter Cake   104
Sirloin Steak cooked in oven   131
Smoked Char (how to serve)   122
Sour Cream and Buckwheat Medivnyk (Honey Cake)   113
Uncooked Rose Petal Preserves   110
Whitefish or Pickerel Bourride   120
Wild Rice   126

British Columbia

General

A brief glossary of food and cooking terms†

Buried eggs — a Chinese delicacy, these are sometimes called thousand-year eggs. They are coated with a clay that preserves and colours them. A small slice of one at the beginning of a Chinese banquet suffices — they are very rich to eat.

Chapati flour — a whole-wheat flour used in India for thin griddle-fried breads.

Doboschtorte — a many-layered Hungarian cake often made with chocolate butter-cream filling.

Galantine — a dish made of boned poultry or meat, stuffed into a symmetrical shape and cooked in stock. *Galantines* are usually served cold, in the same manner as *pâtés* and *terrines*.

Kugelhopf†† — a cake, sometimes made from raised dough, baked in a special mold with curved, swirled sides and a central hole. The mold is frequently lined with dried fruit or nuts before the dough is added. Kugelhopf is considered to be an Austrian specialty, but for centuries it has also been a part of Alsatian cookery.

Mongolian steamer — a covered pot, sometimes called a fire pot, with a chimney rising through the centre from a built-in brazier below. A broth is heated by the burning charcoals below, and various vegetables and meats are dipped and cooked in the broth by the diners, fondue-style.

Pappadums — parchment-thin wafer-life bread that is traditionally eaten with curries. Pappadums are sold, uncooked and vacuum-packed in layers, at many specialty shops. All you have to do is fry them briefly in hot oil and they become crisp, and curly at the edges. A pile of pappadums on a plate looks like billowing brown clouds.

Phylo dough — paper-thin, crisp dough used in Greek pastries. It is difficult to make, so many people like to buy it ready-made at Greek food shops. It is used for all manner of sweet dishes and for cheese and spinach pies.

---

†This glossary includes only those terms which are not explained somewhere in *The Gourmet's Canada* or are not readily accessible in a standard dictionary.
†† There are several alternative spellings for this term, and for a number of others used in *The Gourmet's Canada*.

Ugli fruit — an East Indian fruit that looks something like an orange but is less spherical in shape and has a thicker skin. The taste is insipid, but the fruit has a slightly laxative quality.

Vacherin — a desert whose chief ingredient is usually meringue, which may act as a layer between fillings or as a "crown" into which the filling is poured. Wherever the meringue is placed and whatever the filling may be — from almond cream to chocolate rum — the *vacherin* is a tribute to French civilization. Sometimes *vacherins* are served frozen; they then become a rich ice-cream.

A list of sources of buffalo meat

J. Azaria
Clearbrook Game Farms
Ormstown, Quebec
  and
1440 St. Catherine St. W.
Montreal 107, Quebec

W. W. Belch, M.D.
584 Charlotte St.
Peterborough, Ontario

LBK Buffalo Ranch
RR #2
Oro Station, Ontario

R. Lynn Ross
Mile 147, Alaska Highway
Pink Mountain, B.C.

R. Scheffelmaier
RR No. 3
Coronation, Alberta

Index